POLITICAL PORTRAITS

GENERAL EDITOR
KENNETH O. MORGAN

ARTHUR HENDERSON

CHRIS WRIGLEY

GPC
BOOKS

GPC Books is an imprint of the University of Wales Press, 6 Gwennyth Street, Cardiff,
CF2 4YD

First published in 1990

© C. J. Wrigley, 1990

British Library Cataloguing in Publication Data
Wrigley, C. J. (Christopher John)
Arthur Henderson.—(Political portraits).
1. Great Britain. Politics. Henderson, Arthur, 1863–1935
I. Title   II. Series
941.0823092
ISBN 0-7083-1083-4
ISBN 0-7083-1085-0 pbk

Cover design: T. C. Evans, Logic Graphics

The publishers wish to acknowledge the advice and assistance given by the Design
Department of the Welsh Books Council which is supported by the Welsh Arts Council.

Typeset by BP Integraphics, Bath, Avon
Printed at The Bath Press, Avon

Contents

Editor's Foreword

The aim of this open-ended series of short biographies is to offer personal portraits of several of the decisive figures in the making of British politics over the past two hundred years. It will range over leading practitioners of politics, from Britain and Ireland (and probably the commonwealth/ empire as well) who have vitally shaped our public affairs in the nineteenth and twentieth centuries. Its premise, of course, is that people and biographies are vitally important as explanatory keys to the past. Too often, historians tend to see the course of historical change in terms of vague impersonal factors, evolutionary patterns, underlying themes, even that Scylla and Charybdis of historical understanding, 'forces' and 'trends'. The impact of the disciplines of economics, sociology or anthropology is often taken as reinforcing this tendency, and helping to obliterate flesh-and-blood human beings from our map of the past.

Now, no one would seriously dispute the enrichment of historical studies that has resulted from the stimulus of other disciplines. At the same time, it can hardly be questioned that the role of key individuals, locally and regionally as well as nationally, has been crucial in shaping the rhythms and speed of our political development in the years since the twin impact of industrialization and representative democracy. The growth of our political parties are impossible to visualize without the personal imprint of Gladstone, Disraeli or Keir Hardie. The course of wars, and their consequences, would have been totally different if Lloyd George or Churchill had never lived. Without Parnell or de Valera, modern Ireland would not have emerged in its present form. Even in the 1980s, the dominance of Mrs Thatcher confirmed anew the powerful impulses that can be released by the authority or whim of one determined individual.

So there need be no apology for offering a new series of biographies, brief but authoritative, all written by expert scholars, designed for the intelligent general reader as well as for the student or the specialist, as launch-pads for political and historical understanding. Portraits of individuals, naturally, open up wider social, cultural or intellectual themes. They also help to make history fun—vibrant, vivid, accessible. They may also be a means to a deeper understanding of our world. It should always be remembered that Karl Marx himself, whose influence is so frequently taken as elmininating individuals entirely from history in favour of the rise and conflict of social classes, actually took the reverse view himself. 'History', Marx wrote, 'is nothing but the acitivity of men in pursuit of their ends.' Some of these men—and women—and the ends they pursued, achieved, missed out on, or simply forgot, are illustrated in this series.

Arthur Henderson, whose career is assessed here by Dr Chris Wrigley, an outstanding authority on British labour developments, is a pivotal figure in the emergence of the British trade union and labour movement. Along perhaps with Herbert Morrison and James Callaghan, he has been the central and most representative personality in the British Labour Party's evolution from being a party of protest to becoming a party of power, fit for government. His historical importance is, perhaps, threefold. First of all, he was a major architect of the alliance of the trade unions with the new Labour party. He asserted Labour's proud independence in the unions' transition from Liberal–Labourism to becoming the foundation of a new party. He was the rock-like embodiment of the ethic of solidarity, of what was popularly parodied as 'This Great Movement of Ours'. Secondly, he was Labour's key organization man, the Carnot of victory as party secretary from 1911 to 1934, who created a nationwide constituency structure and the central direction of Head Office to give coherence to the congeries of local bodies that made up the labour–socialist coalition. With Sidney Webb, he created the 1918 party constitution, with all its ambiguities. And finally after the First World War, he was to become a leading figure in the world socialist movement and the attempt to transform the international order through the League of Nations and proposals for disarmament. In all the disappointments of the inter-war years, he was one of Britain's notable Foreign Secretaries, the real embodiment of 'peace in our time'.

All these and many other themes are traced with much scholarship and clarity by Dr Wrigley. He emphasizes Henderson's early skills as trade union negotiator and conciliator for the Iron Founders. He outlines his emergence as an independent Labour MP after the by-election break-through at Barnard Castle, his relations with Hardie, MacDonald and other leaders, and his role in steering a delicate path between co-operation with the Liberals and the assertion of Labour's independence before 1914. He emphasizes particularly the centrality of the First World War for Henderson's career, his rise to government office under Asquith and Lloyd George, his pivotal role as a link with the unions and the importance of his break with Lloyd George over the response to the revolution in Russia in 1917. Never has a 'door-mat' loomed larger in public affairs! After 1918, Henderson's vital leadership in domestic, Irish and above all international affairs are spelt out, culminating in his heading Labour's revolt against unemployment benefit cuts and MacDonald's proposed 'National Government' in August 1931 which has made Henderson one of Labour's acknowledged folk-heroes ever since. He was not an easy man to know: the soubriquet 'Uncle Arthur' is in many ways misplaced. At the same time, there was a rock-solid integrity and honesty of purpose about him which made him uniquely influential in his time. Dr Wrigley shows, too, his roots in late-Victorian working class community life, the importance of his Methodism and his temperance. Henderson was a very British leader of a very British Labour/socialist movement. That was how and why he built to last, and why he deserves his central role in this pantheon of British political pioneers.

KENNETH O. MORGAN
University College of Wales
Aberystwyth

Acknowledgements

I am grateful to Margaret Walsh, Kenneth Morgan, Alistair Duncan and Liz Powell for reading through the whole manuscript and suggesting many improvements, and to Su Spencer for typing it.

Introduction

Outside the circle of professional historians Arthur Henderson (1863–1935) is a less well remembered figure today than several of the other early major figures of the British Labour party like Keir Hardie, Ramsay MacDonald and Philip Snowden. Arthur Henderson was three times in effect leader of the Labour party: in 1908–10, when the chairmanship of the party was a rotating post among leading figures of the parliamentary party; again in 1914–17 and finally in 1931–2, by which time the post was called Leader. On the two later occasions he took over after a major crisis had shaken the party. In 1914 the outbreak of the First World War shattered the Left's hopes of an international general strike preventing such a war, and Arthur Henderson took over from Ramsay Mac-Donald on behalf of the pro-war majority. In 1931 he again took over from Ramsay MacDonald, when MacDonald and several colleagues chose to form a National Government with the Conservative party and much of the Liberal party. In both cases he was the solid, trade-union figure around whom the majority of the party could regroup.

Henderson never became Prime Minister. While some Labour party leaders who never became premier can be seen essentially as socialist preachers—Keir Hardie, George Lansbury and Michael Foot—others have been solid trade-union figures—Arthur Henderson, George Barnes, Willie Adamson and Jimmy Clynes. Of this latter group, Arthur Henderson is the most outstanding.

Those still alive who heard Henderson speak publicly remember him as a good, forceful but not charismatic speaker. Mary Agnes Hamilton in the preface to her 1938 biography confessed, 'I started with the usual view that he was, of course, sound, but alas! dull'. However she went on to testify, 'I learned, very soon, to recognise the bigness and rest on the sincerity of a man with whom one never met disillusionment'. During his lifetime 'Uncle Arthur' became a much loved figure within the Labour movement. More widely, he was seen as the epitome of the respectable, skilled trade-unionist. Remembering his period as MP for Burnley (1924–31), one woman from a textile family background recently told me 'He was a man of integrity who showed how an ordinary working man could achieve a lot in public life. People liked to look up to such figures. They showed what working people could aspire to'.[1]

Henderson also achieved international standing from 1929, firstly as Foreign Secretary during the second Labour Government, and then as president of the world disarmament conference at Geneva. For his ill-fated efforts to provide an alternative to brute force in international relations he was awarded the Nobel Peace Prize in Oslo in the autumn of 1934.

After his death Beatrice Webb paid private tribute to Henderson in her diary. She wrote, three days after his death,

> He had no intellectual distinction; no subtlety, wit or personal charm. Nevertheless he was an outstanding personality, because of his essential goodness, absence of vanity and egotism, faithfulness to causes and comrades, and a certain bigness, alike of soul and person, which made him continuously impressive in all the circles he frequented.

A little over two years later when Ramsay MacDonald died she wrote: 'Arthur Henderson will stand out as the wisest and most disinterested of the labour leaders of 1906–35'.[2] This brief biography reviews Henderson's career, and pays special attention to his Liberal–Labour start in politics and his trade union background. It was from these roots he grew to be part of the solid trade-union trunk of the Labour party.

1

The Liberal–Labour Trade-unionist

Arthur Henderson was a major figure in the Labour party before 1914 because he was a leading trade-unionist. His union was the Friendly Society of Iron Founders, which had been established in 1809 and was one of the major craft unions of Victorian Britain. Henderson joined the Iron Founders on 25 June 1883 shortly before he was twenty.[1]

Precise details of his parentage and birth are not known. The standard account of his background is that he was born on 13 September 1863 in the New City Road, Glasgow. His mother's name is not given. His father was David Henderson, a manual worker who died when Arthur was young. Together with a brother and sister Arthur grew up in poverty in Glasgow, with the family suffering hard times especially after the death of David Henderson. His mother remarried a man named Robert Heath, and the family then moved with him to Newcastle upon Tyne. However, there is a strong probability that he was born on 20 September 1863 at 10 Paterson Street, Anderston, Glasgow. If so, his mother was Agnes Henderson, a domestic servant, who made her mark on the birth certificate. There is no birth registered for the Glasgow Registration District for another Arthur Henderson between 1861 and 1864 inclusive, nor does there appear to be one in the two nearest counties. The Glasgow Post Office Gazettes for the early 1860s list four or five Hendersons in New City Road but no David Henderson. Perhaps Agnes's family lived there.

There is an even stronger probability that Henderson's mother married Robert Heath in Newcastle and not Glasgow. On 9 May 1874 an Agnes Henderson, who made her mark on the register, married Robert Heath, described as a policeman, in the Newcastle Register Office. He was twenty-nine, she was twenty-eight and described as 'spinster'. She gave her father's particulars as William Henderson, deceased, weaver. There appears to be no marriage between a Robert Heath and a Mrs Henderson registered in Glasgow at this time.

The standard account of Henderson's background stems from Mary Agnes (known as 'Molly') Hamilton's biography. She may well have got her details from the family, who might have remembered what Henderson's mother had told them. Arthur Henderson's wedding certificate gives his father's particulars as 'David Henderson, deceased, cotton spinner'. It is just possible that Arthur Henderson's birth was not registered at all and that there were two Robert Heath–Henderson marriages in early 1874; but it is very unlikely that both of these possibilities occurred. If not, then Agnes Henderson may well have had a relationship with a man named David, which never resulted in a wedding. This was not uncommon, especially for domestic servants. This would explain the memories of a man named David who died or left when Arthur was young, the naming of Arthur's brother as David W. Henderson, and Arthur Henderson naming his eldest son David. Henderson himself may well have not known of his mother's relationships when he was married, or may even never have known at all. The probability is that at some time he did know, for there is a surprising lack of information concerning his parents in later publications about him and he would have had some control over information in some of them. Given the disdain for illegitimacy among most of the respectable English working class, and given also the scurrilous use to which such information about Ramsay Mac-Donald was put by the so-called patriotic journal *John Bull* in September 1915, Henderson had no reason to make such information available even after his mother's death.[2]

Two central elements in Henderson's early development were his active role as a Methodist and his involvement in the affairs of his trade union. He came from a Bible-reading household, the family going to Congregationalist chapel on Sundays. When he was about sixteen his religious experience became more intense. This was brought to a head by hearing the young Gypsy Smith speaking at a Salvation Army street meeting. A few weeks later Henderson testified before another such meeting of how Jesus Christ had transformed his life. His elder brother later recalled, 'For Arthur, life began with his conversion. Before that, he was just the ordinary boy'.

Henderson found the Christian fellowship he needed at the Wesleyan Methodist Mission chapel in Elswick Road. It was to be the solid foundation on which he built his life. In 1885 he and Eleanor Watson, one of his friends at the Mission, agreed to get married. This they did at their chapel on 11 March 1889, when he was twenty-five and she was twenty-four. She not only shared his commitment to chapel affairs but also supported his very considerable trade union and political activities. Together they brought up four children, David, Will, Arthur and Nellie.

Henderson was not slow in taking on responsibilities within his chapel. He was a teacher in its Sunday school when he was still an apprentice. According to a man with whom he worked and whom he brought into his fellowship, he 'drew round him a band of young men and women who were inspired and guided by his leadership'. He was involved in all its activities, including visiting the sick and needy of this poor area of the city.[3] Alongside this he abstained from drinking, smoking and gambling. Henderson was to be a noted advocate of temperance, a cause which drew to him much hostility during his political career. In the 1890s he travelled widely as a speaker at North of England Temperance League meetings and mass demonstrations. He was to be one of the most notable teetotallers of the Labour party's leadership.

The second solid base of his life was the Friendly Society of Iron Founders. As with his commitment to Methodism, once he had joined he was not backward in taking an active role. His youth had been spent in the iron industry. He was apprenticed at twelve as an iron-moulder, starting at Clarke's Foundry and moving, after that failed, to the Forth Banks Locomotive and General Foundry Works of Messrs Robert Stephenson & Son. After he had completed his apprenticeship in 1880 he spent just over a year in Southampton before returning to Newcastle and rejoining Stephenson's, where he worked until the summer of 1893. There he was soon a leading figure in branch meetings and an eager recruiter to the union. Before long he was branch secretary.

Henderson's career as more than a local trade-union official stemmed from changes in the structure of his union. Newcastle was an area pressing for reform. One idea in the air was to move the headquarters of the union to the north. Whilst this was not done, in September 1891 the rules of the Society were revised. The changes which came into operation in February 1892 included the organization of the 117 branches into eighteen districts, with elected committees 'to watch over and advance the best interests of the society in general'.[4] In addition, in lieu of full-time paid organizers, each district elected a delegate who acted for the district committee. The nominations for these posts came from the branches and the membership in the district voted where there was more than one candidate.[5]

The district delegate posts were filled from the summer of 1892. Henderson did not arrive at this post 'by the vote of all the lodges extending over a very wide area', as Molly Hamilton claimed in her biography. The union's executive minutes for 27 July 1892 make that clear: 'That the appointment of delegate for no. 6 be confirmed—Mr. A. Henderson —there being no other candidate'. Nor was she correct in writing, 'It was, of course, a whole-time and a salaried post. Its magnificent remuneration, at the rate of some fifty shillings a week, enabled him to leave the foundry'. The union's only full-time officers then were W.H.Hey, the general secretary, and Joseph Maddison, the assistant general secretary.[6] That Henderson was the only nominee for the area covering Northumberland, Durham and Lancashire may have owed as much, if not more, to the fact that it was an onerous unpaid task as to Henderson's personal qualities and the significance of Newcastle as a centre for heavy industry. Among the first district delegates he was not alone in being returned unopposed.

Initially, he continued to work at Stephenson's. In the late summer of 1893 he left to work for the *Newcastle Evening News*, a paper which was being set up explicitly to 'fully recognise and advocate the wants of the workers'. He was one of several trade-unionists who were on the paper's board when it started publication on 2 October. Henderson told a meeting of his district committee in September that 'he had left the trade and ... if the committee thought he should resign, he would do so'. However he put it to them that in his new job he 'occupied a better position for serving the Society than ever he had done'. They agreed, and asked the union's executive to keep him as district delegate, observing that 'having more time at his disposal and with more of an independent spirit, he would be able to meet the employers, he [no longer] working at the trade'.[7]

Henderson was soon to be much occupied with union business and to make a major impact within the union. This was due to his role in representing the union in the major iron-founders' dispute in the North-East which lasted from 21 March to 3 September 1894. It was the most costly dispute to date in the history of the Friendly Society of Iron Founders. They paid out £11,700. 3s. 4d. (£11,700.17p) in strike pay during the year, most of it due to this dispute. As well as being the dispute which brought Henderson to prominence, it is also significant as being one in which his lifelong attitudes to industrial disputes were first clearly displayed. A 24-week strike caused considerable suffering to the families of those concerned. In this case, as the pattern-makers stayed out until 26 November 1894, normal working in the industry was disrupted for over eight months. Henderson wanted to secure peace in industry by both sides of industry—employers and trade unions—coming together regularly, on a formal basis, to try to resolve all issues of discord.

The strike followed the rejection of a wage demand made in early March. The men wanted an increase of 3*s*. 6*d*. (17½p) per week, which would have restored cuts made during 1892–3. When the cuts had been made, the men had accepted them, understanding that they would receive a pay-rise when trade revived. The union's officers later observed of the strike, 'In justification of their action, we may state that there was every indication of a revival in that district when our members put in their claim for an advance'. In all, 1,549 iron-founders stopped work, and they were joined from 7 April by 354 pattern-makers. The chief labour correspondent of the Board of Trade reported:

> As the work in hand in the engine shops reached completion, the absence of castings for further work put a stop to engine building, and large numbers of engineers were gradually thrown out of work... All the lesser branches of these trades, and the unskilled labourers therein employed, suffered at least as great an extent, so that a strike at first directly affecting about 2,000 workers ultimately kept out of work seven times that number.

Unemployment among shipbuilding workers went up from 12.9 per cent in March to 43 per cent at the end of July.[8]

Supervised at a distance by his union's executive, Arthur Henderson acted on behalf of the union throughout the strike. Both sides were well organized. After fourteen firms offered a compromise of 2*s*. (10p) advance, the union held a ballot and the men agreed to this reduced wage-demand. However the Employers' Association rejected this, and so the employers and the men dug themselves in for a lengthy dispute. The iron-moulders could hold out so long because of the financial strength of their union, and because it gained strong support among those directly affected. A very high proportion of iron-moulders and pattern-makers in the region supported the strike, and it spread to shipjoiners and sawyers. In the case of pattern-making, all but sixty workers in the area stopped work, including some non-union men. Pickets travelled to other areas to stop them doing work normally done in the North-East. Other than at Huddersfield and Halifax, then deemed to be 'hot beds of non-unionism', they were generally successful. In the case of the moulders, Henderson tried to boost union membership where it was weak, as at the Elswick works. He also put much effort into trying to ensure that members of other unions did not do 'black work'. The union executive in April urged him 'to appeal to other organisations for assistance whom we have assisted'. The Middlesbrough Trades Council gave both unions support and a platform from which Henderson and W.J. Mosses, General Secretary of the United Pattern Makers Association, could publicize their members' cases.[9]

The employers were especially intransigent. Perhaps this was because, as the *Newcastle Evening News* suggested, they held 'the belief that the funds of the men's society would soon run out, and that the dilemma would have immediately to be faced between a collapse of the union or a collapse of the strike'. The employers clung firmly to the position that they would agree to nothing until the men withdrew their claim for any increase in their wages.

The dispute was marked by two features of industrial relations of the period—offers of neutral mediation and the prospect of setting up a board of conciliation. Mediation by civic, national political or religious figures was common in major disputes. The great coal lock-out of 1893, which lasted sixteen weeks and affected 300,000 miners, had been settled following a conference with Lord Rosebery in the chair. From early on in this dispute there were offers to mediate. On 21 April the Iron Founders' executive resolved that 'Mr. Henderson ... be advised to accept the services of the Rev. Moore Ede as mediator in trying to effect a settlement of the strike'. However, the Rector of Gateshead's efforts were rebuffed by the employers for several months. After attempting unsuccessfully to arrange direct negotiations with the employers, from 3 May Henderson publicly stated his side's willingness 'to meet the employers under a neutral chairman to be mutually agreed upon'. The employers bluntly made clear their objections to a conference chaired by a third party, observing,

> (1) that the gentleman selected, being outside of the trade is often unable to appreciate the merits of the case; and (2) his desire to settle the dispute generally manifests itself by his suggesting some compromise, such as splitting the difference.

However, without this, the union observed, a conference of both sides 'would be a mere farce'.[10] In July, attempts at mediation by the Bishop of Newcastle failed as the employers insisted as a preliminary condition that the men withdraw their demand for a wage increase.

The other major feature of the dispute was the creation of a board of conciliation. This was to be a means to the settlement of the dispute. The employers offered to set one up, early on in the dispute—but, as usual, tied it to withdrawal of the wage claim. Henderson and other union representatives met the employers for further negotiations on 20 and 25 June, but got nowhere. Afterwards he complained that he had not been allowed at the meeting to state the men's case fully, and added that 'when we find the employers attempting to justify the paying of an advance to 'blacklegs' and a refusal to an advance to those men on dispute, we feel that, with a continuance of such treatment, all hope of a settlement must be very remote'. After more efforts at mediation by the Revd Canon Moore Ede in mid-July, Henderson agreed, on 21 July, to a board of conciliation if it were to review all the differences between both sides, and offered a return to work if it were set up. If that were not acceptable to the employers he urged 'a private and preliminary conference' under the Bishop of Newcastle 'to talk over the points of difference'.[11]

From that time the sticking point in a settlement was what would be considered by a board of conciliation. Perhaps Henderson's executive feared that he would move ahead of his members on strike in making concessions for a settlement. For their minutes of 25 July record,

> That Mr. Henderson's report be received as satisfactory; and that it be pointed out to Mr. Henderson that overtures or suggestions to the employers for a settlement must be submitted to the strike hands before they are submitted to the masters.

On 8 and 9 August there were further direct talks between the employers, and a delegation appointed to negotiate by a general labour conference. Henderson as usual was the leading union speaker. At a further meeting on 22 August the employers pressed that the reference to the board should be 'Does the state of trade at this time justify an advance or reduction in wage, and if so, how much'. This was rejected by the moulders as they felt there could be no question of a reduction.

The deadlock appears to have been broken by Henderson. On the 28th he went to the employers offices and talked further about a board of conciliation. He and the employers agreed that a permanent board should be formed. Once that had been formally agreed the men should return to work at their old wage rates; and the first business of the board should be to review the wage rates. The union then put this to a ballot. A majority of 709 to 452 agreed to those proposals, and those who could return to work did so on 3 September.[12] However the pattern-makers rejected similar proposals by 256 to 58 in October and stayed out for several more weeks.

By 1894 many industries had created such boards. They had been set up from 1860 onwards in such industries as hosiery, boot and shoe, and iron. From the mid-1880s the Scottish Ironmoulders had been working with employers under a procedure whereby there should be a month's notice before stoppages, during which time they would try to resolve their differences. In 1893, after a long series of disputes in the cotton industry, both sides had agreed (the Brooklands Agreement) on a disputes procedure which it was hoped would avoid great fluctuations in wage rates as well as lessen industrial conflict. Generally boards of conciliation and other such schemes had appealed to more weakly organized unions, to the more cautious trade-union leaders and to those who believed that, if both sides of industry came together, goodwill would flow. The leading advocate of conciliation in industry in the Newcastle area was Henderson's Liberal mentor, Robert Spence Watson.

The conciliation board set up for the iron industry of the north-east coast comprised eleven employers and eleven moulders, with a standing committee of five from each side. Its published rules laid down,

> The object of the Board is to regulate general advances or reductions in the wages of moulders. But any other general question may by common consent be brought before the Board.

Four weeks' notice was to be given before wage changes. The rules also included:

> There shall be no stoppage of work in the nature of a strike or lock-out; and pending the decision of the Board upon any question, all working conditions shall be those current at the time of notice given.[13]

Henderson appears to have been genuinely enthusiastic about the setting up of the conciliation boards. When working at Stephenson's, he and other union representatives had been trying to get conciliation procedures agreed with management. Such a way of dealing with industrial troubles reflected his Christian beliefs in co-operation rather than conflict in human affairs, as well as his cautious and Liberal outlook. Involved in Liberal politics, he was accustomed to associating with some of Newcastle's leading employers. He hoped to use the conciliation board as a means of resolving differences in the industry rather than going through further lengthy disputes such as that of 1894 which had brought considerable hardship to the moulders and their families. He was well aware of the employers' strength in the Newcastle area, later referring to it as 'the strongest capitalist centre on the North-East Coast', where employers 'have taught all other employers their trade in the matter of organisation'.[14] Before the end of 1894 he was praising the work of the board to union members—pointing out that 'a result of the meeting of the board was that something like 40 men would get advances ranging from 6*d*. [2½p] to 5*s*. [25p]'.[15] The union leadership pressed the case for involvement in the board on the lines of it being a cheap way for the union to achieve wage increases. Its Annual Report for 1896, noting that participation in the conciliation board had cost £19 18*s*. 4*d*. (£19.92), observed:

> This may appear rather expensive, yet we are inclined to believe that it is by far the cheapest method of settling any grievance which may arise between our members and their employers. This expenditure has been incurred through negotiating successfully for an advance in wages of 1*s*. 6*d*. [12½p] per week, involving nine branches and something like 1,700 members, the cost being less than 3*d*. per member.

Henderson was the leading trade-union representative on the conciliation board, acting as secretary of the moulders' side on it. Later he was to praise the board's role in the avoidance of further major disputes in the iron-foundries of the North-East before 1910. In 1909 when a conciliation board was set up for Lancashire, he was also secretary of the men's side on that. As a hard-working union official he was not a naive and unqualified supporter of conciliation boards—but always, even before the 1894 dispute, he was a believer in settling industrial differences by collective bargaining, not trials of industrial might.

The 1894 dispute made Henderson better known nationally within his union. In the July 1894 ballot for three places as delegates to the Trades Union Congress, Henderson came third, his 2,287 votes being 634 ahead of the unsuccessful fourth candidate's vote and only 165 behind that of the second. In 1892, when he had first stood for this he had come eighth of eighteen in the poll with a vote of 593, and in 1893 he had come ninth of thirteen but with 777 votes. In 1894 he received eight nominations, more than any other candidate; whereas in the previous contests he had been nominated by two branches on each occasion.[16] Clearly he had become a significant figure in the union by mid-1894. His position was also strengthened by the accession to the secretaryship of the union of Joseph Maddison, another moderate from Newcastle.

Henderson went to the 1894 Trades Union Congress mandated by ballots of the Iron Founders' membership to vote for labour representation and to support the eight-hour day, with trade exemption. For him, attending that Congress was part of his political education. In 1917 he recalled,

> It was a great gathering and made a deep impression upon us [the FSIF delegates]. The new Unionism had begun to exert an influence and Congress

was the rallying centre where the old school and the new met to settle accounts. Such questions as the formation of a Federation of Trade Unions for offensive and defensive purposes, the independence of Labour on national and local bodies, the application of the principle of Collectivism, and the State Regulation of the hours of adult labour, provided the giants of both schools with material which produced some of the finest debates I ever heard.[17]

However, when Congress passed a resolution which laid down that future delegates to the annual Congress had to be either people working at their trade or salaried union officials, a resolution which was aimed at Keir Hardie and other socialists, Henderson was excluded. It was a brusque introduction to the world of the TUC, for this lifelong unionist.

2

The Liberal–Labour Politician

Arthur Henderson grew up in Newcastle upon Tyne, a town with strong Radical and Liberal traditions. It was represented in Parliament by the prominent Radical, Joseph Cowen, from 1874 to 1886, and by John Morley, one of Gladstone's major lieutenants, from 1883 to 1895. Cowen combined support for European revolutionaries, Home Rule for Ireland, and extension of the franchise to working men with a vigorous belief in British imperialism. He was the proprietor of the *Newcastle Chronicle*, a paper which Henderson read and discussed with his workmates as an apprentice at Stephenson's.

Henderson was the type of socially aware, nonconformist, skilled working man that Gladstonian Liberalism needed to attract to its ranks in the industrial cities. He was a leading figure in his chapel, a man who did not drink, smoke or gamble. An eager sportsman, playing cricket and football, he was a founder of St Paul's Football Club, which was to be one of the constituent parts of Newcastle United. He was also an able speaker, drawing not only on his experience as a lay preacher but also on his time as an active member of the Tyneside Debating Society.

The leadership of his union, the Iron Founders, was predominantly Liberal. During the 1880s it was firmly in the hands of staunch Liberals such as James Jack, Edward Woods, and William Hey. The assistant general secretary from 1886, Joseph Maddison, was from Newcastle and would have known Henderson's qualities as a branch official. Henderson appears to have been one of the 'coming men' of the Liberal part of the union, while Samuel Masterton, the Chelsea branch secretary, was one of the faction more influenced by independent labour and 'New Union' ideas. When Maddison became general secretary in 1894, Masterton defeated eight other candidates to become assistant general secretary.[1]

Henderson was also the 'coming man' among working-class Liberals who wanted Liberal—Labour candidates in elections. As one who combined Gladstonian Liberalism with a degree of municipal socialism he was very acceptable to the more progressive Liberals. By 1895 he had been an active Liberal Party member for several years. He much admired Gladstone, later recollecting being very impressed when he saw the 'Grand Old Man' receive the freedom of the city at Newcastle Town Hall on 3 October 1891. Apparently he was an eager proponent of the Liberals' domestic policies, 'the Newcastle Programme', laid down at their 1891 conference, the occasion of Gladstone's visit. According to Molly Hamilton, 'He carried a copy of the programme about with him, and was often to produce it, on convenient, and, to reactionaries of all sorts, inconvenient, occasions'.[2] He spoke in support of John Morley, Gladstone's distinguished lieutenant, at a big public meeting in 1892.

When he first stood for municipal office in November 1892 he made clear his position as a Labour candidate within the Liberal broad church. His candidature followed on from a TUC initiative to get more working men into Parliament. It had set up the Labour Electoral Association in 1886, which urged working men to form local organizations to get bona-fide working men elected. In practice the Association suggested working with the Liberals.[3] Keir Hardie, in 1888, when fighting the Mid Lanarkshire by-election, had begun with Labour Electoral Association support, but had gone his own way after the local Liberals refused to back him for that seat. In the North-East, the Tyneside National Labour Association backed Henderson for Newcastle Council.

In the council by-election Henderson was presented to the electorate 'as a bona fide working man' and 'as a genuine social reformer who would use his best energies to improve the moral condition of the masses'. Unusually for a council by-election, Henderson had enlisted the help of a local MP, J. Havelock Wilson, who came to speak in his support. Wilson was then in his radical phase, a colourful New Union leader, who had beaten a Liberal as well as a Unionist for Middlesbrough in the July 1892 general election. He was the leader of the merchant seamen's union, one which was prominent in the Labour movement in many coastal areas, especially in May Day demonstrations. Wilson later wrote,

> I happened to hear him speak at Byker, and realised that he had exceptional qualities. I accordingly advised the Liberals at Newcastle to invite Mr. Henderson to second the resolution in favour of Mr. Morley at a great meeting at the Town Hall. My advice was taken and Henderson made a brilliant

speech, with the result that he was immediately regarded as the coming man of politics.[4]

During the council by-election, on 14 November, Havelock Wilson told a crowded public meeting,

> Mr. Henderson had taken a very proper course, seeing that he was a Radical workingman, in allying himself with the Party that was desirous of going further in the direction of reform than the other Party at the present time.[5]

Henderson was at pains to state during this campaign that he 'did not believe in dividing the Liberal and Labour Party when their mutual interests were at stake'.

During the by-election Henderson advocated policies that were both Radical and trade-union orientated. They were in line with those policies being propounded in London municipal politics by John Burns and the more radical Progressives. During the campaign Henderson frequently began his speeches by proclaiming his stand on trade union issues — condemning sub-contracting, 'which led to the pernicious evil of sweating' and calling for the Corporation to be a model employer by paying trade union rates for the job and observing the eight-hour day.

The eight-hour day was an issue which, in the 1880s and 1890s, provided a dividing line between socialists and advanced radicals, and Liberal trade-unionists. The former demanded legislation as the means by which it could be achieved and defended, whilst the latter had the more limited aim of securing it in the public sector and doing so by trade union negotiation. In the London May Days of 1890 and 1891, the legislative approach had triumphed, gaining the support of most on the progressive side of politics. However, after the first enthusiasm of New Unionism had diminished, many Liberal trade-unionists in the capital had gone their own way again. Henderson, in this by-election, took a characteristically moderate position. His union, the Iron Founders, was equivocal as to whether a working day limited to eight hours, a socialist remedy for unemployment, should be brought about by legislation. In July 1892 the membership had responded to the question, 'Are you in favour of the eight hours day being obtained by legal enactment ... or are you in favour of it being obtained by trade union effort' by voting for the latter; in May 1889 they had voted in favour of legislation.[6] However from 1889 the policy of the union was for an eight-hour day, one way or the other; and so, as was customary, Henderson was in line with his union's policy.

He went on in his speeches to urge municipal socialism. He called for the municipalization of the trams, gas and water. 'These public necessities should be in the hands of the public, and as a result thousands of pounds would be saved annually in the rates.' He also called for branch libraries and reading rooms to be opened across the city and for municipal housing to be built and 'let at a rental within the reach of the poorest workmen'. More than that, he urged, that as 'they were in the face of a very serious depression of trade it would be a good thing if they could induce the Corporation to borrow money and proceed with the work, for this would give employment to many when that employment was needed'.

The by-election for the Westgate North council seat caused exceptional interest in the city. It came about very soon after the council elections, as a result of an elevation to the aldermanic bench. The *Newcastle Daily Leader* commented on the electoral struggle between Henderson and J.W. Parker, a butcher, that it aroused 'more than usual interest from the fact that almost for the first time in connection with municipal contests politics had been imparted into the struggle, Mr. Henderson receiving ... the support of the workmen members of the Liberal Association, while Mr. Parker, it is said, received the support of the Conservatives'. The local Conservatives tried to condemn Henderson's candidature on the grounds that he did not live in the ward (he lived at 71 Monday Street, Elswick until June 1894) and that there should be no politics in local government. On the residential point, Henderson could reply that the butcher lived further away in Grangerville! As for no politics in local government, J.H. Rodgers, a supporting speaker for Henderson, vigorously replied that on Newcastle Council, 'They had worse than politics. They had cliques. If they had politics they would know where they stood, and if politics were good for the country, they were good for the city'.

The electorate clearly responded to this political fight. The electoral register had 2,318 names on it: by November 1892 it was old. Yet 1,750 electors turned out to vote in this municipal by-election. In the July 1892 general election 1,732 had voted in this ward, and in the parliamentary by-election following John Morley taking office in Gladstone's government, 1,771 had voted. Hence the local press rightly referred to it as 'proportionately a phenomenal poll for a municipal contest'. Henderson won the seat by 948 votes to 791.[7] In the hour of his triumph Henderson pointed out a clear moral from his success. 'They had', he said 'won a splendid victory and shown what Labour and Liberalism could do'. He called on other wards to do likewise 'until Labour was really represented on the Council'.

Henderson's victory, indeed his very candidature, depended largely on Liberal support. He was invited to stand by two eminent Liberal councillors, Beattie and Carr. They chaired his two main public meetings. He was adopted unanimously by the Liberals of the Westgate North ward, and a Liberal activist, Keith Durham, organized his campaign. The Liberals also gave Henderson guarantees to cover his loss of earnings through attending council meetings. From the Liberals' viewpoint, Henderson was an able and respectable young Liberal trade-unionist. At a time when there were various socialist and independent working-class challenges to the Liberal party, including in Newcastle a campaign directed against Morley, Henderson was a good candidate for them. In the by-election he was supported by a considerable number of trade union speakers, including some men already councillors, by the Newcastle, Gateshead and District Trades and Labour Council (of which Henderson was a member) as well as by many of his workmates.

His success in the by-election was also partly due to the severe recession affecting Newcastle and the North-East. High levels of unemployment were an engine of political change in many working-class areas between the mid-1880s until beyond the turn of the century. This was a major factor in building up pressure for working-class candidates. In areas such as Battersea this had been followed by demands for independent working class candidates and then by support for socialist candidates.[8] During his council by-election Henderson spoke vigorously against the harsh operation of the Poor Law. At a public meeting,

> He noted that at the last meeting of the Guardians a proposal had been made to open the stone yard. He hoped the Guardians present would object to that. The time had gone when they should pauperise the workmen like that. There was not a workman present who would be in favour of sending his mates to work in the stone yard with the result that in a few months he would be a disfranchised citizen. Let them provide relief works where men could labour without the stigma of pauperism, where men could honourably do their work and be honourably paid for it.

Henderson and his family knew about the hardship of unemployment at first hand. He had been out of work for lengthy periods, including for six months in 1884, eight months in 1885 and a shorter spell in 1891. Once on the council, unemployment was the first issue on which Henderson spoke. At his first meeting of the full council on 7 December 1892 he supported a scheme put forward by the city engineer to spend £6,000, employing 200 to 250 men for three or four months planting trees on the Town Moor. He called on his fellow council members to back the scheme 'as a Corporation or else they would have to open their private purses', urging them 'to allow the working men to have a chance to do work which would not demoralise them'.[9]

In Newcastle in the general election the Conservative candidate, Charles Hamond, had topped the poll, John Morley had hung on to the second seat, and James Craig, a wealthy self-made man who had successfully raised funds for the Newcastle Liberals, had been ousted. There had been fears beforehand that Morley would lose. He had incurred the hostility of many in the Labour movement by vigorously opposing Eight Hours Bills, which he described as being part of 'the strong socialist doctrine I hate'. From 1889 there had been a campaign in Newcastle which attacked Morley over this and pressed for independent Labour candidates. There were demonstrations, rallies and meetings, including one in September 1891 at which John Burns, Keir Hardie, Robert Blatchford and R.B. Cunninghame Graham denounced Morley. At the 1892 general election the local labour campaigners called on working men to vote for Hamond.[10] Whether this had a major effect is another matter, but it was a warning of which the Liberal hierarchy took notice.

Hence it is not surprising that in early 1895, with a new general election on the horizon, Morley told the Newcastle Liberal Association that in his opinion the person chosen to be the second candidate to run with him for the two Newcastle parliamentary seats 'should be one in touch with the working classes'. Morley was told 'that this might easily be accomplished, if the Bill for the payment of members were passed. Otherwise some difficulty from a financial point of view would arise with securing such a candidate'.[11]

The key figure in pressing for a working man candidate and in fostering Henderson's political career in Newcastle politics was Robert Spence Watson. He was long the leading Liberal in Newcastle, founding the Newcastle Liberal Association in 1873, and, from 1890 to 1902, being President of the National Liberal Federation. He had presided over the conference which had laid down 'the Newcastle Programme'. He was also a leading figure in promoting conciliation agreements in industry. He had acted as an arbitrator as early as 1864, and between 1884 and 1894 was the sole arbitrator in forty-seven disputes in major industries in the North-East. Watson saw the need for a 'balanced ticket', representing working-class issues as well as Home Rule for Ireland, if Morley was to hold his seat and the second seat be recaptured.[12]

When the time came for selecting the second candidate, the Liberals' executive committee set up a selection sub-committee under Spence Watson. This recommended to the executive that Henderson should run alongside John Morley in the forthcoming general election and made arrangements that Henderson should be funded should he be elected MP. The executive endorsed this proposal by eighty-four votes to three. The *Newcastle Evening News* outlined the case for Henderson's candidacy as follows:

> Councillor Henderson is still young in years, though he has occupied a seat in the city Council for some time. He is a prominent trades unionist, and as Secretary of the Moulders' Union took a prominent part in the recent dispute in that trade. He is a fluent speaker, has been an active Liberal for years, and some time ago was publicly complimented by Mr. Morley for the manner in which he supported a vote of confidence in that gentleman at a meeting in the Town Hall.

However it soon had to note that 'certain Liberals' were 'up in arms' against a trade unionist being second candidate.[13]

Whilst that paper supported Henderson, the leading local Liberal newspaper, the *Newcastle Daily Leader* deplored his selection and called for Craig to return as candidate. In a series of editorials the paper attacked Henderson by a series of 'it is said by many' denigrations of him. Thus in one it reported, 'It is said—and reiterated—with what truth we know not—that Mr. Henderson has not the confidence of his own class, that is the workman class ... It is certain that the recommendation has not the favour of what may be called middle class Liberals'.

Others out to block Henderson managed to suggest both that he offered nothing new and that he was a socialist in disguise. The *Newcastle Daily Leader* in one editorial asserted he offered 'nothing that is not the common property of Liberalism except a legal eight hours day with a trade option, and a larger number of Liberals than we care to think of are already pledged to much more than that'. In contrast Thomas Barker, who had been campaigning as a Liberal–Labour candidate for some time, asserted, 'It is well known fact that Mr. Henderson and others who support him always had an affectionate leaning towards the ILP candidate until Dr. Watson put his foot down'. He added for good measure, 'Messrs Henderson, ILP and Co. would municipalise the public house'.[14]

When the executive's recommendation came before the Liberal Thousand on 22 February they decided to appeal to James Craig to be the second candidate. According to Spence Watson, two-thirds of this body were working men, a view borne out by recent research.[15] Craig accepted their invitation. Robert Spence Watson was left to save his face by observing that the rejection of the executive's recommendation 'surely disposed of the idea. ...that in any sense or shape the Association was the property of the clique'.[16]

Henderson loyally accepted this decision. On the 29 May he sat prominently at the front of Morley's platform in the Town Hall for a major public meeting. When it came to the general election Henderson moved the resolution adopting John Morley and James Craig. The *Newcastle Evening News* described his speech as one of the 'rare merit and remarkable force' and commented that he 'threw his soul into the task of advancing the final choice of the Liberal Thousand'.[17]

The failure of the Liberal Thousand to endorse his candidature must have been very disappointing for Henderson. Yet, it cannot have greatly surprised him. Seven months earlier the *Newcastle Evening News*, the paper for which he worked and on whose board he served, had vigorously condemned the refusal of the Liberals in Sheffield to select Charles Hobson, a well known local trade unionist, to be their candidate in a by-election in the Attercliffe constituency. Its editorial for 3 July 1894 had proclaimed:

> The division between men of the Liberal Party and of the Labour Party is a new phase of our public life...
> Since the Liberal Party thinks fit, in the teeth of its own pledges, to go in for Labour representation in speechmaking, but to resist it in practice, there is no help for it but that the labouring community should take independent action on its own account, and work in defiance, if need be, of the hereditary group.

For James Ramsay MacDonald the Attercliffe by-election was the last straw, and he joined the Independent Labour Party. He wrote to Keir Hardie, 'Attercliffe came as a rude awakening, and I felt during that contest that it was quite impossible for me to maintain my position as a Liberal any longer'.[18]

With the discarding of Henderson, the *Newcastle Evening News* observed of the Newcastle Liberal party:

> It has suffered a serious loss in the Unionist dissenters [i.e. from 1886, over Home Rule for Ireland], thereby being weakened financially and numerically. It cannot afford to lose many of its working class supporters.[19]

Henderson's allegiance to the Liberal party was not shaken in the mid-1890s. Given that as a potential parliamentary candidate he was very much the nominee of Robert Spence Watson and his associates, with their undertaking to arrange the necessary finances for the election and, should he win, for his salary as well, he had no cause to be bitter with the local Liberal leadership. His appearance then as a potential candidate depended on them; later it was to depend on the sponsorship of his trade union. In 1895 when his nomination was obstructed he retired gracefully. He was to offer to do so again later, when, in 1903, his nomination at Barnard Castle ran into difficulties.

In 1895, while still thirty-one, Henderson could afford to wait for other political opportunities, especially given the political weight of his backers. His loyalty certainly helped to get him the well-paid Liberal agent's job later in the year. The Liberal establishment looked after him at this time: indeed he was made a Justice of the Peace for Newcastle just a week before the 1895 general election.

Both Morley and Craig were defeated in the July 1895 election. Morley later observed, 'In attention to Ireland I had been negligent of Newcastle; the eight hours men had their turn, and the running political currents helped them to bring me down'.[20] Morley lost by 308 votes, whilst an independent Labour candidate polled 2,302 votes. (The seats were to be recaptured from the Conservatives in 1906.) Henderson then took up the post of agent to Sir Joseph Pease, MP for Barnard Castle, in December 1895. He received £250 per year but was allowed to continue with his trade union work. The job did require him and his family to leave their home at 30 Croydon Road, Newcastle, and move close to the constituency: they set up home at 45 Hurworth Terrace, Darlington (moving later to Windsor Terrace, Darlington). There Henderson maintained his own political and civic career. He became a Durham county councillor in March 1898, being returned unopposed for a Darlington ward—the one ward where an existing councillor did not stand again. He took over a Liberal seat, and served for the three-year term.[21] Later in the year he was elected to Darlington Council. On 15 June 1911 he was made a Justice of the Peace for Durham county. The election to Darlington Council was another triumph for Henderson. He unseated W.C. Barron, the only retiring member seeking re-election, in the elections on 1 November 1898. Henderson won Darlington South Ward by 480 to 373 votes.[22]

Five years later Henderson, then newly elected as MP for Barnard Castle, was made mayor of Darlington. He was its first Labour mayor, though council elections then were not fought explicitly on party political lines in the town. He was proposed as mayor by Alderman T.M. Barron, the brother of the man Henderson had defeated. Councillor J.G. Harbottle, who seconded the nomination, commented, 'In entering the

Council he wrested the key of the South Ward, which was considered
a great feat ... he came into the Council through a very notable victory'.[23]
However, for all the talk of 'no politics' on the council, Henderson, as
in Newcastle, was clearly there as a Liberal–Labour councillor.

3

Independent Labour MP, 1903–1906

In July 1903 Arthur Henderson became a nationally-known figure because he was the victor in a famous by-election. It was the first that Labour won in a three-way fight. It also made him the fifth MP who acted in an independent group of Labour MPs. He joined Keir Hardie, Richard Bell (though the latter's independence from the Liberals was already doubtful) and two men returned in earlier by-elections, David Shackleton and Will Crooks. Yet until the last there were doubts as to whether Henderson really had separated himself from the Liberals, and indeed these were not really resolved until July 1904.

Henderson's emergence as an early Labour-party figure was almost entirely due to his trade union commitment. Like so much in political careers, the timing also owed a great deal to chance: the chance that a vacancy should occur in the Barnard Castle constituency, that the Liberal candidate was unsound on free trade; and that the Unionist Government's popularity was waning thereby allowing the non-Tory vote to divide and Henderson still to win.

The Labour party was formed, initially under the name Labour Representation Committee (LRC), on 27 and 28 February 1900. Samuel Masterton represented the Friendly Society of Iron Founders at the inaugural conference. The union's membership subsequently voted for affiliation to the Labour Representation Committee by a two-to-one majority. Henderson's union was the fourth largest of those affiliating to the LRC in its first year. With the Taff Vale Judgement in 1901, the Law Lords awarded huge damages to the railway company against the Amalgamated Society of Railway Servants because of a local strike in south Wales. The Iron Founders, like other unions, now realized that trade unionism needed the protection of a change in the law, and this would be assisted

by representation in the House of Commons. The Iron Founders' executive committee minutes of 4 April 1902 record,

> That in the opinion of the EC the necessity of increased Labour representation
> in the House of Commons has been clearly demonstrated by the recent
> decision in the House of Lords, and with a view to assisting in the formation
> of a party independent of either political party, that we pay a levy of 1*s*.
> [5p] per working member annually, the same to be submitted to a vote.
> of the Society.

The union eagerly took up the cause of Labour representation. They
sent members from nearby areas to the 1901 and 1902 conferences of
the LRC. To the third, held in Newcastle upon Tyne, they sent Arthur
Henderson as well as a local member. At this conference Henderson stood
without success for one of the nine trade-union positions on its executive,
coming thirteenth with 253 votes to the ninth person's 308. He also moved,
on behalf of the Iron Founders, a motion concerning affiliation fees.

The Iron Founders' executive committee in August 1902 had resolved,
'That the Labour Representation Committee be informed that the committee suggests that 1*d*. [2p] per member per year is totally inadequate,
and suggest that 1*d*. per member per quarter be charged'. Henderson,
in moving the resolution at the 1903 Conference, drew on his experience
as a Liberal agent. His speech is also notable for his commitment to
strong organization, a commitment which was to be central to the service
he gave the Labour party for the rest of his life. Henderson's speech
to his fellow delegates was recorded in the conference report:

> Surely, if they were going to do something more than simply play a game,
> they must not be satisfied to go on, for instance, depending on a register
> that was made up by the other Parties. He had been engaged for the last
> seven years in connection with registration work, and he happened to know
> what expense was associated with that work. Their own officials had already
> as much work in hand as they could efficiently manage, and voluntary assist-
> ance in registration work was played out. . .
>
> In this movement great strides had been taken during the last three years,
> especially the last six months. They could not tell what might take place
> in the next year. He sincerely trusted that they would take up the only logical
> position, and build up a strong organisation.[1]

The Iron Founders' leadership strongly urged their union's members
to support Labour candidates. The union's *Annual Report for 1902* commented,

> The past year stands out as one of the most eventful in our history, we
> having decided, for the first time since the formation of the Society, to take

part in politics; nor do we stand alone in this respect, as quite a number of trade societies have, for the first time, launched out in the same direction.

Having decided on such a policy your duties do not end with such decision; indeed, this really is the beginning of your duties. It is now your duty to work with unflagging zeal to obtain the object we have in view,viz: to place the law on an equitable basis so far as trade unions are concerned... Wherever any Labour candidate appeals for your votes they should be freely given, no matter what society or organisation he is a member of; he should be regarded as a plank in our platform, and every effort should be put forth to secure his return to Parliament, always remembering that our present action has been forced upon us by the present law makers and law administrations...

It is in this trade union context, not in the realm of ideas, that Arthur Henderson's move to Labour from Liberal–Labour politics is to be explained. In July 1902 David Shackleton had secured the Clitheroe seat in Parliament as a Labour Representation candidate without opposition from other parties. Shackleton, the secretary of the Darwen Weavers, was in similar mould to Henderson, a man of solid Liberal background. In his speech to the 1903 LRC conference, Henderson's comments on great strides made in the previous six months referred back to Shackleton's success. Within a month of Shackleton's election to Parliament, the Iron Founders voted by 4,230 to 2,409 in favour of independent labour representation.

When nominations were invited for the post of the union's parliamentary candidate, Henderson was one of six to come forward. He secured nomination from thirty-nine branches, compared to John Davison's twenty-four and Robert Morley's nine. Davison was a strong supporter of New Unionism, Morley was an ILP activist and an organizer for the Workers' Union, and another candidate, Rees Davies, was a Marxist. In the ballot, which was held in late 1902, Henderson came first. He received 5,619 votes to Davison's 4,242, Morley's 1,411, Davies's 604, Frederick Favell's 600 and James Purvis's 69. Henderson had the blessing, perhaps even the active support, of Joseph Maddison, the union's general secretary, and those of a Liberal–Labour outlook.

The job specification given for the union's parliamentary candidate laid down that the person would be General Organizer of the union while a candidate, receiving £200 a year, but on being elected to Parliament would be 'allowed a free hand ... so long as he votes with the Labour party on matters pertaining to the welfare of the unions' and would receive an additional £100 a year from the Labour Representation Committee.[2] Henderson, in thanking the union's members for electing him to the post, promised to display 'a loyal adherence to the constitution of the Labour Representation Committee' and assured them that if elected to Parliament they could 'rely upon my hearty co-operation with the Labour Group, and on my voice being heard and my vote recorded in support of their policy and programme'.[3]

Inevitably his election to a paid, union job raised questions about the compatibility of this with being a paid Liberal party agent. Indeed it had been raised before. In 1898 the Leeds district of the Iron Founders had complained of his working in a parliamentary by-election at York for a federated employer, Sir Christopher Furness, a shipowner and ship-builder. Now there was considerable ambiguity in his position, being a potential parliamentary candidate for his union under the LRC banner, yet still being a paid agent in the Barnard Castle constituency for the Liberal MP Sir Joseph Pease. Presumably Henderson raised this with his union's executive. Its minutes record for 31 December 1902, 'That Mr. Henderson be allowed a free hand respecting retaining his present position'. The matter was due to come up at the 1903 LRC conference in Newcastle; and, indeed, delegates voted overwhelmingly in favour of a resolution requiring that those who were on the LRC executive, its MPs or its candidates 'should strictly abstain from identifying themselves with or promoting the interests of any section of the Liberal or Conservative parties'.

However, Sir Joseph Pease was elderly and in poor health. At a meeting of supporters at West Lodge, Darlington, in December 1902, he declared his intention not to stand again. Notwithstanding Henderson's election as the Iron Founders' parliamentary candidate, the president of the Liberal Association, Sir David Dale, asked Henderson to stay on as agent for two or three months. On 19 December Pease's son, Jack, who had been elected MP for Saffron Walden in May 1901, wrote to the Liberal party's chief whip, Herbert Gladstone, to say that the local Liberals wanted his father to continue until the next election but would wish soon to select a new candidate. He also commented,

> At the present time Mr. Arthur Henderson is agent and a fund will probably be raised to keep him in the constituency for some time to come. He, however, is obliged to give up his agency whenever he is called upon by his trades union to become the formal candidate for Parliament. As you perhaps saw he was elected by the Friendly Society of Iron Founders for England, Scotland and Wales (by a large majority of votes) as Labour candidate to be run

at the next election. Some of the members are very anxious that he should appear as Labour candidate free from the trammels of any party. He is a very good Liberal and fully recognises that there are only two lobbies in the House of Commons but he may be impelled to adopt very much Mr. Shackleton's attitude.

Jack Pease hoped that Henderson could be fixed up with a Liberal seat elsewhere. Clearly informal approaches were made to him about Salford South. Pease told Gladstone,

> Mr. Keith Durham of Southport, who used to be in Newcastle and knows Mr. Henderson very well, told him recently that the Liberal Association of the constituency which Groves now represents think that they could carry a Labour candidate upon whom the Liberal Party might unite. In 1892 and 1895 with an Independent Labour candidate, the Liberals only lost the election by about 100 votes. Possibly the way could be opened for Henderson's candidature in this constituency.[4]

But Henderson was not tempted.

Herbert Gladstone was very willing to have more Labour men in Parliament—in much the same way as Robert Spence Watson and his associates were in Newcastle when Henderson had first stood for the council and had come near to being parliamentary candidate in 1895. The arrival of more Liberal–Labour candidates was not seen as a threat. Indeed as Philip Poirier has written, many of the supporters of Sir Henry Campbell-Bannerman, the Liberal party leader, who distrusted the Liberal imperialists, 'preferred almost any Labour man to an out-and-out Roseberyite'. On 2 January 1903 Campbell-Bannerman publicly declared, 'We are keenly in sympathy with the representatives of Labour. We have too few of them in the House of Commons'. After further intimations of this attitude from leading Liberals, secret negotiations for a Liberal–LRC understanding in certain seats took place between Ramsay MacDonald and Jesse Herbert, acting on behalf of Herbert Gladstone.[5]

Jack Pease, who advised Gladstone on North-East politics, would have known in broad terms of such moves to reach an understanding with Labour, even if he did not know the details. In the ensuing weeks it appears he would have been happy if the local Liberals had selected Henderson to succeed his father. Sir Joseph Pease announced in February 1903 that he would be retiring, but on 23 June he died, thereby causing an early by-election.

In the meantime Henderson, following his union's policy, appears to have become more committed to independent Labour representation. He had been a delegate at the LRC annual conference in Newcastle of 19–21 February 1903, which had firmly resolved to follow an independent course. That conference had endorsed William Crooks as candidate in a by-election in Woolwich. The Woolwich branch of the Iron Founders asked their executive for help. The Iron Founders' executive endorsed Crooks as candidate, sent £10 to his election fund and asked Henderson to go and help. Perhaps because of his position as a Liberal agent, Henderson asked Ramsay MacDonald if he thought Crooks 'would be favourable to my so doing' and whether he considered it advisable. However his executive soon wired him to go to Woolwich without delay, which he did.[6] Crooks achieved a great victory, turning a Conservative majority of 2,805 in 1896 to a Labour majority of 3,229 on 11 March 1903.

Two days later, the national executive of the LRC endorsed Henderson as an acceptable trade-union sponsored candidate. Henderson now needed a constituency., Ramsay MacDonald had already been making preparations for Henderson to be adopted in Barnard Castle. On 24 February he had written to H.H. Hughes, the LRC election agent in Darlington, to enquire if an affiliated trade union had an active branch in the Barnard Castle constituency which could organize a conference to establish a local LRC for the constituency. Then, 'if a movement is made on behalf of any of the affiliated societies in the division', Henderson could be brought before a selection meeting. Such a meeting was organized of local trade unionists and others supporting independent Labour representation, at Bishop Auckland on 1 April. Twenty delegates from the Barnard Castle constituency attended, 'representing a body of over 3,000 voters'. Henderson was unanimously adopted as prospective LRC candidate.

The next day Henderson went before a special meeting of the executive of his union for them to determine whether he should be candidate for Barnard Castle or for another Durham county seat, Willington. Earlier in the day he consulted MacDonald. At the meeting of his executive, Henderson outlined the prospects in each constituency. On Barnard Castle he also advised them, based on six year's practical experience in the division, that the expenses in connection with keeping the register posted up to date, advertising meetings and other incidental expenses would not exceed £150 per annum. After careful consideration, his executive unanimously agreed that he should contest Barnard Castle. Henderson reported this decision to MacDonald, adding 'The question of registration was fully considered and I am satisfied with the conditions laid down. I am going to begin at once'.

Henderson was first in the field for the impending vacancy. MacDonald had been careful to ensure this. He had written on 20 March of the LRC moves in Barnard Castle constituency, 'The difficulty is that we have not a very firm grip and we have got to move very cautiously lest the Liberals should rush in and anticipate us'.[7] Once Henderson's candidature was proclaimed, the question was whether the Liberals would accept him as an independent Labour candidate or run their own candidate against him. According to Molly Hamilton, Jack Pease offered him the Liberal Association's nomination and was astounded when Henderson replied that his union required him to stand on behalf of the LRC not as a Liberal. Given that she knew Henderson many years later and that her details may not have been precise, it is quite possible that this offer came from Pease, acting on his own initiative, not from the Liberal Association. Henderson would have been faced with agreeing to abide by the Liberal Association's verdict as to whether it endorsed him, and thereby breaking with his union's policy and clearly going against the LRC's very recently agreed Newcastle policy of independence. Having experienced Spence Watson's inability to carry the Liberal activists' endorsement for his candidature in Newcastle in 1895, Henderson would not have been likely to take this course. His actions were based on loyalty to his union and its policies.

Whether Henderson, as the Liberal agent for the constituency, acted in bad faith is another matter. Dr Purdue has argued that for a party agent to stand against the body that had employed him was like 'an accountant who uses his knowledge of his employer's finances to enrich himself and ruin his employer'. He also cited Samuel Maccoby, who later lived in the constituency. Maccoby wrote in his history of Radicalism, 'By the standards of that day Henderson's action was not very straightforward for he had been paid for over seven years to nurse the constituency's Liberalism and Radicalism'.[8] Yet it was Sir David Dale and the other leading Liberals who pressed Henderson to stay on as agent after his selection as the Iron Founders' candidate and after Pease announced his intention not to stand again, and it seems likely that they may have built up Henderson's hopes that he might succeed him as MP. Moreover at this stage of the LRC's development, with Shackleton and Crooks newly elected, men so close to the Liberal and Liberal–Labour outlook, the position was not as clear cut as it would appear after 1918 when Labour was unequivocally not an auxiliary progressive force to the Liberals. That Jack Pease remained on friendly terms with Arthur Henderson, and that prominent North-East Liberals such as Dr Spence Watson and the Revd Canon Moore Ede were supportive, suggest that Henderson's determination to be a Labour candidate was not seen as ignoble by all Liberals, especially when Liberal–Labour accord was in the air.

By mid-April 1903 the Barnard Castle Liberal Association's Selection Committee had decided by eight votes to six to recommend that Hubert Beaumont be invited to address an adoption meeting of the whole Association later in the month. Beaumont was a member of one of the old Liberal families of the North-East. At the adoption meeting thirty-four members tried to get the Association to support Henderson, but sixty-five opposed this. The meeting agreed to adopt Beaumont by fifty-eight votes to thirty-six. In London, Gladstone and his colleagues saw this as a set-back at a time when they were trying to avoid clashes with Labour. One wrote to Gladstone:

> It would have the worst possible effect on the working-class electorate and lay the Liberal Association and Party open to the charge of active hostility to Labour interests in the case of a Labour candidate already in the field. . . the only thing that I can see to do is to bring the strongest pressure on Beaumont himself to induce him to return from a rather undignified position and to avert a worse than useless struggle which would have far-reaching and unfortunate results. Don't let us play Keir Hardie's game for him.[9]

Whilst there was pressure from the Liberal party in London on Beaumont to withdraw, there were doubts as to whether Henderson should stand against a Liberal as well as a Tory. This was considered by the Iron Founders' executive at a special meeting at the end of April, with them deciding that he should continue as candidate for Barnard Castle.[10] Even with this verdict, Henderson appears to have had doubts as to whether he should continue, especially given his experiences in the Preston by-election of May 1903. The Labour candidate there was John Hodge of the Steel Smelters, the current chairman of the LRC. Ramsay MacDonald pressed Hodge hard to appoint Henderson as his agent for the by-election.[11] Henderson had been taking pains to cultivate Ramsay MacDonald. His letters to MacDonald in the spring and summer of 1903 strike a note of friendliness, sometimes even having a somewhat deferential tone. For his part MacDonald appears to have been very willing to tap Henderson's experience as a professional agent. In early May, the political sub-committee of the LRC's national executive made a report which urged that the LRC should produce a handbook on registration and electoral law. It strongly recommended that Henderson's 'long experience of Registration Law' should be used, with him writing that part of the handbook for a fee of £5. Henderson did take this on, preparing it even in the midst of the Barnard Castle by-election.[12]

Henderson had a hard time as agent in Preston. He wrote afterwards, 'it was one of the briefest contests on record'. The Tory mayor called the poll for the earliest date legally possible. Henderson found very poor organization in the constituency—'the register was the worst I have seen'. Shortly before polling day he could only express the hope 'that this Tory citadel will receive a severe shaking'. Hodge was faced with opposition from both the Catholics and Protestants in the area. Moreover as the Labour party was later to find so often, whilst the trade union leaders backed the Labour candidate, this was not the case with ordinary members of unions which subscribed to the LRC, some of whom canvassed for the Conservative candidate. Hodge lost in what was a straight contest. While he polled 1,656 more votes than Keir Hardie had done in 1900, it was a disappointing result after the triumph of Woolwich.[13]

This failure in a straight fight with a Conservative, made Henderson doubtful about even standing in Barnard Castle. After Preston he wrote to MacDonald, 'I am satisfied that there is no possible chance of winning with three in the field'. Like Isaac Mitchell, the secretary of the General Federation of Trade Unions and prospective LRC candidate for Darlington, Henderson was worried that there were too many Labour candidates selected for the county of Durham for any real chance of getting Liberals to agree to free runs for some Labour candidates. Mitchell had demanded on 6 May that the national executive committee of the LRC should give consideration to reducing the number of candidates in Durham. This it did the next day, but decided to take no action. Indeed in that meeting they agreed to endorse Henderson as candidate for Barnard Castle and Frank Rose for Stockton. When MacDonald saw Henderson in Preston during the election he found him 'much less determined to fight' than he had been after his union executive's decision at the end of April. As a result MacDonald got the LRC leadership to agree not to publish its endorsement of Henderson's candidature for Barnard Castle until it was quite clear that he would stand.[14]

MacDonald disagreed with the LRC executive's decision on Mitchell's request. It was increasing not decreasing the number of candidates in Durham county. MacDonald wrote to Henderson on 20 May, 'Of course you know my own private opinion. It is that we are making a great mistake in running so many candidates in your particular corner'. He went on to assure him, 'I am doing all I possibly can to relieve the situation, but as you know these things take a little time'. MacDonald also gave the opinion, 'I do not see at the moment much chance of Stockton being surrendered, and from what I gather I do not [think] that a surrender at Barnard Castle will satisfy the Liberals'.

It is quite possible that Henderson, a skilled trade-union negotiator, was trying to put pressure on the LRC leadership to get a two-way fight. He wanted action from them to get withdrawals elsewhere, notably of Rose in Stockton. There are signs that he was stretching the truth in order to get his way. Hughes informed MacDonald (also on 20 May):

> Henderson tells me that there is a feeling at headquarters that we are making a mistake in contesting so many places in Durham. He thinks that if Rose retired the Liberals would leave D'ton and Bd. Castle alone. He has been at me two or three times to go down to Stockton and try and bring this about. To further spur me on, I suppose, he now tells me—*in confidence*—that if Rose does not retire he will have to—as his ex. will not allow him to contest if he is opposed by a Liberal. I have pointed out to him the harm resulting from such an action on his part, and have suggested that before he takes any steps of that description rep [representatives] from Stockton, D'ton and Bd. Castle should meet and talk the matter over.[15]

Earlier Henderson had told MacDonald himself that his executive might not finance a three-way fight. MacDonald, however, noted that Maddison, the Iron Founders' Secretary, 'gave me to understand the contrary'. From the union's executive minutes it does not appear that they were out to stop Henderson fighting a three-way contest. Indeed in his letter to MacDonald of 19 May Henderson had asked MacDonald for help with his union's executive if he withdrew from Barnard Castle.

In all this Henderson had to recognize that there was great enthusiasm among LRC supporters in the constituency for him to fight the seat. This enthusiasm appears to have stopped Henderson from further equivocation. A very successful meeting on 23 May seems to have been decisive. He wrote to MacDonald,

> We had a splendid gathering and I see no other course than of going full steam ahead. The delegates will hear of nothing else and I am strongly of opinion that we ought to have at least half a dozen good meetings and give the Division a boost in that way...
>
> I have made up my mind to go on and, if I have to move, your Committee and my Executive will have to drag me out by my neck. So I think you had better announce your endorsement of my candidature and make up your mind to give me all the help you can.

MacDonald assured Henderson 'as you have decided to go on you can rely upon our best to back you up'.

It was agreed at the meeting on the 23rd, held in the Temperance Hall at Bishop Auckland, to set up the Barnard Castle Parliamentary Division Labour and Progressive Association. The Association was to have Henderson as its president, two county councillors as its chairman and secretary and a district councillor as its treasurer. It was to have paying individual members, ward committees and an active women's section. Before Henderson's arrival in the constituency there was a flourishing small branch of the ILP at Crook. However most of his votes came from the mining villages and, according to the Liberal *Westminster Gazette*, 'to the Durham miner the ILP has long been anathema, and is looked upon almost with the same suspicion as the Conservative organisation'.[16]

With Sir Joseph Pease's death a month later, Henderson had the benefit of knowing he had enthusiastic support. In contrast, on the Liberal side, the national leadership still wanted Beaumont to withdraw. Jack Pease wrote to Gladstone enquiring,

> whether anything is being done at headquarters to prevent the split of the Labour and Liberal votes ... which must almost inevitably give the seat to the Tories if both Henderson and Beaumont go to the poll. I had a call today from Hubert Beaumont asking for my support for his candidature. I did not commit myself to assisting either himself or Henderson. I pointed out the difficulty of an official Liberal opposing a Labour candidate at the very time when the Liberals were endeavouring to come to an arrangement with Labour reps. throughout the country and how much I was indebted to Henderson's assistance in the Saffron Walden division.

Beaumont, however, was very willing to take on a Labour opponent. He wrote to Charles Trevelyan, 'What I am doing now, all you Liberal members with large working class constituencies will have to do within the next ten years, because if you don't smash the Independent Labour party now ... they will smash the Liberal party as they avowedly say they wish to do'.[17] So Beaumont did not withdraw and Pease did endorse the official Liberal candidate.

However, the campaign was a dire one for the local Liberals. Firstly it was common knowledge that the Liberal party nationally did not want opposition to Henderson and no national speakers came in support of Beaumont. Secondly, Beaumont was harmed by the views and activities of his mentor, Samuel Storey, chairman of the Northern Liberal Federation and former MP for Sunderland. Earlier in the year Joseph Chamberlain launched his Tariff Reform Campaign, thereby challenging free trade, an almost sacred doctrine with Liberals and most of Labour. In the by-election Beaumont followed Storey in welcoming the call for an inquiry into the matter. Henderson was thus able to make much of his unequivocal opposition to Chamberlain's proposals—'every vote given for an inquiry was a vote given for a tax on food'.[18]

Storey also tried to be too clever in twice offering Beaumont's withdrawal if Henderson gave satisfactory pledges. On the first occasion Henderson was invited to pledge support for the Liberal party other than on purely Labour questions. Henderson could not agree to this as he was union-sponsored, and his union's membership held a full range of political opinions. He did, however, promise the Liberals support if they moved to enact his election programme, a set of policies which would have offended very few Liberals. On the second occasion he was challenged to support the Liberal–Labour candidates of the Durham miners. Henderson, who was close to Lib–Lab miners such as Sam Woods, was happy to reply, 'I say emphatically and deliberately that if the Durham miners by their vote return me as a Labour candidate I unhesitatingly promise to go and support the Durham miners' Labour candidates in return'. Storey's attempt to claim that this was not good enough and that Beaumont should not withdraw seemed to many, including the President of the Durham Miners' Association, to be less than honourable and did Beaumont much harm.

In these circumstances Henderson appeared to be the unequivocal champion of free trade against the threat of protection. He also advocated legislative action to remove the Taff Vale threat to the unions and in general terms he condemned 'the aggregation of capital by the formation of the huge trusts, the high pressure of modern industry and its effect on employment, the terrible problem of slumdom'.[19] Overall his policies were likely to appeal to most Liberals in the constituency. This temperance advocate and Nonconformist preacher could hardly be mistaken locally as an extremist, even if some Liberal newspapers chose to suggest his candidature was the work of 'socialist wreckers'.

Henderson was careful to keep Keir Hardie and other ILP leaders out of the constituency, just as had been done in Clitheroe, Woolwich and Preston. Asked by a reporter about Hardie, 'Mr. Henderson snapped out with startling acerbity, "Don't talk to me about Mr. Keir Hardie—I'm not a member of the ILP, and I know nothing about him"'. Later, in the mid-1930s, when Sir Stafford Cripps was being kept away from by-elections, Henderson was to say that he had to do the same with Keir Hardie 'with K.H.'s complete understanding and approval'. However, at the time MacDonald was writing to Henderson to say that Hardie felt hurt at being excluded and warned that the ILP might have to consider 'how far the party can support candidates who deliberately plan to reject its speakers'. In contrast, Henderson was eager to have moderate figures such as Crooks and Hodge support him, and even tried to get John Burns down, who had spoken for Crooks in his by-election but who was drifting away from independent Labour. He was also very eager to have Ramsay MacDonald come to speak for him. When Hodge joined Henderson in pressing MacDonald to speak on the eve of the poll he commented, 'We have so few discrete speakers to rely upon'. Given the problems Beaumont faced and the support given to Henderson, the by-election became very important to the LRC. MacDonald observed on 3 July that 'it will give the movement a very great blow if he should beat Henderson after all in the poll'.[20]

Henderson knew the constituency well and so the organization was much better than the last-minute efforts made in Preston. Henderson had his headquarters at Crook, at the mining and industrial end of the geographically large constituency. His campaign benefited from being sponsored by his union, £800 being sent to him during the campaign.[21] This sponsorship was especially important in a county campaign. While the other candidates had the use of motor cars, he had to rely on the railway and a two-horse carriage. Above all, Henderson was fortunate that the Liberal campaign lacked national support and the candidate's views were suspect, from a Liberal point of view, on what was fast becoming the key issue in British politics. He was also fortunate that the political tide had turned against the Conservatives and that in that constituency the progressive vote could be split without impairing his cause.

The result was announced on 25 July 1903. It showed that Henderson beat Vane, the Conservative candidate, by forty-seven votes, with Beaumont coming third. Henderson polled 3,370, Vane 3,323 and Beaumont 2,809 in a heavy poll on an old electoral register. *The Times* on 27 July laid stress on the good weather on polling day as a cause of Colonel Vane's failure to capture the seat—for, as both its report and editorial commented, 'the result might have been very different, as many farmers and farm-hands would not give up the time to vote'. Others saw the result as a verdict against Joseph Chamberlain's tariff reform campaign. Herbert Samuel, then a newly elected Liberal MP, wrote to his wife, 'The Barnard Castle election is another blow to Chamberlain's policy —and a blow also to "official Liberalism".' Samuel, a month earlier, had been expressing to MacDonald the hope that a Liberal–Labour

deal could be arranged which would cover the parliamentary seats of
county Durham.[22] The main issue was the effect it would have on Liberal
party relations with the labour movement. One of Herbert Gladstone's
colleagues wrote to him.

> The figures are remarkable.
> Henderson will be as right as can be in the House. The question rather
> is—what effect will the B.C. result have on the Labour folk in the North
> of England in particular? It makes for trouble I am afraid.[23]

After the declaration of the poll, Henderson said that the election had
proved 'that the workers of the country had become alive to their interests,
and were determined to do their political work in their own way, believing
themselves to be competent to do it equally well as those who proposed
to do it for them'. That evening he visited several mining areas in the
constituency, including Crook and Cockfield, and addressed his supporters. At Cockfield he declared:

> ... the Progressive forces were united at Woolwich. At Barnard Castle they
> were divided ... but nothwithstanding that fact the cause of the workers
> had secured a splendid triumph. If the Liberal Party were prepared to consider
> the Labour Party then what was accomplished at Woolwich might again
> be accomplished.
> If on the other hand they dared to set aside the will of the organised
> workers they must be taught the lesson that they had been taught at Barnard
> Castle.[24]

Not surprisingly, Henderson's victory was received with bitterness by
some local Liberals. During the campaign some had persisted with the
untrue story that Henderson had kept the Liberal party's marked registers,
in spite of Henderson's clear denial. After the election, the Iron Founders'
executive resolved, 'That Mr. Henderson be allowed to use his own dis-
cretion in the libel case'. Henderson let the matter go then, but when
it was repeated in the 1906 general election, he took action, secured
damages and presented the money to a local charity.[25]

Immediately after his victory, Henderson began preparing for the next
campaign. He raised this work with his union executive, which resolved
on 31 July 1903, 'That the register in the Barnard Castle Division be
attended to as suggested by Mr. Henderson, but it is expected that the
cost of the same will come out of the general election expenses fund
estimated at £150 per year'. However, when he tried to go further and
get agreement for a permanent registration and election agent in Barnard
Castle, costing more than the £150, the executive refused his request.

When he arranged that the matter be voted on by the full union membership, the executive did not recommend support for his proposal. In a vote on the issue the membership rejected it by 3,374 votes to 1,402.

In looking at Henderson's early career, especially before the payment of MPs from state funds in 1911, it needs to be emphasized just how close he was to his union. The terms of his sponsorship laid down that he worked under the supervision of the Iron Founders' executive committee. In September 1903 the executive held a special meeting, the main business of which was 'a very lengthy discussion on Mr. Henderson's procedure in his organising work, and travelling expenses to and from Darlington during the time Parliament is in session'. This ended in an agreement he would be allowed third-class railway fare once every three weeks to Darlington, with additional travel allowances only if urgent business took him to his constituency.

As one of the very few LRC MPs, he was soon in demand as a speaker. Early on, the executive made it clear that his travel expenses to such meetings should normally be paid by the organizers. In October 1903 the executive resolved, 'That Mr. Henderson be informed that all future engagements outside the Society must be made subject to his services not being required by the society, which must have the preference where possible'.[26] The Iron Founders were proud to have Henderson as their star speaker at labour rallies, such as that held in Hyde Park on 26 March 1904 against the use of Chinese labour in South Africa.

Henderson still worked for the union, using his home in Darlington as his office. After his election to Parliament, he investigated irregularities in many Iron Founders' branches, including those at Blaydon, Gloucester and Swansea. He also negotiated with management where the union had special difficulties, as with the General Electric Company at Witton, Birmingham and at Entwistle's, Bolton, and he became involved in organizing the union's response to the introduction of premium bonus systems in Barrow and elsewhere. One of his major functions as organizer was to spearhead the union's membership campaigns. In the later summer and early autumn of 1904 he campaigned in south Wales, where he found several districts 'largely untouched by trade unionism'. He spoke at public meetings in the main towns. He reported back to his union's members of the case that he had made for joining their craft union:

> At each meeting I spoke on 'Trade Unionism and Labour Politics', pointing out that present day industrialism made it imperative that the 'workers' should be combined, and that the principle of combination should be so applied

as to become the instrument for securing to them a fuller share of the fruits of their labour. The claims of our society upon all connected with the 'craft' was urged because of its long and useful history, its financial stability, and its activities in the 'Labour Representation Movement'.

However, as he later observed, he was primarily the union's parliamentary representative and could only fit in such activities as recruitment drives in between parliamentary commitments. When Henderson ceased to be organizer as well, on 1 July 1911, the union appointed two full-time officers who could stay in places for weeks, if necessary, in order to organize recruitment.

The payment of MPs in 1911 led to this change. Henderson, who had become president of the union in 1910, still maintained his close links with the Iron Founders. Its executive maintained the right to use him 'for attending conferences with employers provided his Parliamentary work will permit'. If so, then the terms would be as for any union delegate. The union continued to sponsor his election expenses and to provide 'a sum not exceeding £150 per annum towards registration and meetings in the constituency and clerical assistance for work connected with the Parliamentary position'.[27] In going ahead to select a candidate to sponsor for Parliament, the Iron Founders had laid down loose conditions for that person if elected—he would 'be allowed a free hand ...so long as he votes with the Labour Party on matters pertaining to the welfare of the unions'. Within a year of being elected to Parliament Henderson was in the midst of a major row which shook the fragile unity of the LRC.

Henderson, Shackleton and Crooks were all happy to speak on behalf of pressure groups which often appeared to be adjuncts to the Liberal party. In June 1904 Henderson and Shackleton spoke against the Tory Government's Licensing Bill in Market Harborough, during a by-election meeting organized by the Leicester Temperance Union. Henderson had long spoken from temperance platforms, but this was in a by-election and the meeting called upon working men to support Philip Stanhope. The latter had been the likely Liberal candidate for Clitheroe and had stood aside to give Shackleton the seat. Henderson later warmly praised Stanhope's action. Their appearance in the by-election clearly indicated support for Stanhope.

They compounded this soon after by going with Will Crooks to speak in support of J. William Benn, the leading Progressive on the London County Council, in a by-election in Devonport. In this case they spoke on a Free Trade League platform, this time at the request of the local

LRC. Ramsay MacDonald afterwards wrote to the Devonport LRC and asked,

> How was it that your local LRC handed over the meeting to the Free Trade League? . . . I see no reason why the meeting should not have been held had it not been that the speakers distinctly advised the audience to vote for Benn . . . I am afraid it is going to do us a great deal of harm.

Among many of the ILP and LRC activists the MPs' action caused dismay. Keir Hardie complained of the three MPs revealing 'a tendency to merge in the Liberals'. Condemnation poured in from trades and labour councils, local LRCs and some trade unions around the country. The secretary of the Blackburn ILP reported that at their meeting they had unanimously condemned the three MPs' actions as being 'a gross violation of the spirit of the constitution of the LRC (which expressly provides that its members shall not identify themselves with or promote the interests of either of the two capitalist parties) and one calculated to cause distrust and dissension in the Labour ranks'.[28]

The conduct of the three MPs became a major issue for the LRC executive. Henderson and Shackleton, being members of it, offered explanations of their conduct at a meeting on 30 June. After the meeting the executive issued a press release, saying that it accepted their explanations 'but is of the opinion that inasmuch as such appearances during elections afford opportunities to the press to misrepresent and thereby weaken the LRC movement, it declares that in future the executive must decide what action, if any, should be taken at by-elections'.

At this time, Henderson still had not signed the LRC constitution. The LRC executive in March 1903 had decided to send the Newcastle resolution on independence to all affiliated societies running candidates. Henderson later claimed that he felt that this signature was superfluous since his union had accepted the LRC conditions. Nevertheless, trade union figures such as Henderson and Shackleton had at best been ambiguous in their attitudes to 'independence'. At the 1904 annual conference at Bradford in February David Shackleton had successfully moved the deletion of the words 'or resign' from a clause which had required candidates to pledge themselves to abide by decisions of the Parlimentary Labour Group. In so doing Shackleton had explained the difficulties which might face trade unionists:

> He and two other candidates in Lancashire had been asked 'What is your position on the question of child labour?' As a candidate, whatever his personal opinion might be, if he was to be the nominee of the textile workers,

he was bound to answer in harmony with the decision of the textile workers, and the result was that he could not support the raising of the age of children going to work to sixteen. It was quite possible if the matter came before the Labour group in Parliament, the majority would say 'Yes' . . .

Mr. Henderson had been in that position too. If he had pledged himself to support the Miners' Eight Hours Bill, he would not have been a member for Barnard Castle today.

Keir Hardie seconded Shackleton, observing that they should presume the men sent to Parliament 'were men who in the main endeavoured to perform their duty' and that such threats were unnecessary.[29]

Following the incidents at Market Harborough and Devonport the LRC insisted on signatures. Maddison, on behalf of the executive of the Iron Founders, accepted the LRC decision of 30 June on by-elections. His executive also agreed to 'request Mr. Henderson to sign the constitution of the LRC and accept all responsibility for such signature, in the event of exception being taken in future elections in his constituency'. Henderson now quickly signed the constitution, adding by his signature 'subject to conditions, Ironfounders Executive Committee'. Even after this, a month later in his regular column in his union's journal, Henderson still expressed the view that where there was no Labour candidate standing the LRC should back 'the candidate who is prepared to give us most in return'.[30]

Henderson, Shackleton and Crooks were hauled into line at a time when they were appearing to follow Richard Bell in supporting Liberal candidates. In Bell's case, he revelled in defying the LRC's independent line. By the end of 1904 he had been dropped from its list of candidates. The conduct of Henderson and the others at the two by-elections played into the hands of Bell and his supporters. Indeed, Bell wrote MacDonald a letter criticizing the LRC's press statement of 30 June on by-elections. He asserted that such a policy had been defeated at the 1904 conference and so the question arose as to 'whether the Committee itself. . . is not violating its constitution equally as much as my poor self who has sinned so much against it'.

Their actions also raised a complaint from Will Thorne on the left of the LRC, who had been pressed very reluctantly to abide by the constitution's stipulation that its candidates 'appear before their constituencies under the title of Labour candidates only'. Thorne observed that if they could break the rules 'then I do not see why I should not be allowed to do the same thing by describing myself as a Socialist and Labour candidate, which in my opinion is not such a violation of the LRC constitution as it is on the part of Messrs. Shackleton and Henderson supporting a Liberal hack'.[31] All this was a contrast to Henderson's firm line later in upholding party rules as chief whip in the House of Commons and as secretary of the Labour party. It was to be a case of poacher turned gamekeeper. It must be added, however, that Ramsay MacDonald and Keir Hardie's position at this time was highly unusual—demanding adherence by LRC candidates to an independent line from the Liberals yet themselves having made a secret electoral pact with Herbert Gladstone for the next general election. This reflected the ambiguity of Labour's early years, as did Henderson himself.

4

Working with the Liberals, 1906–1914

Some of the ambiguities in Henderson's attitudes towards independence for Labour disappeared with the scale of Labour's success in the 1906 general election. But, like Ramsay MacDonald, he was to be doubtful throughout the pre-war period as to whether Labour could be truly independent of the Liberal party and hold, let alone increase, its number of parliamentary seats. He saw Labour as a separate party, but for much of the period as one which acted as a pressure group in Parliament for labour reforms in much the same way as the Irish Nationalists pressed the Liberal governments on Irish issues.

He was unquestionably one of the ablest trade-union figures in the parliamentary Labour party before the First World War, along with David Shackleton and George Barnes. Though often relentlessly moderate in his political views, Henderson surpassed them in his dedication to politics and his ability often to readjust his position when it was falling out of line with the Labour movement. He not only represented a trade-unionism which was dedicated to conciliation rather than conflict in industrial relations, but he also reflected respectable working-class nonconformity. Indeed he was the embodiment of what the Labour movement owed to Methodism.

Wesleyan Methodism remained central to Henderson's life when he was an MP. When he moved his family from Darlington to Clapham Park in January 1906, they all went together on Sundays to the Wesleyan Methodist church in the High Street. Henderson became a major participant in Wesleyan Methodist affairs and was sometimes linked with the Liberal Cabinet Minister Walter Runciman in such activities. Henderson travelled miles to preach. Thus in August 1906, after a family holiday at Dovercourt on the East Coast, he diverted to Tredegar on his way

to the Trades Union Congress in Liverpool.[1] As well as being involved
in the main Wesleyan conferences, Henderson was a major figure in its
organizations to alleviate social problems—the Wesleyan Methodist
Union for Social Service and the Brotherhood movement. Henderson
was a committee member of both, and was one of the foremost speakers
at their public meetings.

In in his addresses to such Wesleyan public meetings Henderson blended
the Christian message with the social gospel. Speaking at Bradford at
a large Brotherhood meeting on 16 February 1908 he welcomed the current
situation when

> ... the great organised forces of Christianity recognised, as they never recog-
> nised before, that there was some positive relationship between the affairs
> of everyday life and the principles of their great Master. No longer were
> they satisfied with seeking to lead the individual to patient resignation with
> the things he possessed or did not possess. The doctrine of contentment
> had given way to one of divine discontent.

However he combined this message with the balancing thought that

> ... there was a tendency for the great mass of the workers to be too willing
> to come to the conclusion that all reform must be from without rather than
> from within. If wealth were redistributed it was possible that in some respects
> we might be worse, unless the redistribution was accomplished by moral
> and ethical improvement.[2]

He established himself as the leading Labour man in the Nonconformist
world. He was not alone in the parliamentary Labour party: of its thirty
members after the 1906 general election, eighteen claimed to be Nonconformists and six said they preached at Brotherhood meetings.[3] In May
1910 ten prominent Labour figures, including Henderson, Keir Hardie,
Philip Snowden, John Hodge, Will Crooks and George Lansbury testified
at a series of ten meetings in Browning Hall. The event was 'a *religious*
demonstration' aiming to 'win souls for Christ'. During the week, seventeen Labour MPs signed the interdenominational Fellowship of Followers
declaration:

> Jesus said: 'If any man would come after me, let him deny himself, and
> take up his cross and follow Me'.
>   Meaning so to follow Him, I wish to be enrolled in the Fellowship of
> Followers.

Henderson, who alone made two addresses, spoke to the theme,

> If reformation and reform could have saved the world, the world would

have been perfect long ago. What we want along with our reforms is the spirit of regeneration.[4]

Henderson and other Nonconformist Labour people were crucial in attracting support away from the Liberals to Labour. In places such as Loughborough, the early Labour Party gained able Nonconformist activists impressed by Labour's social gospel. The spread of socialism among Nonconformists was deemed so widespread that a Nonconformist Anti-Socialist Union was set up. Its secretary, who proclaimed himself to be 'a Liberal, a Free Trader, a passive resister', complained in January 1910 that 'there could be no doubt that the nonconformist churches were very largely socialistic' and that 'over fifty per cent of their ministers had socialistic ideas'.[5] Whilst the statement was an exaggeration, the Christian social message put forward by Henderson and the others had a favourable impact among the 'respectable' working class.

Furthermore, Henderson was an avid supporter of the Temperance Fellowship, not only speaking himself but also organizing other Labour MPs such as Keir Hardie into giving support. He was the leading figure in the Trade Union and Labour Officials' Temperance Fellowship which met after the TUC and the Labour Party Conference. At its meeting after the 1909 TUC, he claimed that their Fellowship had played a major role in 'the vast change which had come over officials and delegates during the last few years' and he claimed great progress in their second aim of 'the transfer of the transaction of trade union work from public houses to unlicensed premises'. He himself was one of the 300 of the Fellowship who was a pledged total abstainer.

As such he was an eager speaker on temperance issues from the time he was elected to Parliament. He readily joined with Liberals in attacking Balfour's Unionist Government for its licensing proposals and with the coming of the Liberals to power he was a dependable supporter of their various proposals to tighten up the licensing laws. Indeed his normal posture at public meetings on temperance issues was to argue that the Liberal Government's proposals did not go far enough. Whilst chairman of the Labour party, Henderson appeared at several rallies organized by temperance societies to discuss the Liberal Government's Licensing Bill of 1908, which was eventually rejected by the House of Lords. On 16 May 1908 he spoke at a large rally at the Albert Hall, supporting the Bishops of London and Kensington and Lord Crewe. That October he was a major speaker at a Leeds conference promoted by the Sunday Closing Association. There he called for Sunday closing to cover clubs, and during his speech asserted that he 'was a very strong believer in the principle of entire Sunday closing'. He also was an advocate of local option (the right of communities to decide to prohibit the sale of alcohol in their areas).[6]

His frequent appearances on cross-party temperance platforms and the priority which he gave that cause led to adverse comments from those in the Labour movement less impressed by such a traditionally Nonconformist and Liberal issue. Ben Tillett, the dockers' leader, in one of his left-wing phases, vehemently attacked Henderson, Shackleton, Snowden and other temperance advocates in his pamphlet *Is the Parliamentary Labour Party a failure?*, published in 1908:

> I do not hesitate to describe the conduct of these blind leaders as nothing short of betrayal especially ... in that they have displayed greater activity for temperance reform than for Labour interests ... A great many of the victims to destitution will be in their graves before the Liberal Government will have approached the subject of unemployment ...

Henderson defended himself against Tillett by arguing that the parliamentary Labour party was not restricted to one issue and that on unemployment it was 'adopting different and, as he hoped, saner methods' than Victor Grayson, the independent socialist MP.[7]

The previous year Henderson's temperance activities had been a major cause of an attack on him in his union's journal at the time he was up for renomination as the Iron Founders' parliamentary nominee. Rees Davies, whom he had defeated in the contest for the post in 1902, complained, 'Our member takes great pains to magnify the virtues of the Liberals as compared with the Tories' rather than pursuing a policy of 'A plague on both your houses'. In specifically criticizing Henderson's temperance activities he quoted a newspaper report in which Henderson said 'that the workers had more to fear from the evils of drink and gambling than from capitalism'. Henderson responded by asking, 'Does he object to my using a portion of my time to propagate principles in which I conscientiously believe?' He added that if a majority of the union's membership felt that way he would stand down. He went on to express a view not dissimilar from those he held on Christianity and social change:

> That the workers suffer from the aggregation of private capital is obvious. I agree that the workers must in this as in other respects work out their own deliverance, by securing the legitimate transfer of capital to the use and for the benefit of the community as a whole. What I want to ask is, shall a change of such magnitude be accomplished by a democracy penalised

and paralysed by excessive drinking? My answer is, No. It is because I desire
to see the workers become the effective instrument of their own economic
and social freedom that I desire them not only be independent of the capitalist
and the orthodox politician, but also of the brewer and the distiller.[8]

While such views appalled the Left, they did Henderson no harm in attracting the votes of Liberal working men in a union election and were undoubtedly also in tune with the views of many in the Labour movement.

Henderson was not only an upright temperance supporter, he was also
the epitome of the moderate trade-union leader. When he gave up being
the Iron Founders' organizer in 1911 he proudly told his union's conference that as organizer he had been involved in the most difficult controversies over proposed changes in wage rates or working conditions and that
'in every case where I have been called in the changes have been effected
without a single day's work being lost'. He also claimed the credit for
persuading the union's executive committee to intervene and negotiate
before disputes resulted in 'the men [being] ... on the street'. As he put
it, twenty years of negotiating in the North-East engineering industry
'taught me... that it is pretty well a science to deal with employers successfully in these days'.[9]

He was firmly committed to the use of joint conciliation committees
and arbitration of industrial differences and so avoiding trials of strength
with powerful employers. In May 1908, during a dispute in the North-West
between the Shipbuilding Employers' Federation and their woodworkers,
when another 7,000 men were locked out, Henderson condemned the
employers' action as 'callous and disgraceful and dictated by the desire
that the heel of one party might be placed more firmly on the neck of
the other'. He contrasted this negative stance with the men's willingness
'to go to open arbitration and to set up permanent machinery in the
nature of a conciliation board and referees'. On a later occasion *The
Times* reported his comments:

> ... there were some people who thought that matters would not be put right
> until there was a stand-up fight with capital. That was not his view, and
> he was not going to encourage it. When he undertook a stand-up fight with
> capital he was going to be satisfied that both teams were sufficiently developed
> in the art of fighting and that they were somewhat equally matched. That
> was not the case with some of the industries who were talking about fighting
> today.[10]

Given such views, Henderson was one of the prominent trade-unionists
whom the Board of Trade approached to serve on the panel of worker

representatives on the voluntary court of arbitration which it set up when it changed its arbitration procedures in late 1908. He readily agreed. Shortly afterwards, when he was negotiating on behalf of his union the creation of a conciliation board for Lancashire, he pointed to this system and warmly recommended its use if local procedures failed to achieve agreement. He claimed to have been influential in getting the new system set up:

> ... I have pressed it upon those ... at the Board of Trade that no machinery ... is effective that does not provide for some final reference to a neutral authority instead of allowing all the conciliatory machinery to break-down and having recourse to strike or lock-out ...[11]

He must also have seemed to be a trade union leader more likely than most to support co-partnership in industry. When in the autumn of 1908 Sir Christopher Furness, a leading Liberal employer, made major proposals for such a scheme between workers and shareholders in his West Hartlepool shipyards, Henderson was very willing to listen to his plan. Furness's letter of invitation to Henderson and some of his parliamentary colleagues to the launching of his scheme began:

> Referring to our brief conversation some time ago at the House of Commons with reference to sectional strikes and your expressed readiness to promote any well considered scheme to secure more harmonious relations ... after very full and matured consideration I have evolved a set of proposals which ... I propose placing before the various trades unions represented in the shipbuilding yards on the North East coast.

In the event, both of Furness's options, namely selling his yards to the unions to work on a co-operative system or making the work-force limited co-partners, with special shares, participation in a works council but no strikes, were rejected by the unions. Henderson did no more than write a letter proclaiming the use of a board of conciliation with a final reference to a court of arbitration as his favoured way of resolving industrial disputes in the shipyards.[12]

Before the outbreak of serious labour unrest in 1911, Henderson declared in the House of Commons, 'There is ... a most encouraging tendency on the part of even our most highly organised trades to apply the principle of conciliation, but they desire to apply it altogether on the voluntary principle'.[13] Nevertheless, during the ensuing labour unrest, he joined Crooks, Barnes and Charles Fenwick (a miner who refused to join the Labour party) in tabling a bill in the House of Commons which would make strikes illegal unless thirty days' notice was given in advance and which laid down fines of between £10 and £200 as a penalty for anyone who 'incites, encourages or aids' a strike or a lock-out. At the September 1911 TUC, Crooks's Labour Disputes Bill was unanimously condemned and Congress reprimanded the four for putting it forward 'without the consent or authority of either the trade unionists of the country or the Labour Party' and stating that 'we desire to make it clear that we will, by every means in our power, resist every attempt to prevent or hinder the right of workers to strike at any time when they consider such action necessary in defence or furtherance of their rights'.

It is strange that Henderson could join in an action which so misjudged the overwhelming view within the trade union movement, in which he was so firmly rooted. In the 1911 TUC debate miners condemned the bill as failing to understand their industry, for in the case of a dispute over working in abnormal places 'the whole work would be finished before the dispute could start'. Marsland of the Cotton Spinners acidly observed, 'We must have discipline both inside as well as outside of Parliament, and members of the Labour Party must be given to understand that they are not at liberty to introduce Bills on their own responsibility'. He added later, 'I can understand a Bill of this sort coming from an employers' association, from those who are interested in keeping the workmen down; but I cannot understand it coming from trade unionists'.[14]

In justifying himself to his union's membership, Henderson observed that whilst gains had been made by recent strike action, in the past strikes had caused widespread suffering. He went on to claim,

> It ought never to be forgotten that one important factor in setting the relations between Capital and Labour is ... public opinion. Now today this ... is in favour of better social and economic conditions, a fuller and more whole-some life for the workers then ever before.

He added that the bill provided the machinery to expose bad conditions.

> Of this I am convinced: if the democracy of this country are going to pin their faith to the policy of strike, strike, strike they will before long experience a rude awakening ...
>
> All workers are not prepared, just as all employers are not prepared, to confer, to reason, to recognise. So I think, before involving others in loss and suffering, the law should compel them to let the light of day in upon their position.[15]

Thus his position was at the other end of a spectrum of trade-union thinking from syndicalists, Marxists or even ILP activists.

It is, therefore, not surprising that later in 1911 when the Government set up an Industrial Council to help deal with industrial unrest, Henderson was one of the prominent trade-unionists invited to be a member. The Industrial Council was set up to consider and inquire into such disputes in Britain's major industries as the Government referred to it. It had no compulsory powers and the Government took pains to emphasize that the Government did 'not desire to interfere with but rather to encourage and foster such voluntary methods or agreements as are now in force'. In setting it up, the Liberal Government was soothing the electorate by marshalling together centre opinion in British industry. Places on the Industrial Council were filled by government invitations; not by election or nomination by the TUC, employers' organizations or any other such bodies. The TUC's Parliamentary Committee was divided as to whether its members who accepted the invitation should be congratulated or condemned.

The Government's commitment to such a national conciliation body proved to be neither great nor lasting. As Sir George Askwith, who was both its chairman and the Government's Chief Industrial Commissioner, later wrote, 'When the crisis of acute strikes had passed, they quickly dropped it, without referring any more questions to its judgement, or maintaining its existence for possible emergencies'.[16] In spite of being on the largely ineffective Industrial Council, Henderson would be involved after the First World War with the similar National Industrial Conference.

During the pre-war labour unrest, Henderson also served on a Royal Commission established by the Government to try to resolve trouble on the railways. This stemmed partly from the breakdown of a conciliation scheme set up in 1907, when a dispute on the railways had led to intervention by Lloyd George, President of the Board of Trade. Henderson and other leading Labour figures had tried at that time to help achieve a settlement. Henderson had been critical of the 1907 conciliation scheme from its outset, observing,

> I am a strong believer in the principle of conciliation as a factor in the settlement of our industrial difficulties, but I fail to see why, if this method had to be adopted, it should not have carried with it ... recognition of the railwaymen's unions ... I trust the men will continue their efforts to increase the number of those in the union for, unless they do, there is danger of the machinery being used to bring about the undoing of their organisation. If great care is not exercised it may prove to be a case of signing the agreement in haste and repenting in leisure.[17]

When unrest erupted on the railways in August 1911 Henderson was once again one of the Labour party leaders involved in trying to reach a settlement. Along with MacDonald and Roberts, he urged the railwaymen to accept the Government's offer of a small Royal Commission to investigate the conciliation scheme. Henderson enjoyed good relations with Jimmy Thomas, the assistant secretary of the Amalgamated Society of Railway Servants and, from 1910, a Labour MP; and he had supported the union and Labour's policy of nationalization of the railways.[18] Given this and his long commitment to conciliation and arbitration, he was an obvious choice to go on the Commission as a person in whom the railwaymen would have confidence.

However his role was to immerse him in controversy again. In early November, two weeks after the Royal Commission's Report was presented, he described his position on the Commission as 'the most difficult, if not the most dangerous, he had ever been called upon to fill'. The problem for him was that calling off the strike and the acceptance of the Royal Commission in the first place was deemed by some militant railwaymen and socialists as 'the greatest betrayal of modern times'. Worse still, was that the railwaymen were bitterly disappointed with the Commission's report. It failed to recommend outright union recognition and it involved making some changes which the Amalgamated Society of Railway Servants felt were detrimental. The unions rejected the report and held a ballot to resume a national strike.

Henderson was enraged by Hardie making irresponsible comments about the Commission before its work began and by the strength of Hardie's and other socialists' condemnation of the report. Hardie was appalled by the Liberal Government's use of troops in the interests of the railway companies, especially when at Llanelli troops killed two people when crowds threw stones. However in condemning the Government in a leaflet *Killing No Murder: the Government and the Railway Strike*, published in September, he wrote that when the union leaders accepted the Royal Commission they were told that 'it would be so loaded so as to make sure of its findings being in favour of the men'. Not surprisingly Henderson was outraged, and wrote to MacDonald that 'it almost involves us in a breach of faith ... It is going to be impossible for any of us to conduct negotiations for the party if this sort of line is going to be followed'. When the Tory press made much of it, he wrote again to MacDonald stressing the seriousness of it to them and the Labour party as a whole, 'Strongly as I felt a week ago, my feelings then were nothing in comparison to what they are now'. Henderson, MacDonald and Roberts responded by issuing through the Labour party's office a lengthy statement of what had been promised to the railway leaders, including a comment that their confidence that the men would benefit from a Royal Commission was 'based not on the biased character of the Court, but on the justice and reasonableness of the men's claims'.[19] Perhaps this incident encouraged Henderson to compromise more with the employers' representatives on the Commission than he might have done.

He responded to the hostility expressed by the railwaymen, Hardie and other socialists by making several speeches around the country. He put the case for the report's recommendations and the justifications for his not submitting a minority report. When in December 1911 the railway unions reached an agreement, Henderson could say that it was 'what I have been working for ever since the report of the Commission was published' and he claimed that 'the representatives of the railway companies, once they had had the experience of recognition of the unions, would see, as so many other employers have done, the wisdom of settling differences with the officials of the unions'.[20]

However, it needs to be emphasized that Henderson did not recommend that labour should renounce the strike weapon. Indeed on occasions when he felt the employers were being aggressive, he supported militant action. Thus, when there was a dispute in the south Wales coalfield in 1909 over the owners' interpretation of the Eight Hours Act, Henderson declared

> The struggle, once entered upon, could not be confined to that section of organised labour which was represented by the Miners' Federation. It would be essential that the whole body of organised labour should stand behind the men directly affected, and ... organised labour, when it recognised the menacing position which the coal owners were taking up, would do everything in its power to assist the miners to obtain the fruits of victory.

Henderson's usual moderation as a trade union leader and his various roles in conciliation schemes, however, led to speculation that he might follow David Shackleton and other trade union officials into a Whitehall post. Shackleton accepted the post of Labour Adviser to the Home Office in late 1910 and did not stand in the December general election. When being adopted in Barnard Castle for that election, Henderson issued a denial that he was 'going to get an appointment' and stated 'that no position that this government or any other government could offer him should be accepted, no matter what the remuneration was'. When in 1911 Shackleton vacated his Home Office post to become a National Insurance Commissioner, Henderson felt it necessary to issue to the press the disclaimer:

> Mr. Henderson states that he has no intention of abandoning his work in
> the Parliamentary Labour Party, and, if the position of Labour Adviser to
> the Home Office were officially offered him he would feel bound to decline
> in order to continue his present work.[21]

He saw his work in Parliament as being part of a pressure group to
achieve reforms for the Labour movement. He also saw his own role
very much as one of encouraging trade-unionists to back the Labour
party. He expressed his view of the Labour party's particular functions
very lucidly in a circular to affiliated trade unions after the passage of
the 1913 Trade Union Act. In it he wrote,

> In these days Parliament touches Labour interests at many points, and
> whether the legislative concerns itself with the operation and insurance, piece-
> work particulars, factory and workshop conditions, general trade union
> rights, or the larger questions arising out of industrial disputes on a national
> scale—in these and all similar matters the experience of recent years has
> demonstrated that even a Labour minority of 40 in a House of Commons
> of 670 members has been able to affect administration and legislation in
> a manner that otherwise would have been impossible.

This broadly summarizes Henderson's own parliamentary activities on
labour matters. He also made clear in the circular that trade union action
was no longer enough 'so long as employers continue to supplement their
industrial influence by political power'. He observed, 'When capital
throws away its political weapons it will be time enough for Labour to
consider whether its interests lie in exclusive reliance on the strike and
industrial negotiation'.[22]

Before the 1906 general election Henderson had still been keen to promote such 'Labour issues' through united action with the Lib–Lab MPs
in Parliament. In his union's journal in April 1905 he had expressed the
hope that before long there would be 'all the Labour Members sitting
together giving each other that mutual help and consideration which
would make them individually and collectively more influential and effective'. Such a development would 'demonstrate the solidity of Labour
inside the House must tend towards the success of Labour in the country
and at the polls'. In 1905 he had set as a target getting 'the working
population' to elect 'forty or fifty members in the name of Labour', by
which he meant Lib–Labs as well as Labour party. Yet he also quoted
with enthusiasm in 1905 an appraisal of the parliamentary Labour party
published in the *British Weekly* which stated they were 'men who may

find models in the [Irish] Nationalist Party rather than the familiar "Liberal and Labour" combination'.

After his target number of 'Labour' MPs was met in the 1906 general election, Henderson became less equivocal about the viability of an independent Labour party. He told *Reynolds News* that Labour's success was 'little short of phenomenal' and as a result 'British politics knows for the first time a separate, distinct and highly organised Labour Party'. As president of the party conference in mid-February 1906 he proclaimed Labour's role in Parliament as one whereby it would 'give support when it is possible and oppose where it is necessary', keep 'the government up to the scratch of their professions' and 'promote legislation to heal the deep social wounds and to right the industrial wrongs from which people suffer'.[23]

The parliamentary Labour party of 1906 was dominated by trade-unionists. Twenty-three of its members had been nominated by unions and only six by the ILP. Six of the trade-unionists, however, were also active ILP members. Thanks to their abilities and experience in the previous Parliament, Shackleton and Henderson became Labour's leading trade-union figures. Shackleton, beaten by one vote by Hardie in the election for the chair of the parliamentary party, became vice-chairman. He was to win the warm admiration of his colleagues in Parliament and the members of the Joint Board (an important Labour body made up of representatives from the Parliamentary Committee of the TUC, the executive committees of the General Federation of Trade Unions and the Labour party which had been set up in November 1905) for his leading role in improving the Trade Disputes Bill during its passage through Parliament in 1906.[24] Shackleton's prominent role became even greater following Keir Hardie's breakdown in health in April 1907 and he led the parliamentary party for the rest of the year.

Henderson's position in the parliamentary party also became stronger during this period. He was always happiest when he had his hands on the levers of power within the Labour party but was not the titular leader. The post of Chief Whip, which he took on first from February 1906 until January 1908, suited him well—as did the post of secretary of the Labour Party which he later held. Like Shackleton, Henderson carried out functions that Hardie preferred to delegate. Snowden later recalled that Hardie 'left the arrangement of business, which must necessarily be carried through by conversations with the Government Whip, largely to Mr. Henderson'. Unlike many of the trade-union MPs, Henderson was willing and able to put in long hours at the House of Commons being there usually from the early afternoon when it was in session. As Chief Whip, Henderson was firm with his colleagues. John Hodge told one of Henderson's sons, in the latter part of the First World War, 'Your father is a dictator. He has to have his own way'.[25] Both as a trade-union official and as Chief Whip, Henderson was prone to display intolerance of dissent.

In this period Henderson also developed links with the TUC, though in this he was very much in the shadow of Shackleton, who had the rare honour of being chairman of the Parliamentary Committee of the TUC for two terms from 1907 to 1909.[26] Henderson was the fraternal speaker from the Labour party at the TUC in 1906, 1907 and 1908. On the first occasion he assured Congress,

> It was for them to create and develop public opinion so far as great industrial questions were concerned, and it was for the Labour Party to seek to give legislative expression to the needs of Congress on the floor of the House of Commons ... No greater traitor, no greater 'scab' could exist outside the Labour movement and outside the trade union movement than the man who might be inside, and who might by word or act to seek to make ineffective and to render asunder that unity and that completeness which had demonstrated itself in the movement during the present year.[27]

He measured the Labour party's success in terms of delivering legislation, both for the trade union movement and for the wider working class. This approach to politics made many in the ILP uneasy. Snowden later regretted the way that the 'character of the Labour propaganda had been changed'. He observed that the Party had become concerned 'only with material reforms' and that with the abandonment of 'the old socialist propaganda ... a good deal of the idealism had been lost'.[28] Such tension between the trade union and the ILP wings of the parliamentary party was to be long in evidence.

At first Henderson, Shackleton and the other trade unionists were vindicated. Henderson triumphantly observed in his union's journal at the start of 1907,

> Notwithstanding the carping criticism to which the Labour Party has been subjected, its achievement in the first Parliamentary session since its creation is such as all who assisted in its return may well feel greatly proud. I admit they have done nothing of a very revolutionary character. For this purpose they were not elected.

He then listed at length the parliamentary Labour party's achievements, in particular the Trades Disputes Act, which reversed the Taff Vale Judgement, the Workmen's Compensation Act and the Education (Provision of Meals) Act. However, popular enthusiasm for Labour appears to have reached its peak in the summer of 1907, with Labour and Socialist victories in by-elections at Jarrow and Colne Valley. After all the bragging of the achievements of 1906, Henderson had to confess in September 1907 that 'Labour has fared badly this Session, it having been practically a blank from the industrial standpoint'. At the start of 1909 he was admitting of the previous session, 'From the Labour standpoint it cannot be claimed that the harvest is plentiful ... The meagre output of an eight month's session is another evidence of the slowness of the Parliamentary machine'.[29]

Thus when he succeeded Hardie as chairman of the parliamentary Labour party on 28 January 1908 the policy of working with the Liberal Government and extracting legislative concessions was already beginning to look like a failure. He was soon being criticized by leading ILP figures such as Bruce Glasier for 'playing the Liberal game'. Glasier complained to MacDonald in November 1908, 'His eternal appearances on Temperance and Methodist platforms and the absence of a single proclamation from him of a leadership order gives countenance to those miserable hints and accusations in the Dispatch and elsewhere that the party is becoming merely a Liberal tail'. Ironically Glasier in early 1906 had urged Hardie to decline the chair, arguing,

> If Henderson, Shackleton, or even Barnes accepts the position you nevertheless will be the fighting front. Besides, though this is comparatively unimportant, if a trades unionist takes the post it will tend to keep the trade unions in the country loyal to the movement. If you and our men can lead the socialist line, then in a few years the party will be a socialist party ... [30]

As chairman Henderson lacked Hardie's charisma and socialist fervour. But he also lacked Hardie's erratic and unmethodical ways. Whereas Hardie had followed his own path, failing to consult with Shackleton, Henderson and MacDonald, Henderson acted much more as a spokesman. Snowden later observed,

> The Labour Party had always set its face against a permanent chairman, and had insisted that the Sessional chairman should not be regarded as the 'Leader'. It was considered to be undemocratic. The party must not permit one man to dictate the policy of the party. The chairman was simply the mouthpiece of the party, stating its decisions to the House of Commons. The party in turn was expected to take its directions from resolutions of the party conference.

Henderson, more than Hardie or MacDonald, carried out this role as a party functionary. Snowden, often a vitriolic critic, was much more appreciative of his performance than of Barnes, his successor. He wrote of Henderson,

> ... without being brilliant he discharged his difficult task with efficiency. He was not loquacious. He never spoke except when the occasion required, and then made a clear, business-like statement.[31]

As chairman, Henderson pressed for action on unemployment and various labour issues. In responding to the King's speech in January 1908 he spoke of unemployment being the most grave and menacing issue before the country and warned that if nothing were done 'you will have an almost uncontrollable army of unemployed'. He called on the Government to back Labour's Right to Work Bill if it had no measure of its own. With the economy in recession and the numbers of unemployed growing, the issue was taken to the streets in a series of tumultuous demonstrations and meetings.

The parliamentary Labour party came under increasing attack for ineffectiveness. Their lack of fire on the issue could be contrasted with the actions of Victor Grayson, who highlighted unemployment on 16 October 1908 by making a scene in the House of Commons and getting himself suspended. To the dismay of all Labour's leading parliamentary figures Grayson's activities were warmly received by many socialists in the country. Thus one ILP branch complained to MacDonald,

> The lives of the people are far more important than all the other questions that Parliament is 'gassing' about, and we ... feel that consideration of the unemployed question should be given precedence to all other business.
> ... If the Labour Party could not muster up sufficient courage to support him in his protest they could, at all events, have voted against his suspension ...
> In our humble opinion, the Labour Party have been too tame, too humble and submissive and content to patiently wait the time of the government.

In fact, with regard to Grayson, Henderson appeared to be an arch reactionary, for he had insisted after his election that he be not welcomed by the party at the House of Commons and later, when carrying out a procedural agreement with the Government to end a House of Commons debate at a certain time, moved the closure when Grayson was trying to speak.[32]

The same day that Grayson was suspended, Henderson warned the Liberal Cabinet that he would be unable to restrain extreme supporters of the Right to Work Council unless the Government did something. The Government responded by consulting him. He suggested that local authorities should be empowered to levy a penny rate to pay wages. But this was too radical for most of the Cabinet. Instead Asquith announced a relatively small package of extra relief measures in the Commons on 21 October. These measures were deemed inadequate by most in the Labour movement. When Henderson responded to the King's speech in February 1909, he condemned the Government for failing to find 'an effective and permanent remedy for the unemployment of starving, workless people that in tens of thousands are walking about the streets of the country'. He also emphasized that its proposed labour exchanges would provide no work, though he welcomed their more limited purpose and later called them 'a beginning in taking out ... the Right to Work Bill in penny numbers'. Overall, indeed Henderson was less than dynamic on Labour's prime issues of that period. Writing at the end of the year to Bruce Glasier, Hardie gloomily reflected, 'we are in for another year of Henderson's chairmanship which means that reaction and timidity will be in the ascendency with disastrous effects on our side of the movement'.[33]

Henderson also raised the issue of sweated labour in both of his responses to King's speeches as chairman. He and Shackleton both worked with Sir Charles Dilke in his attempts to eliminate sweated labour. In 1907 Henderson took up the same bill to secure joint boards with statutory wage fixing powers in sweated industries that Dilke had been promoting in earlier parliamentary sessions. Despite MacDonald's opposition, he successfully pressed the issue at the 1908 Labour party conference. In 1909 he welcomed the Government's Sweated Industries Bill but he complained that it was 'more of a permissive character' than the bill he had introduced, as it left the Board of Trade to determine which trades should be covered rather than specifying them. The bill once enacted, however, did not meet with trade union favour, because it did not ensure an adequate minimum wage. At the 1910 TUC, one delegate complained that 'if you wait until your Shackletons, Ramsay Macdonalds and Hendersons get you a 30s. [£1.50] minimum, you will have to wait for another sixteen years'.[34]

Henderson welcomed the Liberal Government's reforms but pressed for their scope to be wider. He had been at the forefront of Labour's efforts to secure school meals and had unsuccessfully introduced a bill in 1905. As chairman he tried to amend the Liberal's 1906 Act which permitted local authorities to provide school meals for necessitous children to be in line with Labour's earlier proposals to compel local authorities to make such provision. Again, at a special Labour party conference on pensions in January 1908 he moved the executive's resolution demanding a pension scheme which was 'non-discriminatory, non-contributory, and applies to those who have reached the age of sixty five or who are rendered unfit earlier'. Henderson called for such a scheme to be paid for 'by direct taxation on large incomes'.[35]

His stance was often indistinguishable from that of advanced Radicals. When Lloyd George introduced his radical budget in 1909 Henderson's words of praise were hardly the measured ones of a leader of an independent party. He told a miners' demonstration at Mountain Ash on 21 August,

> Mr. Lloyd George, instead of going to the already over-taxed working man ... was going to those who enjoyed the luxuries of life, to the owners of undeveloped land and the beneficiaries from unearned increment ... The people had created the value, and Mr. Lloyd George in this budget ... said that the people must enjoy a share of that which they had created. This was the most popular and most democratic budget ever introduced. When in the past they had pressed for social reform they had been met by the question—Where was the money to come from? Mr. Lloyd George had demonstrated where it could be obtained and, also, the potency of finance under a free trade policy.

Henderson had complained after the 1907 budget that 'the poor have no reduction in indirect taxation which presses so heavily upon them'. Lloyd George's 'People's Budget' was one which was in the general direction of the taxation policies agreed at the 1909 Labour Party conference. Henderson saw taxation changes as the major means of redistributing wealth. He was to attack Lloyd George's 1913 budget on the grounds that it did not abolish indirect taxation and he called for 'the entire system to be changed ... not only on account of the departure ... from the principle of ability to pay, but it makes the question of the physical well-being and social and economic necessity matters of secondary consideration'.[36]

His reception of the 'People's Budget' was not an isolated case of Henderson's expressing warm admiration for Lloyd George. At the beginning of the year he had informed his union's members 'I remain unconvinced that the government as a whole are determined to face the issue of the Lords' but added, 'I believe that some of the younger members of the

Cabinet, such as Lloyd George and Winston Churchill, are ready to push the battle to the gate'. Little wonder that Beatrice Webb observed in November 1910,

> The big thing that has happened in the last two years is that Lloyd George and Winston Churchill have practically taken the limelight, not merely from their own colleagues but from the Labour Party. They stand out as the most advanced politicians.[37]

Before the January 1910 election, Henderson bluntly declared in the Commons, 'we . . . will take our stand in favour of the whole of the principles contained in the budget'. Keir Hardie, speaking with Henderson at the south Wales miners' demonstration in Swansea in late September, also declared that 'the Labour Party intended to support the budget to the finish'. But he added, 'That must not be taken to mean that Labour had merged their independence and their identity in the Liberal Party'. In elaborating that remark Hardie asserted that Labour would make its own choice of where it ran candidates, and in any resulting three-cornered fights, they would leave 'the other parties to sink or swim as circumstances might dictate'.[38]

Henderson soon after carried out one of his characteristic political juggling acts, whereby he maintained maximum support for forces opposed to the House of Lords while able to tell party activists that no deal had been made with the Liberal party. Henderson stated in a series of speeches that Labour wanted more than clear runs for their existing MPs, an offer made by the Liberal Chief Whip; and he asserted that Labour was under-represented in the House of Commons. However, he floated the notion that a special Labour party conference could allow the executive to bend the constitution on independent action 'in order to expedite a victory for the budget'. This suggestion was not taken up, but the ILP's national council and the Labour party's executive did withdraw some thirty candidates where they felt there was little chance 'from the standpoint of organisation and money to fight with success'.[39]

So whilst Henderson could assert that the withdrawal of some Labour candidates was not a pact, Labour was very clearly helping the Liberal party. In truth, Labour did not bargain with the Liberals: it made outright concessions. Henderson and the *Labour Leader* urged voters in constituencies without Labour candidates to vote against supporters of the House of Lords. As a result Liberals such as Sir John Simon were pleasantly surprised to gain ILP support, without accepting the Right to Work Bill, and trade union support, without pledging to reverse the Osborne Judgement (which had sought to prevent the use of trade union funds for political or other non-industrial purposes).[40]

After the January 1910 election Henderson followed Hardie's precedent and stood down as chairman of the parliamentary party after two years. He was succeeded by George Barnes, whose leadership for a year from January 1910 was generally regarded as unsuccessful. Barnes tended to act impulsively and without consulting his colleagues. On several occasions he threatened to pursue independent action which might have brought down the Government. He received little support, except from Keir Hardie who himself was prone, as MacDonald put it, 'to regard himself as a free-lance when it suits him and as a member of a team when it suits'. T.D. Benson, the treasurer of the ILP, complained to MacDonald in early January,

> Barnes is making an absolute mess of the position of Leader and is saying all that he ought not to say and giving the show away as far as it can be done ... if the truth were stated it is Barnes himself more than any one else who is responsible for our troubles at the present moment.

In a further letter he urged MacDonald to take the chair, observing that Hardie was too individualistic and that 'Except for Henderson you have no leader'.

Henderson was also highly critical of Barnes's performance. Indeed at the start of 1911, when Barnes complained in his Parliamentary Report of his colleagues' slackness, timidity and failure to pressurize the Government, Henderson was incensed. He wrote to MacDonald that Barnes had struck a major blow against the parliamentary party since his criticism would be taken up by others including left-wing critics such as Victor Grayson and by the Tory press. Henderson said he would not support Barnes for re-election, observing, 'He has proved a conspicuous failure and now seeks to blame the party for all the failures and blunders of leadership'. Henderson continued, 'We must face the difficulty or the party will be broken. You ought in spite of all the drawbacks to throw yourself into the breach and accept nomination'.[41]

In pushing MacDonald towards the leadership, Henderson was in large part responding to the need to fill a vacuum at the top with a capable colleague. He was eulogistic in reporting MacDonald's election in his union journal.

> His services as secretary of the party he has assisted so much in making, his commanding influence and eloquence upon the conference platform ... his rapid progress to the front rank of Parliamentarians during the past

four years, alike testify to his fitness for his new post ... I am hoping that Mr. MacDonald will lead with such conspicuous success that when the time comes his unanimous election for a longer period than two years may be secured.[42]

He had found MacDonald to be a moderate ILP man, whose political views were usually similar to his own. MacDonald also was keen to secure social reforms through maintaining the Liberals in office. He, too, was irritated by the radical wing of the ILP, whom he termed 'phraseologists', and was willing to take a firm line against socialist dissidents such as Grayson. MacDonald's last address as ILP chairman in April 1909 expressed views that Henderson shared and was to express himself in similar terms when later condemning 'Direct Action':

> I sometimes receive resolutions beginning in this way, 'seeing that the unemployed are more important than the rules of the House of Commons'—you know the rest ... The opposition between Parliamentary procedure and the question of how to deal with the unemployed is purely a fictitious one. The unemployed can never be treated by any Parliament except by one which has rules of procedure and these rules must prescribe majority responsibility. Every facility given to the minority to impose its will upon the majority is a facility which any minority can use, and not merely a Labour or socialist minority. To protect the conditions and existence of democratic government is just as essential to the building up of the socialist state as is the solution of the problem of unemployment.[43]

However, their personal relationship had fluctuated in the past from extremely bad to quite good, and was to do so for the rest of their lives. MacDonald was highly sensitive about perceived slights, quick to fall into pained self-justification and evasive in arguments. Henderson himself was touchy, prone to be overbearing if he had majority support for his views, yet not one to hold grudges for long. Neither took kindly to criticism and both were capable of sulking if rebuffed. It was inevitable that they would on occasion clash.

Their most serious pre-war dispute took place in 1910 over Henderson's appointment to supervise the Labour party office when MacDonald went to India for the last three months of the year. Henderson sent in his resignation from the Labour party's executive committee in a huff over comments made by MacDonald and tried to make its withdrawal conditional upon MacDonald's comments being formally looked into 'in the interests of the harmonious working of the committee'. In a letter to the executive's chairman he complained, 'I understand that he intimated to members of the executive that he regarded my appointment as a personal insult. I felt this very much and considered that it was deserving of a personal explanation'.[44] MacDonald's remarks were unwarranted and unfair, but Henderson's response was hardly in keeping with his position as a leading politician. In an earlier clash, at the 1908 Labour party conference, MacDonald had been enraged when Henderson had vigorously refuted MacDonald's views on fixing minimum wages. According to one account, 'If MacDonald had a gun, he would have shot Henderson'. Apparently he did call him a 'bloody liar'.[45]

However in the years following the 1910 elections they usually worked together in harmony. As well as admiring MacDonald's abilities, Henderson felt that there was no acceptable alternative. In August 1912 when MacDonald was thinking that Snowden might challenge him if he continued beyond two years in the post, Henderson wrote, 'There is not the remotest chance of Snowden's election. You must buck yourself up and go through with it'. For Henderson, MacDonald was the leader who might control what he saw as the excesses of the ILP and so could maintain the balance between the trade union wing and the socialist wing of the party. Henderson supported him loyally through several party controversies—but he did warn him not to incline too much towards the ILP.

For Henderson, MacDonald was also an ILP figure who would work in Parliament to gain concessions from the Liberals. The January and December general elections had not made this task easier. Labour had gone into the elections as auxiliaries of the Liberals, and Labour had come out of them as such. For after the two elections the Liberal Governments depended on the support of the Labour party if the Irish Nationalists abstained, or just on the Irish Nationalists. But far from becoming more powerful in determining legislation, Labour became tame supporters of the Government. As Snowden later put it, 'To have recklessly turned out the Liberal government on some minor question would have been egregious folly. If a general election had followed upon the defeat of the government the result would have been that every Labour candidate would have had to face Liberal opposition, and not half a dozen Labour members would have been returned'. From 1911 Henderson and MacDonald expounded this case and warned of the problems of funding another early general election. Henderson, for example, when urging the Leicester Labour party not to run a candidate in a by-election 'repeatedly stated that we must keep this government in till next January because of the Trade Union Act, Home Rule' and other such considerations.[46]

In the December 1910 election Labour had attempted to differentiate itself more from the Liberals than it had done in the January contest by emphasizing its prime commitment to repeal the Osborne Judgement. On 18 November 1910 Henderson stated that 'until the Osborne Judgement is satisfactorily dealt with it cannot and will not be subordinated to any other question, no matter how important that question may be in the eyes of other parties'.

However after the election he and MacDonald took the pragmatic view that it was better to take what the Liberals offered, which was payment of MPs and some degree of improving trade-union law, than nothing at all. Indeed before the December election, speaking as the fraternal delegate from the Labour party at the TUC on 14 September—amidst heckling as to Labour's independence—Henderson had called upon delegates to remember that it had taken five years to get the Taff Vale decision reversed and had stated, 'If we secure payment of members it will be our best weapon in assisting to keep our movement together until we accomplish our ideal'.[47] MacDonald and Henderson were also willing to support Lloyd George's contributory National Insurance Bill. At his union's conference Henderson said,

> ... if we can adapt ourselves to the new circumstances, instead of this Bill being a hindrance or prejudicial to the union, I am convinced that it may be instrumental in advancing the interests of the Society. In fact I believe the object of the promoters—especially the Chancellor of the Exchequer—is, by attaching certain disabilities to those who go in for the Post Office scheme, to bring pressure to bear to get men into the trade unions or friendly societies.[48]

The trade union movement showed its support at a conference organized by the Joint Board in June 1911. Henderson's prediction that it would boost trade union membership was very much the case in some less organized groups of workers such as shop assistants. There was also the appeal that his union represented one of the industries covered by unemployment insurance.

Most socialists were highly critical of the majority of the Labour MPs supporting a scheme which did not redistribute resources to the needy. Several Labour MPs campaigned strongly against the Bill, and abused MacDonald in the process. Henderson complained in his union's journal of 'The unfortunate and unseemly wrangle in our ranks and amongst our own leaders':

> On a great and complicated measure like the Insurance Bill there must be differences of opinion amongst men who have learned to think for themselves.

> What there is no room for is the turning of the Labour Movement into a fighting arena, to enable our leading men to go for each others' throats. The annual conference or the weekly meeting is the proper place for discussing differences... The fact is, the elementary lesson of party discipline has yet to be learnt by men with large hearts and great intellects.

He was especially enraged by Hardie's speeches at public meetings, in which he made such comments as, 'It was evidently hoped that the measure would so placate and pacify the Labour Party that no more candidates would be run'.[49] He demanded that the next parliamentary Labour party meeting should clearly lay down a common policy on the Insurance Bill. Even when they had met and confirmed their support for the Bill, Hardie, Snowden, George Lansbury and six others still voted against it in the House of Commons. Henderson then determined to toughen up party discipline. Meanwhile he and the majority of the Labour MPs spent long hours securing a string of concessions on the Bill as it proceeded through the House of Commons.

There were also serious clashes within the parliamentary party as to what priority was given to securing votes for women. There had been major differences when Hardie was both chairman and the leading advocate of the issue within the parliamentary party. The matter came to a head again in October 1912 when Lansbury tried to press on the parliamentary party the policy of voting against the Liberal Government on everything until it granted women the vote. Lansbury resigned his seat and lost it when he fought the subsequent by-election on the suffrage issue.

Henderson had long been sympathetic to women's suffrage, but he wanted to achieve it alongside universal male suffrage. Hence he was a member of the Adult Suffrage League, and also worked closely with Mrs Fawcett and the moderate National Union of Women's Suffrage Societies. At the 1910 Labour party conference he successfully argued that Labour should not adopt the stance of refusing any electoral reform bill that did not include women's suffrage. In 1913 he was to do the same with regard to a bill to abolish plural voting, a measure which he felt would help Labour in the next general election. At the time he wrote to MacDonald, 'Personally I was fully prepared to take the responsibility of refusing to vote for further enfranchisement of men until the claims of women were recognised, but I must decline to apply this position to a Bill for the removal of plural votes'. Not surprisingly, after Henderson had carried the Labour party with him on this, he was subjected to considerable heckling by the militant suffragettes.[50]

Henderson used Lansbury's actions as a cause for tightening up discipline in the parliamentary party. He was one of the emergency sub-committee of the Labour party executive which interviewed Lansbury before the by-election and ascertained that he would not accept the Labour whip if elected. In the interview Lansbury agreed that in the circumstances of the by-election he was not entitled to expect 'either the collective or individual support of the Labour Party'. When Hardie, Snowden and two others ignored the executive's instructions that party speakers should not assist Lansbury, they were reported to their sponsoring organizations. Henderson won the support of the 1913 Labour party conference for a procedure whereby the whip could be withdrawn from MPs who got badly out of line. After this Henderson was happier about discipline, although after the parliamentary party meeting where he won the vote on the Plural Voting Bill, he complained to MacDonald,

> We had Members in the discussion ... saying that they were not bound by the Annual Conference resolutions; others that they were expected to carry out the decisions of the ILP conference; and others stating that they were bound by nothing but the decisions of the Party. And one or two of them went so far as to say they claimed their freedom against the decision of the majority of their colleagues. You can see that we do not improve.[51]

Henderson's eagerness for MacDonald to be chairman of the parliamentary party was also in part due to his wish to take over the post of secretary of the Labour party. It is highly probable that in early 1911 they made an agreement that if MacDonald took the chair Henderson would do all he could to extend MacDonald's tenure beyond the usual two years. Henderson would also give up his post as treasurer and secure it for MacDonald, thereby enabling MacDonald to stay ex officio on the party's executive committee. MacDonald would then vacate the secretaryship at the party conference in January 1912. This arrangement was to dominate the Labour party for two decades. Henderson had been a competent, but rather timid, leader of the party; whereas MacDonald was a better speaker and had more charisma. MacDonald had been a capable secretary of the party; but Henderson was to be more methodical and a better organizer of the party's national development.

Henderson enjoyed being secretary of the Labour party, supervising the central administration of a political party and improving its local organization. He had considerable experience for the task, both as a former paid political agent and a trade union organizer. But he had also been involved in the administration as treasurer from February 1904 and had acted on several occasions from July–August 1904 onwards as Mac-Donald's replacement when he was away. The payment of MPs released Henderson from his constant travelling on behalf of his union. However, he now continued this well-established life-style with similar expeditions around the country but organizing for the Labour party. It was an arduous mode of living, and not one many family men like Henderson would have taken on. It also did much to make 'Uncle Arthur' much more aware of party rank-and-file feeling than most of the Labour leadership. Kenneth Morgan has commented, 'As a peripatetic one-man link between Westminster and the grass-roots, he developed a national vision of the movement that was unique'.[52]

Henderson worked hard to help foster the local organization necessary to get Labour candidates elected to Parliament. From the time of his efforts to get Hodge elected in Preston in 1903 he had been acutely aware of the problems of trying to win elections in constituencies lacking adequate ILP, trade union or other Labour organization. In the years immediately before the First World War, therefore, along with Arthur Peters, the national agent, he not only put considerable effort into by-elections but also laid the foundations of better organization in many constituencies, especially in 1913 in those which Labour would have been likely to fight in the expected 1915 general election.[53]

With MacDonald he put considerable effort into building up trade union support for the party, both in organizational and financial terms. In 1910, as vice chairman of the Joint Board, Henderson supported moves to amalgamate the TUC and the General Federation of Trade Unions (GFTU) with the Labour party, a proposal which had been gaining support since 1907. The 1910 Labour party conference backed the move, but the TUC, by a narrow majority in that year, rejected it. Henderson, chairing a meeting of the three national committees in April 1910, urged that they try to accomplish something practical, observing that 'The Congress resolution was defeated by 29,000 a majority certainly not very large and indicating a growing feeling among the trades for a closer union of forces'. After lengthy silence it was clear that no one advocated outright fusion, but MacDonald and Hardie were enthusiastic for the three organizations to have offices under one roof, to develop a central Labour Club which could put up delegates from the provinces 'after the style of those in Germany and other countries', and to avoid duplication of conference agendas.

Henderson used the Joint Board as a forum to stress the Labour party's primacy in political issues such as the operation of labour exchanges.

He pressed that where consultation took place with the Government, delegates should be sent from both the Joint Board and the Parliamentary Committee of the TUC.[54] Shackleton had resisted such moves in 1909 but when he resigned as chairman of the Joint Board on 22 November 1910 Henderson succeeded him. As a result Henderson was in a stronger position to steer the trade union movement Labour's way, as well as strengthening further his own position in the movement.

He and MacDonald put much effort into trying to ensure that Liberal-inclined miners' unions broke their close link with local Liberal parties and set up separate electoral organizations for Labour. It was a policy which was likely to expand Labour's number of parliamentary seats, but in the short run it led to several clashes with the Liberal party in by-elections. Like Henderson's efforts in boosting Labour organization locally, and thereby greatly contributing to expectations of more Labour candidates standing in general elections, this policy would take Labour further down the road of independence from the Liberals.[55]

The logic of the situation was becoming very apparent by 1912. Whilst Labour awaited legislative concessions from the Liberal Government, it was confined to its existing seats. However when Enoch Edwards, the president of the Miners' Federation died in June 1912, the Liberals claimed his Hanley seat. MacDonald and Henderson were outraged. MacDonald warned, 'If they will not allow us to retain our present numbers in Parliament, we must take steps accordingly'. They responded immediately by putting up a Labour candidate at Crewe, where polling was due thirteen days later. There Henderson stated the argument he was to make several times in succeeding months: that while some Labour MPs held their seats because of Liberal votes, the same applied to many Liberal MPs and 'in view of the long line of front presented to Labour attacks the Liberals had most to lose'. Speaking with Snowden at Blackburn, he assured a Labour meeting that 'their policy in fighting elections would be dictated solely by what were the interests of their own movement ... whenever there was the slightest chance of winning ... the attack would be made'.[56] Henderson's prominent role in challenging the Liberals not surprisingly led to retaliation against him. *The Times* on 22 August 1912 reported that his activities had 'deeply incensed a number of leading Liberals' in Barnard Castle who were now determined to put a Liberal candidate up against him.

Even before the death of Enoch Edwards, Henderson had been responding to threats of Liberal candidates in Labour seats with warnings that 'Labour would take up the challenge'. Speaking on May Day in

Wolverhampton, where the local Liberals had said they would contest all seats, Henderson had declared, 'If the Liberals thought that the Labour Party was to remain for an indefinite period forty two strong ... they were making a great mistake'.

However, as a thoughtful party organizer Henderson was aware that repeated bad results would lead anti-Tory voters to plump for the Liberals. During the by-election in Crewe he expressed his fears to Jim Middleton, 'I feared from what I saw we might have another slump'. In October 1913, when there was pressure to fight a by-election in Keighley arising from the local Liberal MP accepting ministerial office, Henderson resisted. He argued, 'I anticipate a considerable falling away of our previous support and this will weaken our position in the constituency and damage us in the country'.[57] Although more willing to fight the Liberals from 1912, his attitude remained pragmatic as to whether particular seats should be contested when by-elections occurred.

Overall, Henderson's attitude towards the Liberals appears to have hardened between 1910 and 1914, perhaps because he was more in touch with rank-and-file feeling than many of his colleagues in Parliament. In January 1914 a special Labour party conference devoted a morning to debating the parliamentary party's performance. There were calls for the Labour MPs to 'put more life and spirit into their work and not consider other parties'. W.S. Sanders, a member of the party's executive commented, 'They had to get back to the old position of fighting in public and forcing things from the government, otherwise they would be looked upon as a mere body of people who followed in the wake of Mr. Lloyd George instead of making Mr. Lloyd George follow them'.[58] Soon after, when speaking with Beatrice Webb, Sanders contrasted the attitudes of Henderson and the other Labour MPs. Unlike most of them, Sanders told Webb, there was Henderson 'who feels that the Labour members ought to take a more distinctive line and whose uneasiness has a bad effect on his temper'. In particular Sanders commented adversely on MacDonald's closeness to Liberal ministers and his opposition to striking out in 'a constructive socialist direction'.

Henderson appears to have been uneasy about MacDonald's close political and social contacts with leading Liberal politicians in these pre-war years. In 1921 he told Beatrice Webb that some ten years earlier MacDonald had 'proposed to enter a Coalition Cabinet with Lloyd George and Balfour (to oust Asquith) and [had] offered him (Henderson) an undersecretaryship'. She noted, 'Henderson refused decisively and declared that any such action would destroy the Labour Party and that he would not consent to it'.[59] While it is unlikely that Lloyd George made a formal offer to MacDonald to join a cross-party coalition in the late summer or autumn of 1910, it is quite possible that he flattered him with details of his secret proposals and MacDonald may well have sounded out Henderson to see his response. Certainly after the 1910 general elections, when the Liberals were dependent on Labour and/or Irish Nationalist support; and Labour was eager to avoid another election and was dependent on the Liberals for legislative concessions, there were repeated suggestions from the Liberals to Labour to join the Government, with a Cabinet place for MacDonald. Lloyd George, the Liberal Chief Whip, and others made informal approaches to MacDonald in at least October and November 1911, March and June 1912, June 1913 and March 1914.

In March 1914 Henderson as Labour Chief Whip (a post he had taken again that January) accompanied MacDonald for further discussions with Lloyd George and the Liberal Chief Whip. Lloyd George said that he was speaking on behalf of the Cabinet and the reason for calling the meeting was that they were preparing for a possible election over Home Rule for Ireland. He offered for discussion the possibility of the Liberals conceding 'a substantial increase' in Labour MPs by withdrawing Liberal candidates from constituencies where Labour might beat the Tories— and Labour doing the same so far as they could; a programme for legislation if the Liberals formed a new government after the elections; and representation in the Cabinet. MacDonald was clearly attracted to such proposals, but there is no sign that Henderson was. Indeed, he had vehemently condemned Will Thorne at the special Labour conference in January 1914 for suggesting that MacDonald was making secret bargains with the Liberals and stated that if Thorne's charge was correct 'the chairman of the Parliamentary Party ought no longer to occupy that position'.[60] The Labour party's executive committee did not take up Lloyd George's proposals, presumably as most of them were aware that the rank and file would not stand such a deal. Independence had become a prime concern of Labour party activists, regardless of whether seats were lost or the Liberals lost office.

If Henderson's stance towards working with the Liberals had moved gradually between 1906 and 1914, his political thinking had changed hardly at all. He remained very much a stalwart of the trade-union wing of the Labour party and was often highly critical of ILP activists in private. He was very sensitive to ILP hostility to him during his time as chairman. Yet, by 1914 he was happy to pay tribute to the role of the ILP when

he spoke at its conference as the fraternal delegate from the Labour party.
Then he declared,

> It had been largely instrumental in bringing about the great revolution which
> had taken place in the public thought and outlook in regard to social and
> economic questions. It had also done more than any other separate organisa-
> tion to create and strengthen the Labour Party and it had helped to revitalise
> some of the older trade unions.

Other than as a matter of convenience, Henderson did not become
a socialist before the First World War. Then it was a matter of joining
the least demanding affiliated socialist body. When he became secretary
of the Labour party on 24 January 1912 the position brought with it
international socialist responsibilities. Snowden later commented with
scorn, 'It would have been incongruous for the British Secretary of the
Socialist International not to be a member of a socialist body, so Mr.
Henderson joined the Fabian Society!'.[61]

During the 1912 clashes with the Liberals in by-elections Henderson
was often challenged to define the difference between his and the Liberals'
position. At Wolverhampton he had replied that Labour 'stood for full
citizen rights for both men and women, while the Liberals went for one
man one vote'. He further claimed that the Liberals' economic policies
were closer to those of the Tories. Later that year, speaking in the Midloth-
ian by-election, he observed 'that when they wanted to tackle monopoly
in land, monopoly in railways, and monopoly in mines they could not
find much difference' between the Liberal and Tory candidates.

As a trade union official Henderson was critical of changes in industry
which intensified the exploitation of labour. He wrote in 1908, 'There
can be little doubt that the modern tyranny known as "speeding up" is
accountable for much of the wastage of life rampant today'. At the Labour
party conference on 27 January 1909, when moving a resolution on unemployment, he argued that it was nothing to do with free trade but stemmed
'from over-organisation for the production of profit to be utilised for the
individual'. By 'over-organisation' he meant the introduction of labour-
saving machinery which not only dispensed with labour but enabled
capital 'to bring greater pressure to bear on the remaining workers'.[62]

Although he was often the spokesman of the craft trade-unionist, care-
fully expounding the view of such 'steady men' on matters like National
Insurance, he could be critical of a narrow craft point of view.[63] Once
trade-unionists had secured the reversal of the Taff Vale decision, he
urged that they should look to those in need. He wrote,

There is a great gulf between those who have and those who have not. To narrow and, if possible, to remove this gulf is the work to which we, as trade unionists, should devote our best energies. No instrument can assist so effectively in this beneficent work as a highly organised, well equipped, independent Labour Party, caring for the social and industrial needs of the wage earners. Seeking to so alter our commercial organisation as to give a fuller and more complete opportunity to the many as well as the few.[64]

In his concern for social reform, and even his emphasis on taxation as a means for redistributing wealth, his views were no different from those on the Radical wing of the Liberal party. Where he parted company from someone such as Lloyd George was in his criticisms of industrial capitalists' activities in reorganizing industry and in his advocacy of the concerns of organized labour. Henderson did argue the case for Labour party policies on nationalization, though again such policies as nationalizing the railways were not exclusive to Labour. The First World War was to demonstrate that wide ranging state control and direction of industry in Britain could be more than just a distant aspiration. Unexpectedly, Henderson himself was to be involved in helping the industrial war machine to run.

5

Oiling the War Machine, 1914–1917

Henderson was one of the major Labour figures to speak at a large rally in Trafalgar Square on 2 August 1914. Here, the Government was called on not to support Russia 'either directly or in consequence of any understanding with France' and to 'rigidly decline to engage in war'. But after war was declared on Germany on 4 August, he soon became the leading figure of the Labour movement to support Britain's war effort, being active in both the recruiting campaigns and the Government's efforts to ease labour supply problems in the munitions industries. His involvement in the Government's munitions policies and his eventual support for the Military Service Bills brought him into conflict with major groups within the Labour movement. There were clashes between his loyalties to Labour and to the Cabinet long before he fell out with Lloyd George in the summer of 1917 over the proposed conference at Stockholm.

The rally was an attempt to carry out the Second International's policy of preventing war by organizing demonstrations of working class hostility. The previous day Keir Hardie and Henderson, as president and secretary of the British Section of the Second International, had issued a manifesto calling for 'vast demonstrations against war in every industrial centre' and declaring that, 'The success of Russia at the present day would be a curse to the world'. It concluded with the appeal,

> Workers, stand together ... for peace. Combine and conquer the militarist enemy and the self seeking Imperialists today, once and for all ...
>
> Proclaim that for you the days of plunder and butchery have gone by; send messages of peace and fraternity to your fellows who have less liberty than you. Down with class rule. Down with the rule of brute force. Down with war. Up with the peaceful rule of the people.[1]

Such rhetoric of international socialism would not have come readily to Henderson. But his deeply-held Methodist convictions moved him towards mediation for international problems as did his long pursuit of conciliation not conflict in industrial relations. As Lloyd George showed on several occasions it was easy to move from such appeals in industrial disputes to similar ones in the sphere of international relations. Henderson's Radical background also made him critical of jingoism. Like other leading figures in his union, he had denounced the Boer War. He spoke of it as 'an iniquitous war—which has produced such a vast harvest of reaction and of demoralisation in our national affairs'.[2]

When the British National Committee had been set up in July 1905 as a means whereby a wider range of British socialists and trade-unionists could have links with the Second International, Henderson had been one of its first group of four trade-unionists. While two of the others, Will Thorne and Ben Tillett, were notable New Unionists and socialists, Henderson (who represented the LRC) and Hodge were from craft unions and were moderates.[3] Henderson may have seen this as a significant area of Labour politics and, as a very prominent trade-union MP, one in which he should be involved. His career clearly reveals his eagerness to hold simultaneously many of the strings of power and influence within the party. His membership may also have owed something to the long tradition of radical working-class hostility to the tsars of Russia and other absolute monarchs.

His main interventions in foreign issues before 1914, other than on armaments and relations with Germany, concerned Russia. After the 'Bloody Sunday' massacre in St Petersburg in January 1905, the 1905 LRC conference agreed to set up a fund for the widows and orphans. When Henderson acted as treasurer for the fund it brought him into contact with Prince Kropotkin and some other Russian exiles and developed his awareness of the adversities faced by opponents of the tsarist regime. In August 1906 and January 1907 he was associated with further appeals to British trade-unionists for funds to help those involved in the struggle against the autocracy in Russia.[4]

Henderson also played a part in the parliamentary opposition to links with the tsarist government. From 1905 onwards Keir Hardie, Will Thorne and other Labour MPs raised a series of anti-tsarist issues. Before the Anglo-Russian Entente was signed at the end of August 1907, Henderson questioned Sir Edward Grey as to 'whether his negotiations with Russia relate to matters other than boundaries and are concerned with general political relationships'. The Labour MPs did not pursue the matter, however, when the full extent of the Entente was revealed.[5]

When it was announced in May 1908 that King Edward would visit the Tsar at Reval, the ILP and the Labour party led a vigorous campaign against this occurring. Henderson, as chairman of the parliamentary party, asked for a debate on the visit. This took place a week later, with Keir Hardie and Grayson condemning it strongly. The King responded by removing their names from the list of those invited to royal garden parties. Whilst neither was likely to accept such an invitation, Henderson and the parliamentary Labour party made it a major issue of principle, requesting that all their names should be removed until Hardie's was restored. Henderson devoted much of one of the 'Parliamentary Notes' for his union's members to rebut the inevitable hysteria which this aroused in the right-wing press. After providing details of the incident, he ended on a Radical note:

> ... to submit to a form of ostracism which imperils the liberty of free speech would be positively discreditable to any Party, but more especially to the Labour Party. For to them is committed the task and responsibility of fighting unpopular causes and for declaring for rights that may involve the privileges of those in high places. To shrink from an obvious duty in such a situation would but prove our unworthiness to succeed to the great heritage of liberty which others have won, and to be representatives of those who believe that there are great fights yet to be fought before social and economic freedom can be secured.[6]

A year later, when it became known that the Tsar was to make a return visit to Britain, the Labour movement launched a further campaign against this link between monarchs. Henderson, when rebutting the attacks on this campaign made by the Liberal and Tory press, especially the *Daily Mail*, again defended the actions of the Labour movement with an old Radical plea:

> The number of people who had been done to death or exiled from their own land was ... sufficient justification for demanding this visit should not have the official benediction of the government. The country that received Garibaldi and Mazzini, the country which above all others had been an asylum for those who fled from religious and political persecution could not depart from its ancient tradition.[7]

When Henderson condemned the visit in Parliament he drew heavily on Prince Kropotkin's pamphlet *The Terror in Russia* for details of tsarist atrocities and repression. This pamphlet had been sponsored by the Anglo-Russian Committee, a predominantly Radical body formed after King

Edward's visit to Russia. Henderson was also one of 180 who signed a lengthy letter condemning the visit which the Russian Parliamentary Committee drew up and sent to the press. Whilst this campaign owed much to Radical dissent from Sir Edward Grey's foreign policy, Labour joined in wholeheartedly and made much impact, particularly in organizing a protest rally which was attended by six to seven thousand people in Trafalgar Square on 25 August.[8]

Henderson and the other leading Labour figures also shared common views with the advanced Liberals in Parliament on the issue of armaments. He repeatedly warned that more armaments would increase the dangers of a war taking place with Germany. Indeed he often expressed opinions that echoed the 'Peace, Retrenchment and Reform' views of the old Cobdenite creed. When responding to the King's Speech in February 1909 he roundly dismissed the need for increased naval expenditure, observing that the working classes of Germany and Britain had no desire 'to get into entanglements or into a great international war', and chided the Liberals:

> I hope that there have been present those who still have some regard for the old Liberal watchword of 'retrenchment'. We do not hear it so much spoken ... [on] Liberal platforms as we did a few years ago, and many of us begin to ask whether, after all, there is any difference between the two orthodox parties so far as expenditure for Navy purposes is concerned.

He was to revert to this theme of the Liberals' abandonment of 'Peace, Retrenchment and Reform' a month later when he attacked the Government's proposed increase in the naval estimates, proposals which he deemed to 'represent the beginning of the triumph of the Navy League'.[9]

Henderson and his parliamentary Labour party colleagues also joined with radical Liberals in criticizing provision for the army. In 1906 they complained of 'enormous expenditure', called for better conditions for ordinary soldiers and demanded that the 'upper ranks should not be the exclusive possession of those who had wealth, position and influence'. The following year they criticized Haldane's army reforms. Henderson warned the members of his union against the Government's bill because 'in the end it will almost certainly lead to compulsory military service'. He also commented, 'Many Liberals have quietly complained against the possibilities of militarism they fear it contains'. He added that it fell to the Labour party to take a decided stand.

His case against large expenditure on armaments owed much to old-fashioned radicalism and a little to the Second International. He argued,

... our alleged need for a great Army in addition to a powerful Navy is
the result of our present national policy of aggression and of the state of
militarism which obtains throughout civilisation, coupled with our own
method of ruling subject races by force and by refusing them self-government.
With the component parts of the Empire and of the world self-governing
and self-supporting, and with the rise of the International Labour Movement,
the need for great armies disappears. Further, to sanction this scheme would
seriously hamper the efforts of those who are seeking to bring about universal
disarmament.[10]

Beyond calling for the curtailment of armaments expenditure and encouraging links between the working people of different countries, his main
answer to international conflict was arbitration. Such a policy again fitted
in well with the old radicalism and recalled Gladstone's handling in 1871
of the dispute between the USA and Britain over the American Civil
War actions of the Confederate commerce raider, the *Alabama*. Thus
Henderson was very much at home when speaking at the predominantly
Liberal International Arbitration League's dinner in March 1909, a week
after the Government had published its increased naval estimates. As
well as expressing strong support for the principle of arbitration, he gave
his often expressed view that working people were hostile to war and
made much of a delegation of thirty Labour MPs going to Germany.
'If they could demonstrate the good will between the working classes',
he told the diners, 'it would be difficult for officials ... to embroil them
in what would be the greatest calamity of either of their histories'.[11]

Henderson went to Germany at least twice before the First World War.
In late 1908 he travelled extensively with George Barnes, studying trade-
unionism and German policies towards the unemployed, the elderly, the
sick and the disabled. In September 1912 he went on another major tour
with a delegation made up from the Labour party's National Executive
Committee and the parliamentary party. That took place after another
naval scare in Britain during which MacDonald had been attempting
to rebut Winston Churchill's arguments for increased naval expenditure.
MacDonald dubbed the visit 'a pilgrimage for knowledge and a crusade
for peace'. He led the group, but Henderson, as party secretary, took
it upon himself to keep them to schedule. As a result of being hurried
on, Pete Curran responded, 'All right, Uncle Arthur, we'll all be there'.
The nickname 'Uncle Arthur' stayed with him for the rest of his life.[12]

While Henderson would proclaim international working-class abhor-
rence of war, he was horrified at Keir Hardie's efforts from 1910 to get
commitments from British as well as other European socialist parties

to the anti-war strike. Hardie, in trying to take Second International policy from mere hopes of preventing war to serious consideration of means of preventing it, pushed the proposal that a 'particularly efficacious' way of doing so would be by general strikes 'especially in the industries that supply war with its implements'. Dr Newton has cogently argued that Hardie hoped that the threat of such action would give the various ruling classes cause to be cautious about war.[13] If so, such a position involved much higher stakes than that shared by MacDonald, Henderson and other Labour leaders, that demonstrations of international working-class mutual goodwill would curtail rash actions by diplomats.

An anti-war strike obviously would involve the trade union movement. Henderson's objections probably centred on his belief that the craft unions, at least, would be very unlikely to approve political action of that kind and also that such a policy would be impractical. Given the improbability of even the powerful German socialists, let alone the French or British, being able to stop a war in their country, calls to take part in such a strike were likely to be a failure and were also unlikely to alarm the ruling classes. In fact his stance matched that of the German trade-unionists who, within the German socialist party, successfully opposed the adoption of the policy of a general strike against a European war.

Whatever his reasoning, Henderson took the unusual course of refusing to move the National Executive Committee's resolution at a special Labour party conference on disarmament held at Leicester on 31 January 1911. He did so on the grounds that Hardie, who had also declined to move the resolution, intended 'to move an addition to the Armaments resolution which, I could not accept, and it would mean dividing the conference against the position taken by the majority of the committee'. At the conference, Henderson vigorously condemned Hardie's proposal as a distraction from parliamentary action and succeeded in defeating it. At the 1912 Labour party conference Henderson again made clear his opposition to such a policy, but did not recommend opposition to an inquiry.[14]

Thus before August 1914 Henderson was an opponent of the strike against war. Moreover, those who did support such an action, recognized that to have a chance of being effective it needed to be done when war threatened, not when mobilization was already underway. When Britain entered the European war on 4 August 1914 the war machines of the continental powers were already in action, unhindered by general strikes. Hence Henderson felt, after the attempts to rally popular opposition to war on 1 and 2 August, he was in a new situation after 4 August. Just as a trade union official he had often had to compromise and act in the best interests of his members according to an industrial situation, so now in August 1914, although the situation was not as he would have wished, he came to terms with the reality of a major war in progress.

Henderson can have had few doubts that the war would gain popular support, especially given the German invasion of Belgium. Indeed the famous anti-war rally at Trafalgar Square was at best a qualified success. Whilst the *Manchester Guardian* reported the speeches and the cheers of those hostile to war, The Times gave an account which stressed the mixed reception given to the speakers. That evening, dining with three Liberal Cabinet ministers, Ramsay MacDonald had confirmation that British entry into the war was inevitable. Lloyd George made much of the neutrality of Belgium: Sir George Riddell, their host, noted that he 'understood Ramsay MacDonald to agree that if Belgian neutrality were infringed, this country would be justified in declaring war upon Germany'. However he also recorded MacDonald as saying that entry into the war was a mistake and that, 'In three months there will be bread riots and we [the Labour party] shall come in'.

The next day in Parliament, MacDonald, speaking to a policy agreed by the parliamentary Labour party, called for Britain to remain neutral. In answer to Sir Edward Grey's account of commitments made to France, MacDonald argued that Britain's honour was not at stake, though he did make qualifications to the effect that Grey would gain Labour's support if Britain was in danger or if the conflict was confined to saving 'a small European nationality like Belgium'. MacDonald also tried to widen the debate to include tsarist Russia, so long the object of hatred to radical working people.[15]

The following day, 4 August, Henderson as secretary of the Labour party, called a meeting of the National Executive Committee for the morning of 5 August to decide the party's response to the international crisis, and as chairman of the Joint Board he called a further meeting in the afternoon of Labour leaders from a wide range of working-class organizations 'for the purpose of considering the formation of a National Peace Emergency Committee' which would urge the case for neutrality, work for permanent peace and 'render all possible assistance to necessitous citizens by the provision of food etc.'[16] However, by noon on 4 August the British Cabinet was aware that large numbers of German troops had invaded Belgium, and at 11p.m. (British time) its ultimatum to Germany expired.

So when the National Executive Committee met on 5 August its task was to respond to a war already in progress. It passed resolutions which condemned secret diplomacy and the pursuit of the balance of power for causing the war and asserted that the Labour movement's 'duty now is to secure peace at the earliest possible moment on such conditions as will provide the best opportunities for the re-establishment of amicable feelings between the workers of Europe'.[17] Although these resolutions were not carried unanimously (eight to four), they were resolutions behind which all could unite. But the assertion of future policy was vague. All should seek an early peace—but was this through a British military victory? The answer could not be fudged by the parliamentary party.

That very evening MacDonald and his parliamentary colleagues discussed whether or not to vote in favour of the Government's request for £100 million war credit. MacDonald urged that they should abstain on the vote, but in the debate reiterate their condemnation of Grey's policies which had led to war. In an acrimonious debate the trade-unionists and many of the ILP members made it clear they would not accept this suggestion. John Hodge, who stated bluntly he would vote for the credit, argued that he 'was no believer in a policy of sitting on the fence— either we were for our country or we were against it'.[18] MacDonald was in a small minority, supported only by Keir Hardie, Tom Richardson and Fred Jowett (Philip Snowden being in Australia), and he resigned. Henderson was elected chairman 'temporarily', while staying on as Chief Whip.

Between then and mid-October, Henderson and other members of the parliamentary party made approaches to MacDonald to resume the leadership. MacDonald nursed his wounded pride, deluding himself that he had left the leadership because 'the men were not pulling together, there was enough jealousy to spoil good feeling'. Yet MacDonald himself was a prey to conflicting ideas. Later in August he could write to Henderson of his wish to take up 'as others have done on other matters, the right of following my own beliefs without forfeiting my general loyalty to the party'. A few days later he was writing to him to urge that the parliamentary party should fall into line with him:

> Is it to throw itself out of action altogether and allow each individual to drift whether it seems good for him? Or is it to attempt to take up a distinctive position which will be in due course the rallying centre for those who will wish that this war shall not have been fought in vain. If it is to do the latter, it must think things out from now onwards and it must be prepared to operate with outside organisations with which it agrees in this respect.[19]

MacDonald then was already involved in the formation of such an 'outside organization', the Union of Democratic Control, which was to become a major vehicle of anti-war dissent.

For all of MacDonald's complaints of lack of discipline within the parliamentary party and his other attempts to explain the real issue away, both in letters and in his own diary, the reality was that he lost the leadership because he would not unequivocally support the Government wage a war that was already in progress. The majority of his colleagues felt that in these circumstances to continue to criticize the policies which Labour deemed to have brought about the war was to pursue a secondary issue. For them, after 5 August, that was all so much water under the bridge.

The other meeting which Henderson summoned for 5 August was of representatives of a wide range of labour, socialist, co-operative and women's organizations to consider forming a National Peace Emergency Committee. At the Labour party's Executive Committee Henderson, Turner, Wake and Twist were appointed as a sub-committee to draw up recommendations for what was now called the War Emergency Conference. Their proposals were endorsed by the Executive Committee and later in the day by the conference. There it was agreed to establish a committee to co-ordinate action aimed at minimizing working-class suffering arising from wartime economic dislocation. They quickly agreed to press the Government 'to maintain the aggregate volume of employment' (including the possibility of additional public enterprises), to control the price and distribution of food, and to ensure supplies of milk for those most in need.[20]

The following day the creation of this new body, the War Emergency Workers National Committee (WEWNC), was warmly endorsed by the National Executive Committee of the Labour party, which called on 'all Labour and Socialist organisations' to concentrate their energies on 'detailing measures to mitigate the destitution which will inevitably overtake our working people whilst the state of war lasts'. Henderson served as chairman of the WEWNC until he entered the Cabinet, and was very willing to press unemployment, consumer and social welfare issues in Parliament and Whitehall. This was a continuation of his pre-war role in Parliament when, as a trade union MP, he had diligently raised time after time health and safety issues on behalf of his and other unions.

The WEWNC did much to establish Labour as the champion of working people generally. It took up the issues of high food prices, lack of coal and poor separation allowances for the dependants of soldiers and sailors.

These were areas in which the Labour movement made much headway. When the Committee organized district conferences across Britain on poor levels of separation and other allowances Henderson, as its chairman, highlighted the issue both in the press and in Parliament. Interviewed by the press, he linked this issue with problems of getting sufficient volunteers for the Army and argued that 'the public conscience has been educated to such an extent that there is a gratifying willingness to shoulder the responsibility for wives whose husbands have fallen or for men who are disabled'.[21]

In pressing these matters Henderson and the Committee were explicitly trying to represent more than organized labour. He presided at a public meeting organized by the WEWNC on 12 March 1915 to discuss the need to control the prices of wheat and coal:

> It was not for the highly skilled and organised workers the conference was interested, they could look after themselves and were doing so. They were claiming and, he was glad to say, in many cases obtaining substantial increases in wages. They pleaded for the great body of the unskilled, unorganised and detached bodies of workers ... The men had left their homes to fight for their country, and upon their kith and kin left behind fell the hardships and sufferings from high prices which might have been avoided or minimised had the government taken action.[22]

This was one of a series of such conferences the WEWNC organized across Britain in the early part of 1915.

Wartime inflation and the industrial truce made these very powerful issues by early 1915. In the House of Commons on 2 February, Henderson linked his complaint against the recent lengthy parliamentary adjournment—in spite of the war—with 'the most serious issue with which the civil population had been confronted since the opening of hostilities ... the terrible prices now ruling for food and coals and other commodities'. He dubbed them 'almost famine prices'. He secured a debate on the issue the following week, when Clynes spoke for Labour, vigorously criticizing the Government for leaving supplies 'to the mercies of those who are exacting the highest prices according to the laws and practices of their trade and business'.[23]

Early in the war both the Labour movement and the Government feared serious unemployment. This was an issue which the WEWNC, and Sidney Webb in particular, took up vigorously from its inception, making strong representations to the Government. As well as its impact on those unemployed and their families, there was also the lesser concern about the

impact on trade unions. By late August 1914 unemployment was having
an extremely serious effect on the trade unions' finances, especially those
in the textile industries because they were paying out unemployment,
sickness and death benefits. Henderson was soon demanding state financial assistance. He wrote a report on this crisis for the Joint Board. At
its meeting on 24 August it agreed to Henderson's suggestion to send
a deputation to the Prime Minister, requesting that the Government

> ... take steps through the provision of an appropriation grant for subsidising
> the unions or by giving the necessary assistance through the local Relief
> Committees, which will enable all working class citizens to obtain uniform
> assistance and incidentally enable the unions to continue the payment of
> sick, superannuation and similar benefits.[24]

Henderson observed, when writing on the 26 August to the Secretary
of the Bradford Trades Council, that 'in view of the assistance which
has already been rendered by the government to the banks and financiers
of the country, it is only fair that trade unions, who have done so much
in the past, should receive some considerations'.[25]

When Henderson and two colleagues saw Asquith on 27 August they
emphasized the impact of the war on Lancashire textiles and such trades
as hat-making. They stressed that 'no union in existence has ever made
any preparation for an emergency such as we are in now', but failed
to press hard for a government subsidy. Asquith made it clear that he
did not like the idea of an appropriation grant, but undertook to consult
his colleagues on other points. Eventually the Government did make a
special grant to those unions badly affected by unemployment provided
that they imposed a special levy on their members still in work. This
was better than nothing—but it only covered a part of the huge losses
suffered in the early part of the war, notably by the cotton unions.[26]

The Joint Board at its meeting on 24 August also made the recommendation,

> That an immediate effort be made to terminate all existing trade disputes,
> whether strikes or lock-outs, and whenever new points of difficulty arise
> during the war period a serious attempt should be made by all concerned
> to reach an amicable settlement before resorting to a strike or lock-out.

This recommendation was also sent to Asquith when the Joint Board
asked that he receive a deputation. G.D.H. Cole, writing a few months
later, argued that Henderson and the others should have made such a
recommendation conditional on the Government granting the financial
assistance that the unions sought.[27] During the debate on the Second

Reading of the Munitions of War Bill, Henderson made high claims for the impact of this call for an industrial truce. In reality, however, the Joint Board's call was a recognition of what had already been happening spontaneously across British industry. The Joint Board was realistic enough not to try to negotiate with what it did not control. It only took a few months of soaring prices and rising profits to end such unqualified patriotic goodwill being shown at work-places across the country.

The industrial truce was followed by the political parties agreeing to an electoral truce and to the party machines being utilized for the recruiting campaigns. The electoral truce gave the Labour party a clear run at any by-election involving a seat which it had previously held. The parliamentary party agreed the same day that its whips should join the committee of a joint Parliamentary Recruiting Campaign. The following day, 29 August, the Labour party's executive agreed unanimously to the electoral truce and, by seven votes to four, to the party's involvement in the recruiting campaign. It urged local affiliated bodies to support recruitment locally.[28] Arthur Peters, the National Agent, subsequently devoted his time to recruiting.

This was a crucial decision. Later, when criticized for entering Asquith's coalition Government in May 1915, Henderson defended himself by arguing that 'it was consistent with the position that the majority of the National Executive and the majority of the Parliamentary Party took up in the early days of the war'. He referred to this decision in particular. Indeed it is notable that Asquith wished to reward the three Chief Whips (Percy Illingworth, Lord Edmund Talbot and Henderson) with Privy Councillorships in the New Year's Honours list at the start of 1915.[29]

The recruiting campaign further divided the majority of the party from the minority. The ILP felt that, if Labour politicians and trade-unionists were to engage in recruiting campaigns, they should at least not join platforms with speakers of the other parties. In MacDonald's case, whilst he consistently condemned the diplomacy leading to the outbreak of the war, he prevaricated until September as to whether he would support the recruiting campaign or whether he would come out unreservedly in support of the Union of Democratic Control. Instead of appearing in person at a recruiting meeting in his constituency on 11 September, he sent the mayor of Leicester a letter to be read out. Amidst much verbiage, he asserted in it, 'Victory ... must be ours ... we cannot go back' and he urged the 'serious men of the trade union ... and similar movements to face their duty. To such men it is enough to say, "England has need of you"'. This annoyed many in the ILP but encouraged those who hoped he would resume the leadership. Henderson responded warmly to it, writing to him,

> Nothing has given me so much satisfaction for a long time. It enables the movement to see that we are not apart as some imagine... I am convinced that whatever our views we ought not to stand apart at the critical moment.[30]

However MacDonald's recruiting message was not a first step towards rejoining the majority, and by October Henderson was tiring of his colleague's ambiguities. When Henderson spoke at a recruiting meeting in his constituency on 7 October he made a point which he would repeat in many speeches over the next few months—that the time for doubts had passed:

> ... that when the war began there might have been some room for differences of opinion, but the experience we had passed through had blown to the winds every shred of argument advanced in support of neutrality. The German Chancellor had said that the wrong they were committing they would endeavour to rectify when once their military goal had been achieved ... We wanted no new pledges from those who refused to honour their old pledges, and the German Chancellor was only aggravating the national crime to which he was a party when he endeavoured to throw so much dust into the eyes of the civilised world.[31]

His lead was followed by the majority group of Labour MPs and many leading trade-unionists. Their manifesto on 11 October argued that, before war broke out, 'the German military caste were determined on war' and that the violation of Belgium 'was proof that nothing, not even national honour and good faith, was to stand between Germany and the realisation of its ambitions to become the dominant power of Europe, with the Kaiser the dictator over all'. Their statement went on to absolve Grey's foreign policy of any blame for the war (contrary to the party's policies of early August) and to assert that 'combatants and noncombatants must be supported to the utmost'. This was indeed a stark contrast to the policy of the ILP, whose National Administrative Council on 13 August had reiterated its condemnation of British foreign policy, reasserted the hopes and ideals of international socialism, and stated that the German Socialists were 'no enemies of ours but faithful friends'.[32] The majority group's manifesto of October ended all likely bridge-building with the minority for the foreseeable future. It also ensured that MacDonald firmly declined to resume the leadership.

When MacDonald protested to Henderson about the manifesto, Henderson was conciliatory. He wrote back,

I only signed the manifesto after a good deal of thought. I had nothing to do with its drafting as I was busy in Barnard Castle when the proof was sent forward. It was represented to me by two or three members of the Executive and the Parliamentary Party that a very bad impression had been created in neutral countries and that it was desirable that some statement should be made that might exercise a counteracting influence.

But he did complain, as he had done before the war when faced with ILP minorities going their own way in spite of majority votes,

From some of those with whom you have been acting, especially members of the N.A.C. [National Advisory Council, ILP], some of us have received no word except that of discouragement and censure from the moment that we decided upon the recruiting campaign. In fact, I consider their treatment, and especially some of the things that have been circulated through the *Labour Leader*, have been nothing less than shameful. It appears to me that it is always right to rush into print if one line is taken, but it is never right... even to attend a recruiting meeting or to make a public reference if it be opposed to the policy which some people have adopted.

Henderson urged that 'much unpleasant feeling might be avoided if some of us who do not see eye to eye on all points but who largely agree on fundamentals could occasionally come together'.[33]

MacDonald and Henderson kept in communication, with Henderson still trying to get MacDonald to resume the leadership. But MacDonald, whilst distancing himself from the *Labour Leader's* vitriolic comments on the recruiting campaign, maintained his independence. At first he declined to see Henderson and the other officers of the parliamentary Labour party. On 18 November he did see them but, as he noted in his diary, 'declined to allow my name to be considered for chairmanship, and further declined to make any promise as to future action'. On 10 December he saw them again and once more firmly declined to stand for the chair. He noted,

Henderson first asked me to bind myself to go back after the war. I declined. After some explanatory talk it was agreed that Henderson would agree to act on condition that it was known that it was to be temporary. This was confirmed at the meeting, Henderson stating that he wished to retain his Secretaryship and the right of reversion to Chief Whipship. Some did not agree.[34]

So Henderson continued as chairman, and Frank Goldstone succeeded him as Chief Whip.

Henderson combined a commitment to maintaining the strength of

the Labour party with dedication to British victory in the war. In his
letter to MacDonald on the October manifesto, he had written,

> I am apprehensive that we are dividing ourselves off into small groups which,
> unless care is exercised, can only have a destructive effect upon the influence
> of the Labour Party. I have done what I could to follow the line which
> would leave the Labour Party at the end of the war as strong, if not stronger,
> than we were when hostilities broke out.

This concern for the Labour party's post-war strength remained a central
consideration with him throughout the war. It was a major point dis-
tinguishing him from many of the Labour movement's super-patriots.

By mid-autumn 1914, he was giving strong support to the war effort.
In his response to the King's Speech on 12 November, he gave an early
version of 'the knock-out blow' policy. Speaking as chairman of the parliamentary Labour party, he declared, 'Believing as they did that in proportion to the completeness of the victory would be the permanence of peace,
they would continue to give the government their united support'. He
went on,

> ... there is only one supreme consideration upon which Parliament must
> concentrate its attention. All our energy and all the capacity and experience
> of the nation, both civil and military, must be so applied as to enable us
> to prosecute this war to a successful issue.[35]

He subordinated any qualms that he might have had as a Methodist
in supporting war to what he felt to be national duty. When speaking
on retiring as president of the National Brotherhood Movement in September 1915 he gave what probably was his considered view. He said
of its members away at war, 'They had gone forth, not because they
hated war less; they had gone under a deep sense of obligation because
they felt it to be their duty to stand by national honour, public right,
liberty, justice and free democracy'.[36] All three of Henderson's sons had
volunteered for the army in the autumn of 1914, and the eldest, David,
was to be killed in action on 15 September 1916 on the Somme.

Henderson was not immune to the rhetoric of hate. Thus the *Yorkshire
Observer* on 1 January 1915 recorded him as having told one audience,
'There are some people who thought it did not matter... whether England
or Germany came out victors in the war... Was any man going to see
his child butchered and his wife dishonoured without retaliating? He did
not believe it'.[37] However unlike some of the other leading pro-war trade-
unionists, it was very rare for him to make such crude statements.

The October manifesto of the Labour movement's pro-war majority had not ended on a negative note. It promised:

> When the time comes to discuss the terms of peace the Labour movement will stand, as it has always stood, for an international agreement among all civilised nations that disputes and misunderstandings in the future shall be settled not by machine guns but by arbitration.

Henderson truly believed this, and he expounded it in various speeches. He joined the Union of Democratic Control, only resigning from it when he entered the Government. He had no difficulty in agreeing with its four-point charter which called for democratic control of foreign policy, reduction of armaments, an international body to arbitrate when disputes did occur and no territorial changes without plebiscites.

Nevertheless, whilst in Asquith's Government Henderson was opposed to peace negotiations before Germany was defeated. Speaking at a conference of the Federation of Shipping Trades in Aberdeen in May 1916, after there had been peace suggestions, Henderson said, 'If the choice of twenty two months ago was between honour and infamy, so the choice today was between dishonourable terms in seeking a premature peace and the concentration of all the resources of this great Empire on final victory'. A month later in Northamptonshire he said he was ' convinced of the utter futility and the actual danger of talk of peace at the present moment'. *The Times'* report recorded him going on to declare in a manner which Lloyd George could not have outdone:

> Great and eternal principles had been outraged by our enemies . . . He took his stand on a sentence once used by *The Times*: 'We must go to the German people and say, This workship of war must cease and the sword you have forged must be broken'. That must be our position if we were determined to destroy. . . the blighting, ruthless spirit of militarism.[38]

Given the views of the majority of the parliamentary Labour party on supporting the war effort, it was only a matter of time before their involvement in the war effort extended further than the recruiting campaign. Henderson's entry into Asquith's Cabinet in May 1915 was preceded by his taking on several government appointments. Early in 1915 he accepted two positions from Herbert Samuel, both concerned with employment. In early January he was made a Commissioner with the task of finding work for Belgian refugees, along with the Labour London county councillor, Susan Lawrence. In mid-February, along with John Hodge, he joined a committee set up to look into ways of providing employment for soldiers and sailors disabled in the war.[39]

More significant than Henderson's acceptance of these tasks was his involvement in helping Lloyd George and the Government increase munitions output. Henderson was the leading trade union spokesperson at the conferences held by Lloyd George at the Treasury in March 1915. Following on from these he accepted the chair of the National Advisory Committee (on production) and also became a member of Lloyd George's Munitions of War Committee. At the end of 1914 it had become apparent there was developing a serious shortage of labour, especially skilled labour, in the economy. By now 1,186,357 men had joined the armed forces since the initial mobilization. By December delays in the supply of shells and a shortage of skilled men forced the Government to intervene and try to achieve agreement between employers and unions as to how to accelerate production. On 4 February 1915 the Government appointed a committee of three under Sir George Askwith, the Chief Industrial Commissioner, to investigate the problems and advise 'as to the best steps to be taken to ensure that the productive powers of the employees in the engineering and shipbuilding establishments shall be made fully available'. From 21 February this Committee on Production became an arbitration tribunal, and through its decisions was to lay down a pattern of wage restraint.

By February 1915 the cost of living had risen by twenty-two per cent since the outbreak of war. This resulted in renewed industrial unrest, notably among engineers on the Clyde where the employers had stalled for months over a wage claim. The first case that the Committee on Production heard as an arbitration tribunal was a demand made by the Boilermakers and Iron and Steel Shipbuilders' Society for a 2s. (10p) per week increase. In considering this case earlier, in his capacity as Chief Industrial Commissioner, Asquith had felt that the unions would give way if the patriotic card was played. Thus in a letter to Walter Runciman, President of the Board of Trade, he advised that

> ... a brief statement of the absolute necessities of the nation, particularly during the next few months, and the claim of the nation to demand temporary sacrifices in her hour of need from all her people would have the best chance of success.
>
> From close knowledge of the trade union leaders I have sufficient confidence in them to think that they would never allow themselves to hinder the government should such an appeal be made.[40]

In essence this was to be the approach that Asquith, Kitchener and Lloyd George adopted on several occasions. However, the Government's use of the patriotic appeal whilst allowing working people only small wage rises at a time when prices and profits were soaring inevitably led to serious industrial unrest. It is a measure of the extent of working-class support for the war that the unrest was not far worse.

Until the summer of 1917 Henderson was to be the key trade-union figure to facilitate the co-operation of Labour with the Government's manpower policies. In early 1915 his efforts were directed towards getting more trade-union participation in decision making. After Asquith made a speech on 1 March on the need to avoid loss of work through industrial disputes, Henderson told him:

> ... the Parliamentary Labour Party desire me to assure you that they are exceedingly anxious that all questions of wages and hours and other conditions should be so amicably arranged as to prevent any cessation of work. We are strongly of the opinion that in order to minimise the risk of disturbances the employers should be willing to confer with the representatives of the workers and every effort made to secure a satisfactory settlement on the lines of conciliation.

He went on to call either for two trade union representatives to be added to the Committee on Production or that

> ... an Advisory Committee of five, appointed say from the workmen's panel of the Industrial Council or other representatives, should be set up with the authority of the government for the period of the war ... It should be clearly understood that in all cases this Advisory Committee should be consulted by the workers before any stoppage was attempted.[41]

Thus, building on his pre-war experiences of joint committees, Henderson was proposing before the Treasury conference, trade union involvement in either the Government's arbitration tribunal or a compulsory conciliation procedure. Lloyd George did not make concessions on these areas. His main concern was with securing co-operation in the increase of output.[42]

Henderson led the trade union delegation at the conference organized by Lloyd George, Chancellor of the Exchequer, at the Treasury from 17 to 19 March 1915. The Treasury conference was intended to get agreement on the speeding up of production on war work in engineering workshops and shipyards. This involved very sensitive changes in work practices and, when introduced, led to major industrial unrest in some cities.

At the Treasury conference Henderson left the airing of a wide range of worries about the Government's proposals to others. He stated that all present were 'anxious to assist the Government to the fullest possible limit with regard to output' and acknowledged that with regard to wages and working practices, changes would probably be necessary. Thereafter he devoted most of his comments to the need for the trade unions to be more involved in decision making than was the case with the railways (which had been under state control since the outbreak of the war). He complained that the Government had 'left the management entirely in the hands of the railway managers, and left them contemptuously to ignore the trade unions'. 'Something different to the treatment the skilled men have received from the railway companies will have to be meted out to all the unions represented here today' he warned 'if we are going to ... help the government to keep the peace and secure the output'.[43] The Government was very willing to involve leading trade-unionists such as Henderson in supervising changes in working practices. He was to face bitter criticism for his role as chairman of the National Advisory Committee on production which was set up to help implement the agreement.

Henderson also joined Lloyd George's Munitions of War Committee which met from 12 April 1915. It was Lloyd George's instrument for by-passing the War Office and 'mobilising industry in the interests of increasing our output of warlike equipment'. Through this Committee, Henderson became involved in proposals for legislation, including such sensitive matters as restricting labour mobility between armaments firms.[44] Thus along with Arthur Balfour, the former Unionist leader, he was involved in an important, war supply committee before a coalition government was formed.

The only notable source of friction between Henderson and Lloyd George, at this time, was the issue of drink. Relations between the trade-union leaders and the Government were damaged because Lloyd George persistently claimed that the drunkenness of a minority of munitions workers was seriously harming overall output. At the Treasury conference he had declared that as 'a war emergency measure' the Government would 'have to take drastic action'. The unions objected that he exaggerated, but Henderson, on their behalf, did agree that they would consider any official statistics on drunkenness. As a deeply committed temperance man, he was sympathetic to tighter controls on drink. Indeed, a week later he told a deputation from the National Temperance Conference that he personally would be in favour of greater restrictions on the sale of alcohol if the Government declared them to be 'a matter of military necessity'.[45]

However when the Government published a White Paper based on evidence collected only from employers and government officials the

Labour movement was furious. On 3 May 1915 Henderson wrote to Lloyd George on behalf of the National Advisory Committee complaining that its offer of investigating cases brought forward and making recommendations to remedy any problems substantiated had been ignored. He demanded a committee of inquiry.[46] The next day in the House of Commons he warned that '. . . until some method is found whereby the other side of the case can be stated, it will be impossible for the government to expect from us a continuance of that solid support which we have endeavoured to give during the whole period of the war'. In the face of widespread scepticism and strong opposition from Labour, Lloyd George had to weaken his proposals and set up a committee to look into the charges of bad timekeeping through drunkenness and other causes.[47]

Thus Henderson had been active on behalf of the Government before he joined Asquith's coalition and had been a voice of moderation within the trade union movement. When Asquith saw Henderson on 19 May 1915 and offered him a place in the Government, it was clearly on the understanding that Henderson would continue to act as a major government trouble-shooter for industrial relations. Henderson was pleased to take on such a role. He proudly told a meeting of his supporters in Barnard Castle, 'If industry is to be thoroughly organised, there will be a risk at any rate of disturbance, and I will do everything my experience will assist me in doing to prevent those risks being realised by actual stoppage'.[48]

Earlier on 19 May, Henderson had put Asquith's invitation to Labour to join his Coalition Government before the parliamentary Labour party. By nine votes to eight they decided against acceptance. Later this was reversed at a joint meeting with the party's executive committee, which approved joining by seventeen votes to eleven. They asked Henderson to secure for Labour either two Cabinet posts or one Cabinet post and two lesser offices[49]: Asquith offered the latter. Henderson joined the Cabinet as President of the Board of Education while William Brace and George Roberts took lesser posts.

From the outset Henderson wished he had been given a ministry directly concerned with labour matters. There had been rumours, perhaps encouraged by him, that he might go to the Board of Trade or the Local Government Board. He appears to have seen Bonar Law, the Unionist leader, to discuss his position in the Cabinet at the time when the Government was being formed. Arthur Steel-Maitland, an influential Unionist, informed Bonar Law,

> He says unless Labour is mobilised properly, an adequate supply of munitions
> cannot be made and he will give you instances. His further attitude is that
> it is no use his joining the government (and it might create more trouble
> than advantage) unless he were in a position to help directly in this mobilis-
> ation.[50]

Henderson had to make do with the special additional post of Labour
Adviser to the Government.

Henderson's backing of the Government's industrial policies both
added to the issues on which he was at loggerheads with the majority
of the ILP leaders, and lost him support from many left-wing, trade union
activists. The ILP MPs, other than Jimmy Clynes and James Parker,
crossed the floor of the House of Commons to the Opposition benches
when the coalition Government had been formed. Snowden, in particular,
frequently denounced Henderson for his support of a range of government
policies. In June 1915 he vigorously condemned him and other trade
union leaders for supporting the Munitions of War Bill, claiming that
'they did not speak with the authority of the rank and file trade unionists'.
He said of the Bill that it threatened more 'than trade union rights and
liberties', it raised 'the whole question of the civil rights of the people
of this country'. On that occasion Henderson responded with equal vigour.
'For daring to support a Bill like this', he observed, 'the trade union
leaders have been chided by one of their colleagues... in a way that
I will venture to say it has not been my lot to listen to during the twelve
years I have been in the House'. He hit back with the observation that
none of the ILP manifestoes which Snowden supported had been ratified
by a vote of the party members.[51]

As Labour Adviser in the period before the autumn of 1916 Henderson
operated without a department or assistance of any kind. He acted in
a purely advisory capacity to the Ministry of Munitions or to any other
department which wished for his assistance. An early and major instance
of this role concerned unrest among the south Wales miners. On 1 April
1916 they had given three months notice that they wished to terminate
their 1910 wages agreement. Brace, a former south Wales miners' leader
who had entered the Government as Under-Secretary at the Home Office,
had discussions with two of the miners' leaders and suggested concessions
to settle the dispute. On 30 June all three of the Labour party ministers—
Henderson, Brace and Roberts—went to Cardiff and negotiated a settlement, which was narrowly accepted (123 votes to 112) by a miners' delegate
meeting.

When the South Wales Miners' Federation pressed for a wider interpretation of this agreement than that accepted by the Government, Lloyd George had the threatened strike proclaimed illegal under the Munitions of War Act. When 200,000 miners actually went on strike Lloyd George, accompanied by Henderson and Runciman, travelled to Cardiff on 20 July. The three ministers spent several hours negotiating with the coal owners and the miners in separate rooms in the Park Hotel. When a settlement was put to a miners' delegate meeting, the miners called for speeches from Henderson and Runciman as well as Lloyd George. Henderson's speech in which he addressed them as 'fellow trade-unionists' appears to have gone down well. He was called upon again on 31 August, when the timing of the payment of a bonus under the settlement was contested and thereby brought a further strike in late August. Henderson saw both sides of the dispute at the Board of Trade and took a central role, first by himself and later with Lloyd George and Runciman, in eventually achieving agreement.[52]

Even more valuable to the Government was his work, as chairman of the National Advisory Committee and later of the Central Munitions Labour Supply Committee, in assisting the reorganization of working practices in the munitions industries. Lloyd George was determined to push ahead with dilution (the use of unskilled or semi-skilled labour on parts of work usually done by skilled workers). When challenged as to what he would do if faced with resistance, he replied that if shortages of skilled labour made it necessary,

> ... I should be a traitor to the men at the Front if I did not insist upon it ... I prefer that an adjudication should be made by a Labour Committee, but I mean the thing to be done, otherwise ... the sooner we make the peace the better.[53]

Lloyd George offered Henderson and the other trade union leaders the choice of co-operating to make voluntary methods a success or facing the introduction of industrial conscription. He explicitly posed this choice (or threat) both over gaining greater labour mobility and over dilution. For the Government, the co-operation of the leading trade-unionists made the application of policies which were likely to be very unpopular in many workshops much easier and also helped to avoid some industrial unrest.

Henderson and his colleagues on the National Advisory Committee were eager to be involved in increasing the output of munitions. Christopher Addison, Lloyd George's Under-Secretary at Munitions, noted in September 1915 that they had repeatedly complained 'that they have never been asked to help'.[54] The price of their help was to try and ensure that whatever was carried out was done in a way most favourable, or least offensive, to their union members. Perhaps the high point of their success was the brief period from November 1916 when the Engineers and several other skilled unions were given the power to issue cards of exemption from military service to their members. However the cost of gaining concessions on the way government policies operated was to bind themselves to policies such as dilution which proved to be extremely unpopular on the shop-floors.

On 13 September 1915 Lloyd George chaired a conference between Henderson, two other members of the National Advisory Committee and officials of the Ministry of Munitions. He claimed that the voluntary scheme of gaining mobility of skilled labour, the War Munitions Volunteer Scheme, had failed and he also pressed the need for dilution. Henderson spoke strongly against compulsion, observing that it was 'something which... will be strongly opposed by every trade unionist in the country' and even if it were introduced he was 'not satisfied that you would get very many more skilled men placed at your disposal'. Henderson then offered to help make dilution effective. He said,

> ... we should ... make another attempt to dilute labour by putting a skilled engineer in charge of ten or twelve semi-skilled or unskilled men and women ... and probably have 500 to 1,000 supervisors to 10,000 or 20,000 workers ... in my judgement there is no engineering establishment in this country that ought not to be running its machines twenty four hours.

To ensure the success of such a dilution programme, Henderson urged that 'it would be essential that we should bring together the whole of the executives [of unions involved in munitions production] and throw upon them the responsibility for carrying out this scheme'.[55] This was done under the auspices of the National Advisory Committee on 16 and 17 September, with Henderson in the chair. Following Lloyd George's address, that conference agreed resolutions on various aspects of munitions work and set up the Central Munitions Labour Supply Committee, with Henderson as its chairman, to advise on the implementation of dilution and settling any disputes arising from that policy.[56]

So Henderson was much involved in the preparations for the introduction of the much-hated dilution programme. His proposals at the conference on 13 September had been pre-arranged with Lloyd George. As for the latter, a month earlier he had informed his officials responsible for the implementation of dilution,

... if there is real trouble, you must call the Ministry in, and we must make it a national issue. If the trade unions resent it, if they carry it to the extent of threatening to strike, then... the whole influence of the government must be brought to bear upon it.[57]

Thus Henderson's role was to ease along a tough policy on which Lloyd George had already embarked. In reality the consultation with the sub-committee of the National Advisory Committee and then with the trade unions was not about alternative policies but was to try to achieve their co-operation in the wholesale implementation of dilution. For the trade union leaders it marked another stage along a route on which they had started at the Treasury conference.

Henderson took a very active role in the implementation of dilution. An account of his visit to Newcastle in June 1916 records, 'At each estab-lishment the deputation centred its enquiries on the question of lost time, the possibility of increasing the mobility of shipyard labour and the rea-sons for delay in the application of dilution'.[58] His most famous expedition, however, was in December 1915 when he accompanied Lloyd George to Newcastle and the Clyde. Henderson and J.T. Brownlie, chair-man of the executive committee of the ASE, had pressed Lloyd George to go to these engineering centres to explain the policy to the local rep-resentatives of the trade unions. They can have left with few illusions as to the strength of feeling which the implementation of dilution aroused. One civil servant accompanying them recalled that at Newcastle they

... had met with a very hostile reception from among the trade unions and the extremists among the shop stewards at the Elswick works ... The trouble was that Lloyd George relied solely on his eloquence and the patriotic appeal; he could not cope with the workers' problems or with the technical side of dilution. Henderson ... was not much better, and Lloyd George kept on telling him so. In fact there was no love lost between the two during the whole trip.[59]

Worse was to follow in Glasgow. There they received a hostile reception at a series of meetings. On 23 December when they visited the Parkhead Forge, David Kirkwood, a leading shop steward, pointed to Henderson and said to Lloyd George, 'Henderson! We repudiate him as we do Brown-lie, as we have told him to his face'. Kirkwood, speaking of this meeting later, claimed that the workers he represented

... distrusted Mr. Lloyd George. It seemed to them that his public policy was dictated by the spirit of the 'Servile State'... By joining the Cabinet

Mr. Henderson had lost their confidence. He had been elected to be independent. They thought he should have remained independent.

On Christmas Day Lloyd George and Henderson were heckled vigorously
by part of the audience at a meeting held in St Andrew's Hall. Henderson's
observation that 'The scheme of dilution ... did not come from any
employer. It came from a Committee upon which there were seven trade
unionists' received interjections such as 'Traitors'.

In spite of such hostility to dilution the Government pressed ahead
with it in 1916. On the Clyde the shop stewards' resistance was broken
when the Government between 26 and 30 March deported Kirkwood
and nine others from the area without any form of trial. Henderson's
participation in dilution and his tenure of office in a government which
carried out the deportation of active trade-unionists ensured that he faced
very serious criticism within the Labour movement.

Kirkwood appeared at the January 1917 Labour party conference and,
on rising to speak, was given 'an unparalleled ovation'. He received very
warm support for his speech in which he complained of these arbitrary
deportations and of the fact that in the ensuing nine months his wife
and six children had only received £5. 5s. [£5.25] from the State. The
deportation of trade-unionists was an especially sensitive matter politically
given the British Labour movement's active campaign during 1914 on
behalf of nine South African trade union leaders deported by the South
African government in January of that year. Henderson got a hearing
only with difficulty and was then seriously criticized in the ensuing debates.
He called for an inquiry into these deportations saying that he did so
not only because he 'and other members of the government were involved,
but the whole of the management of the ASE, and the whole of the
methods of the trade union movement were involved'. He also observed
that the demonstration of support for Kirkwood 'had revealed to him
that the conference was not in the frame of mind to do justice to men
like himself'.[60]

The conference did set up a committee of inquiry, under Robert Smillie,
the President of the Miners' Federation of Great Britain. In the debates
at the conference Smillie had been vigorous in his criticisms, raising the
point that 'while it was Kirkwood and his friends in the past, they did
not know who it would be tomorrow'. The committee set out to look
firstly into the circumstances of the deportations, but after that to investigate:

Whether Mr. Arthur Henderson was a party to this action. Whether the

Amalgamated Society of Engineers acquiesced in it; and whether ... [their] action ... was in anyway inimical to the interests of trade unionism.

The findings of the committee when it reported at the end of October 1917 stated,

With regard to the action of Mr. Arthur Henderson, the facts that we have set forth show that, although as a member of the government he could not escape the collective responsibility which rested upon it..., he would not have advised the policy which was adopted in his absence on 24 March 1916. Subsequently he did all he could to get the men returned to their homes and he obtained subsistence allowances for their families in respect of the period during which they were unemployed. We made special enquiries of the deportees regarding Mr. Henderson, and their general view was that they had no complaint to make against him.[61]

The available government sources also suggest that Henderson was not directly involved in the deportations. Addison in early March 1916 had told Lloyd George that Henderson would not be effective in pushing through dilution in the face of trade union opposition. He noted in his diary,

I pointed out to him that in the two critical struggles with the ASE we had had to stand firm, but that Henderson had wanted to give way. It amazes me that LG should expect that Henderson could see a thing like this through against the dogged and open hostility of a number of men in the shipyards.[62]

The decision to deport the men followed a request from Lynden McCassey and his fellow Clyde Dilution Commissioners, and was made by Lloyd George and Addison in consultation with representatives of the War Office and the Scottish Office. After the deportations, Addison recorded that on 30 March 'there was a little unpleasantness in the afternoon owing to Henderson making trouble because I had not consulted him sufficiently'. However on finding out about the deportations, Henderson's immediate thoughts appear to have been to help stop the resulting strikes on the Clyde from spreading further. In the Cabinet on 30 March he 'offered to use his best efforts to enlighten his friends as to the true state of affairs' proposing to address a meeting in Glasgow 'not with the idea of making terms with the strikers but to prevent others joining them'. However he was stopped from doing that lest it in anyway 'gave the appearance of negotiations'.[63]

Another issue on which Henderson received condemnation from much of the Labour movement was military conscription. He remained in office when conscription was introduced in two stages in January and May

1916, in spite of several clear-cut decisions by the Labour movement against conscription. On the latter occasion, when challenged in the House of Commons by Frank Goldstone on his clash of loyalties between being secretary of the Labour party and a member of the Cabinet, Henderson bluntly replied, 'If being Secretary of the Labour Party is in any way to preclude me from doing my duty to my country in this crisis, I want my hon. Friend and others to know that I choose my country before my party'.[64]

Henderson's position on conscription was similar to Asquith's. He did not want conscription, wished to achieve the necessary manpower for the armed forces by voluntary means, but if these failed he would accept conscription. Thus, after he had supported the first Military Service Bill, he wrote to his agent in Barnard Castle, 'My opinions have not changed, but they have been overborne by the conviction that some measure of compulsion is required on the grounds of absolute military necessary'.[65] After entering Asquith's Coalition Government, Henderson had vigorously supported the recruiting campaign, and in so doing had said it was the way to avoid compulsion. In the House of Commons, when rebutting criticism from Snowden that the setting up of a National Register to gain details of the distribution of manpower in the country was a prelude to conscription, Henderson demanded to know what Snowden had done to make the voluntary system a success.[66] At the TUC in September, Smillie and other speakers against compulsion received warm applause. By a large majority Congress passed a motion condemning conscription and promising support and 'every aid' to the Government in recruiting men for the armed forces by voluntary means.

However, already by that time many leading pro-war trade-unionists had been making public pronouncements that they would accept conscription if the Government announced it to be essential. Henderson himself in effect had taken this position on the War Policy Committee, a Cabinet committee set up in August 1915 by Asquith to review Britain's manpower resources. He had told them, 'I am prepared, as a last extremity to accept compulsion for a definite and publicly stated object . . . ' but he had made it clear then and during the rest of 1915 that he felt voluntarism must be tried thoroughly first. He advised his Cabinet colleagues,

> The unity of the nation is in danger. Our aim must be to handle the situation so that compulsion, if it comes, comes by the action of the people themselves. On the alternative of conscription or defeat they will be united again. But they cannot be brought to that alternative suddenly, or apart from the conviction that it is a military necessity.[67]

Following the TUC's vote against compulsion the Labour party's executive organized a joint meeting with the parliamentary Labour party, the parliamentary committee of the TUC and the GFTU in order to place 'the emphatic decision of organised Labour before the government' and to decide on action 'to counteract the subversive agitation' in favour of conscription. When the meeting took place on 27 September at the Board of Education, with Henderson in the chair, it agreed to his suggestion that Kitchener and Asquith should address the conference. As a result of their speeches the joint conference unanimously agreed 'to assist the government in every possible way to secure men for service in the navy, army and in munitions works, and for this purpose is willing to organise and to co-operate in recruiting campaign throughout the country'. Given the past criticism of Labour MPs appearing on Parliamentary Recruiting Campaign platforms with Tories and Liberals, it was also agreed that this voluntary recruiting drive would be 'conducted on Labour platforms only'. This Joint Labour Recruiting Committee worked hard to support the scheme of Lord Derby, the Director of Recruiting, whereby eligible males not engaged in essential work were encouraged to attest to their willingness to serve in the armed forces if called upon to do so. At a meeting at the Board of Education on 28 October, again chaired by Henderson, Lord Derby 'expressed his hearty satisfaction at the co-operation that organised labour was giving'.[68]

Among MPs of all parties there was a widespread belief that Derby's scheme offered the last, and not very great, hope of voluntary methods meeting the armed services' needs without conscription. Lord Edmund Talbot wrote to Bonar Law on 16 October that it was not worth precipitating an early general election in order to win a mandate for conscription before Derby's scheme had its chance as there would be 'great bitterness, with a strong and violent opposition in the new House, and the certainty of strikes in the labour world outside'. He reported,

> During the past week I have had frequent opportunities of meeting the most active labour and trade union leaders both in and out of the House.
>   I am clear they one and all accept this as a final effort. I think most of them think it will fail, that when and if it does, they are prepared to accept and support compulsion.[69]

Henderson was probably one of the people whom he had consulted. By early November he was publicly stating that his personal belief that 'we can get all the men we need without resorting to compulsion' was of little importance as 'the immediate need is to get the men'. Lord Derby's report on the response to his scheme was first considered by the Cabinet on 22 December 1915; but the ministers present delayed their decision until Lloyd George and Henderson returned from their dilution trip to Newcastle and Glasgow. Then Runciman observed, 'Henderson has tumbled into LG's basket, tickled by the flattery of Curzon and company'.[70] In reality Henderson had long been resigned to conscription being introduced before the Cabinet decision to do so on 29 December.

However whilst he was convinced of its inevitability, a large majority of the Labour movement was certainly not yet convinced. Hostility to conscription was reaffirmed at a special National Labour Congress held at Central Hall, Westminster on 6 January 1916. The previous day Henderson had chaired a meeting of the Labour party's executive and the leaders of the TUC and GFTU which prepared a resolution for this conference. Their resolution reaffirmed the TUC's resolution of the previous September, welcomed Asquith's pledges that married men would not be called up until most single men had attested, and left Labour MPs free to vote as they wished. Henderson had convinced them at their previous meeting that resistance to Asquith's 'minimum measure of conscription' was rash. Beatrice Webb was told by her husband that 'Henderson told them that the alternative was a general election and that if that took place every Labour MP would lose his seat—certainly every member who was against military service'. Probably they did not need much convincing. The special Congress declined to accept the resolution prepared for them. Instead it declared outright hostility to the Military Service Bill and recommended that the parliamentary Labour party should oppose the measure in all its stages. During the Congress Henderson clashed again with Snowden. Beatrice Webb wrote of this in her diary,

> Henderson, after beginning well by asserting that he should resign from the government if the Labour Party decided against the Bill, lost his temper, owing to unmannerly interruptions, and challenged the ILP MPs to resign their seats as he intended to, so as to test the wishes of the constituencies. Snowden could not resist taking up the challenge, and was understood to say that he would resign his seat at Blackburn if Henderson would fight him.

The Labour party executive and the parliamentary Labour party met immediately after the special Congress had ended and agreed that 'the Party can no longer remain part of the Coalition government'.[71] Henderson wrote to Asquith:

> In consequence of the decision of Organised Labour to oppose the Military

Service Bill I have no alternative but to tender you my resignation. I had hoped that the National Government as constituted in May last, would have continued as a symbol of unity and determination of our country until our efforts, with those of our Allies, had culminated in a final and lasting peace ... I supported the Military Service Bill in the Cabinet; I shall continue to do so in the House as the representative of my constituents, on the ground of military necessity.[72]

Yet although Henderson carried out the decision to tender his resignation, he appears also to have suggested a way in which Asquith could enable the Labour ministers to stay. Runciman informed his wife, 'At the Cabinet Henderson described the seriousness of the labour situation and showed that unless the PM can announce great changes in the Military Service Bill his clients would be irreconcilable and Labour must withdraw from the coalition'. Asquith requested to see the Labour party executive and parliamentary party and gave assurances which they deemed to be

> ... to the effect that there would be no extension of compulsion to married men, that the Bill was to operate during the War only, that amendments would be introduced obviating any possibility of industrial compulsion, that tribunals would be civilian and not military courts, and that opportunity would be afforded to Parliament to strengthen the clause exempting conscientious objectors.[73]

With these assurances the meeting agreed by twenty votes to eleven to rescind their decision of 6 January and, by twenty-five votes to eight, that the ministers withdraw their resignations pending the Labour party conference at Bristol later in the month.

At the party conference there was an acrimonious debate, with Albert Bellamy, president of the National Union of the Railwaymen, condemning the disregarding of the special Congress decision and saying, 'Let them abide by the decision of the majority or else, for God's sake, get out of the Movement altogether'. Henderson responded that it was 'the most momentous discussion' that had taken place at any Labour party conference he had attended and he emphasized the seriousness of Britain's situation in the war, warning that the wrong decision could bring 'the most lamentable defeat that this country and the allied cause has ever experienced'. The conference declared its opposition to the Military Service Bill but, by a small majority, declined to agitate for its repeal.[74]

When in April 1916 a further political crisis developed over the extension of conscription to married men Henderson again was on the side of slowing down the onset of general conscription. By 17 April, Lloyd

George and Bonar Law were pressing Asquith hard to do as the military members of the Army Council wanted, to extend conscription. Lloyd George was willing to stop short of an outright general conscription bill. Henderson again supported Asquith and exerted some pressure against the outright conscriptionists. C.P. Scott, the editor of the *Manchester Guardian*, saw Lloyd George several times during the week from 13 April. He wrote of this,

> It now became a question of how far George would consent to go. Henderson, on behalf of the Labour members, refused to accept his first compromise terms—i.e. the immediate passing of a Bill for general compulsion to come into force automatically a month hence unless meanwhile the full number of men required ... were forthcoming from among the unattested married men alone—and proposed a slight modification—i.e. that the Bill should not be passed now but only at the end of the period of grace in case the required men had not been forthcoming. Asquith agreed to accept this and George could not easily decline. Had he done so the bulk of the Unionists in the Cabinet would have gone with Henderson and Asquith ...[75]

Henderson used Labour's opposition to extending conscription as a lever to extract such minor concessions in the Cabinet meetings. He also used such manoeuvres as a means of getting his party to sanction his and his colleagues staying in office. Henderson kept the parliamentary Labour party and the Labour party executive informed of the developing crisis. He got them to call upon the Government 'to arrange for a secret session of the House of Commons in order that the necessary facts of the situation should be communicated to Members prior to the introduction of any extension of the Military Service Act'. This took place on 25 April. The next day, at a meeting chaired by Henderson, Asquith, Kitchener and Bonar Law addressed a large meeting of the leaders of the Labour party, the TUC, the GFTU, the ASE, the Miners' Federation of Great Britain, the National Union of Railwaymen and the Transport Workers' Federation. Following this meeting the TUC and GFTU supported the Government's proposals. On learning of their support the Labour party executive agreed, by seven votes to two, not to call a National Labour Conference to discuss the extension of conscription.[76]

Henderson's efforts, however, did not delay general conscription. For the government was so vigorously criticized in Parliament, both in the Secret Session on 25 April and on the following day when it attempted to introduce a compromise measure of conscription, that it was forced to bring in general conscription.[77] But Henderson had helped Asquith to hold his coalition Government together for some months longer. He had also delivered Labour support for something the movement had emphatically opposed. Those favouring outright conscription, such as Lloyd George, had every reason to be pleased with the outcome of Asquith's and Henderson's manoeuvres; as one of Lloyd George's Liberal supporters had observed on this issue, 'nothing really matters if you can get the trade unions on your side'.[78]

For much of his time in Asquith's coalition Government Henderson served as President of the Board of Education. He found trying to combine this role with his major work on behalf of the Government in industrial relations impractical. That his role in education would be subsidiary was clear from the outset. Frank Goldstone, who was a Labour MP sponsored by the National Union of Teachers, wrote then,

> Unfortunately his term of office may be short and ... he may not have adequate opportunity for devoting his energies to educational reform ... The sooner the Board of Education ceases to be regarded as the 'Cinderella' of government departments the sooner will it be found that Presidents remain there sufficiently long not only to develop a policy but to see it mature under their hands.[79]

Henderson was well aware when he took the post on that he would have limited time to devote to education. He tried to secure as his Parliamentary Secretary Christopher Addison, who had served his predecessor. Asquith even asked Lloyd George to release Addison from working with him at the Ministry of Munitions as Henderson wanted his experience and that would 'enable him [Henderson] to be free to help with labour'.[80] But Henderson ended up with one of Lloyd George's main friends among the Welsh MPs, Herbert Lewis, who was also new to the Board. At the Board of Education such impact as Henderson did have reflected his trade union and local government background. While he was President, the Board was beginning to review aspects of education as part of the groundwork for the major reorganization of the education system. Henderson favoured the establishment of committees rather than getting a Royal Commission appointed. He approved the setting up of three to review science, modern languages and the education of young persons after the war, paying particular attention to the problem of those who had been abnormally employed during the war. In making appointments to these committees he took care to include some people favoured by the teaching unions.[81] After his resignation Goldstone commended him for promoting improved relations between the Board and local government:

His term of office will be gratefully remembered because of the increased accessibility accorded to members of local authorities and representatives of the teachers ... Mr. Henderson extended the admirable practice, established by recent predecessors, of consultation with those who have the practical carrying out of the Board's policy. As a direct result of the more liberal regime, the relations between the various partners in the educational alliance have tended to become more cordial.[82]

However in the midst of war Henderson did not see education as a priority for scarce resources. In 1915 he told the TUC, 'It is clear that both legislation and additional state aid for education are out of the question so long as the war lasts' and he advised male teachers that the needs of the armed services were 'paramount', even if their departure resulted in 'a depleted education service, with makeshifts taking the place of the normal organisation and with volunteers taking the place of teachers under arms'. Many in the Labour movement were critical of Henderson's actions as first Labour minister in cutting, rather than expanding, scholarships and other provisions. Ramsay MacDonald won considerable acclaim in the House of Commons on 16 July 1916 for criticizing a range of the Board of Education's policies as being unenlightened.[83]

Soon afterwards Henderson made such criticism a major reason for resigning that post while still staying on in the Cabinet. He wrote to Asquith,

... at a time when public interest in our educational future is keener than it has been for many years, the Department should not be left to a Minister who is necessarily in large measure an absentee, who is not in a position to lay plans for the future, and who appears in Parliament (and his own Party) principally as the defender of reactionary policies inherited from his predecessor.

He went on to observe that his participation in the Government had seriously prejudiced his position in the Labour party:

Through my association with the Military Service Acts and with the labour policy of the Munitions Department, I believe I have permanently forfeited the confidence of certain sections of the organised workers. I am now faced with a much more serious consequence ... of losing a greater measure of the support of the Labour Party ...

If, as I believe to be the case, it is desirable to retain the Labour Party in the Coalition, I should be happy to take a position in the Ministry without Portfolio and without ministerial salary. This would set me free to devote myself wholly to labour questions and would leave me more time to keep in touch with the Labour Party.

In spite of such a letter from a leader of a party in his coalition Government, Asquith did not find the time to discuss the matter with Henderson. On 8 August 1916 Henderson, complaining that his position was becoming 'more and more anomalous', firmly tendered his resignation whilst making clear his availability to discuss his position with Asquith.[84]

Henderson's demand to be released from the Board of Education was not only due to lack of time. It was also part of his manoeuvring over a long period for more powers and recognition for his position as a special labour adviser. In the autumn of 1915 there had been several occasions when there was friction between Henderson and civil servants in the Ministry of Munitions over his role. Thus, for example, in October 1915 Addison noted 'trouble brewing between Beveridge and our Labour offices and Henderson's Committee', which he ascribed to the former being 'rather tactless' in his dealings with the National Advisory Committee. In early 1916 there appears to have been some consideration of setting up a separate ministry for Labour matters under Henderson, but by 8 March Addison felt that this had 'faded out'. Henderson may well have hoped to have succeeded Lloyd George as Minister of Munitions when he went to the War Office on 6 July. According to Addison, before the debate in the House of Commons on the Education Estimates, Henderson had gone 'to the P.M. and raised a storm and said that he had been kept out of the Labour Department and insisted on being given a more prominent position'.[85]

Henderson rightly thought that Addison was against him. Several of the Liberal ministers were willing to use Henderson to try to tame labour while not giving him any major responsibility. Thus Addison noted of a conversation he had with Montagu, who had succeeded Lloyd George as Minister of Munitions,

> ... he agrees with me that he could not give him any executive work. He said that he was a failure at executive work, but we shall give him as much talking to do as possible, so as to please his vanity which is considerable.

However, Henderson's letter to Asquith requesting to leave Education put pressure on Montagu who 'had tried to temporise, by a letter setting out what he could do ...'. This letter angered Henderson, who wrote to Montagu demanding more powers.

Montagu, probably prompted by Asquith, replied to Henderson on 4 August,

> ... I cannot consider any re-arrangement of this office which would have as its result the impertinent proposition that you should be to all intents

and purposes my Under-Secretary. The proposal I shall make seems to me to be more in accord with your status and prestige.

I will ask you to assume the position of Labour Adviser to the Ministry of Munitions and to give us the benefit of your advice in such a way as to be most useful to us.

If you will accept this office I would give instructions that labour cases involving points of principle or departures in practice, or illustrating important aspects of the administration of the Labour Department of the Ministry shall be referred to you for your opinion as Labour Adviser at a sufficiently early stage. I shall also express my desire that you should be regularly informed of the subsequent history of any decision in which you have been interested.

Montagu went on to promise that 'if at any time you have reason for complaint, you will, of course, at once make representations to me and I can assure you that I will use every effort to put the matter right'.[86]

Following Henderson's firm letter of resignation from Education, the contents of which he had allowed to become public knowledge, Asquith removed him from that post. He was then given the post of Paymaster General, which involved fewer departmental responsibilities, but nevertheless involved some responsibilities for pensions. Before making that appointment, Asquith let the press know that Henderson would not be Minister of Labour. The reason given was that it 'would involve too great a rearrangement of departmental duties at this time, and would raise questions such as the creation of a Ministry of Commerce, with which the government are not prepared to deal at this present time'.[87]

Immediately he was released from Education Henderson set to work to organize a department to back up his role as Labour Adviser. By early October 1916 he was installed in his own offices close by St James's Park, with a staff and a second minister, George Roberts. Henderson, to the wrath of Sir George Askwith, claimed (wrongly) that, unlike the Board of Trade, his department would intervene in anticipation of a strike or lock-out. Moreover, in effect, he appealed for problems to be brought to him. Askwith and other civil servants long involved in industrial conciliation feared that this would have the effect of encouraging trade unions to ignore existing arbitration procedures and re-open cases.

Henderson used his position to foster the role of representative bodies of employers and trade unions in assisting the State to extract the maximum output from industry. He set about 'to lay the foundations for a regular and definite system of co-operation and communication between industry and the government' by appointing consultative committees for employers, trade-unionists and for women's labour. Henderson promised, 'Where it is necessary to consult any industry or branch of industry from either the employers' or workmen's standpoint, full opportunity will be given to the representatives of the industry to submit any considerations which appear to them to be material'. Thus Henderson in government office was very much the leading trade-union protagonist of corporatist policies. If the state was to be deeply involved in running British industry, then it should do so in partnership with the employers and the unions. 'Trade unions, quick to realise the value of the new department', ran one press story, 'inform it of matters in dispute, and the machinery of government is at once set in motion'. He also let it be known that the 'department is clearly capable of great expansion'.[88]

Yet despite all this 'puffing', Henderson's role essentially remained as an advisory one to other departments and was not executive. Perhaps Asquith shared Addison's prejudices against a Labour politician being given powers over both sides of industry. Addison observed of Henderson, 'He does not realise that we should have the employers from one end of the country to the other absolutely on their hind legs at such a proposal and that it really would not do'. More revealingly, he also wrote in his diary that 'he would simply take the part of the trades unions, as I am quite sure he would not dare to oppose them at a pinch and the office would be up in arms about it, although I do not think the latter would count much'. Some employers were indeed hostile to Henderson taking posts involving industrial decisions.[89] But it has to be said that there appears to have been far less anxiety by most Liberal politicians about businessmen being put in charge of commercial matters in the Ministry of Munitions and other government departments.

Henderson continued to act as an industrial relations trouble-shooter for the rest of Asquith's Government. He acted frequently for the Ministry of Munitions, and for other departments. Thus in September and October he worked with Runciman and the Board of Trade in settling a potentially serious dispute between the railwaymen and the employers over the men's demand for a further war bonus to their wages. Having reached a settlement granting the men 5s.(25p), Henderson then became involved in getting an agreement for the men working in the railway workshops—a more complex matter because of the problems of links between their wages and those of engineers working in other engineering trades.[90]

His activities on behalf of Montagu and the Ministry of Munitions led him into another major controversy, the possible use of black labour in the building trade. Montagu referred to Henderson the suggested use of 'five to ten thousand African native labourers ... under their own white overseers for employment on navvy work in the south of England'. Henderson agreed to consult the building trade unions on the problem of finding adequate labour for a new explosives factory. Following a Central Munitions Supply Committee meeting he also agreed 'that if the supply of labour in this country appeared to be insufficient ... [he] would recommend to the unions a proposal to introduce 10,000 Kroo boys for the purpose'.[91] Given the uproar over the use of Chinese labour in South Africa after the Boer War, this was an extraordinarily delicate political issue. The building unions refused to agree to the proposal. At the 1917 Labour party conference Henderson was strongly criticised for his role as Labour Adviser in this controversy.

His ministerial responsibility for pensions was also controversial. As Paymaster General from 19 August 1916 he was in charge of part of the administration of pensions. When he took over the post, MPs had been severely criticizing the way the Chelsea Commissioners were dealing with disabled soldiers. Henderson was soon making a public commitment to eliminate the often very lengthy interval between the end of a disabled soldier's military pay and the start of his disability pension.[92]Immediately after his appointment suggestions were made that the administration of pensions should be reorganized. Lord Derby wrote to Lloyd George,

> Henderson now becomes head of the Chelsea Commission. Why should we not give over the whole of the pensions to him, abolish the present board and give him a new and much smaller one? He would be answerable to Parliament and have to fight out any financial question with the Treasury.[93]

Henderson then became embroiled in a political wrangle as to whether he could combine this new position with his post as Labour Adviser. Faced with serious criticism from the Unionists, Henderson informed Asquith that if forced to choose between Pensions and being Labour Adviser, he would take the latter. However, he felt that he could success-fully combine the two posts, for now as Labour Adviser, unlike his service in Education, he had staff to support him.[94] Unionist criticism was osten-sibly aimed at possible inefficient administration. But there were deeper electoral considerations as well. One Unionist MP clearly stated that the objection was not limited to Henderson. He asserted that he and other Unionist MPs

> strongly protest against a member of the Labour Party being appointed to a post which, by maladministration, might prove nothing short of disastrous to our party at the next election if it be contested on the old party lines.

> It would, in the opinion of many of us, result in our losing not only all
> the dockyard seats, but many others which are at present safe Unionist seats.[95]

The Unionists were feeling vulnerable at a time when radical ex-
servicemen's organizations were being formed and were agitating for a
better deal for soldiers and their dependants. In the autumn of 1916 they
were eager to get the Pensions appointment for their party. When, at
the end of November, it became apparent that the Minister of Pensions
would be in control with the Board acting only in an advisory capacity,
the Unionist Chief Whip, Lord Edmund Talbot, wrote to Bonar Law
complaining that 'the whole thing becomes a labour show' and urging,
'please remember that all this makes it of paramount importance that
the new Under Secretary should be and must be of our choosing'.[96] The
fall of Asquith's Government shortly afterwards ended this issue as far
as Henderson was concerned; though he had to face Snowden's sneers
as to his performance in this post at the 1917 Labour Party Conference.

Henderson's entry into Lloyd George's Government in December 1916
was to be a major source of controversy within the Labour movement.
The new Government rested on Unionist support. At the 1917 Labour
party conference Henderson was to be strongly criticized for joining a
government whose leading members included such arch-imperialists as
Lord Milner and Lord Curzon. Snowden, amidst a wide ranging denunciation of Henderson's actions, dubbed Lloyd George's coalition 'the
Northcliffe government'. More worrying for Henderson than the attacks
of ILP and British Socialist party critics were the harsh words from leading
trade-unionists. Ernest Bevin, after savaging Snowden for cheap gibes,
expressed grave concern at Labour joining in a government incorporating
such men with anti-trade union records as Lords Rhondda, Devonport,
Derby and Milner.[97]

Henderson undoubtedly had admired Asquith and warmly supported
him over such issues as conscription. On 1 December, less than a week
before Asquith resigned, Henderson made a major speech at Northampton
intended to boost support for Asquith's Government. He urged that he
should be able to take back a message of encouragement to the Prime
Minister and proclaimed, in words that would haunt him in the coming
weeks,

> ... I say this fearlessly—there is no statesman who possesses the same power
> to reconcile and unite divergent political interests than he does ... Mr.
> Asquith ... is the indispensable man to lead us to the end of this war and
> lead us successfully.

Ten days later, he was struggling with his words to justify his new position:

> I was compelled to say that national duty demanded that I should face a
> personal danger, I mean in the risk of being personally misunderstood ...
> I do not withdraw a single word I then said ... But in the present state
> of affairs I determined to put national considerations before all.

He reassured his Methodist audience with the thought that the new
Government was 'headed by a very prominent Nonconformist and a very
ardent social reformer'.[98]

Henderson had remained loyal to Asquith until Asquith resigned the
premiership on 5 December 1916. He was invited to a meeting of Liberal
former ministers in Asquith's Cabinet, which agreed only to serve in a
government headed by Asquith, but he himself declined to take this position. At the time the King conferred with leading Unionist and Liberal
politicians as to constructing a new coalition, he was still pressing for
the inclusion of Asquith. Balfour noted, 'Henderson, for his part dwelt
upon the difficulty he anticipated in including organized labour to associ-
ate itself with any government of which Asquith was not a member'.
Henderson was said to have expressed his willingness to serve under Balfour, Bonar Law or Lloyd George.

On 7 December Henderson went to Lloyd George to ask him to see
a deputation from the parliamentary Labour party and the Labour party
executive. Lloyd George later told C.P. Scott that when Henderson asked
him what representation he would give Labour if he formed a government,
he replied that when Asquith's coalition government had been formed
he (Lloyd George) had 'advocated the inclusion of two representatives
of Labour in Cabinet instead of one and intended now considerably to
increase the representation of Labour in the Ministry'.[99] Henderson
appears then to have pressed Lloyd George for specific commitments.
He wanted Labour representation in the War Cabinet (thus giving Labour
direct involvement in the running of the war, not being excluded as was
the case with Asquith's War Committee of seven) and Labour in charge
of those areas which he had been keen to control under Asquith—a
Labour Ministry, which consolidated the labour departments of the Board
of Trade and the Ministry of Munitions, and a Ministry of Pensions.
The previous night the president of the GFTU, James O'Grady, had
made a speech at which he had come out in favour of entering Lloyd
George's Government provided that Labour was offered 'responsible positions' and were not treated as 'mere office boys' as under Asquith, while
'doing a tremendous amount of work, in keeping the organised Labour

movement in this country loyal to the government'.[100]

Lloyd George offered Labour these and minor posts, promised that the mines and shipping 'should be nationalised as far as possible' and undertook to appoint a Food Controller. After tense discussion, the parliamentary Labour party and Labour party executive agreed, by eighteen votes to twelve, to join the new coalition. The majority felt that, as it was later put, 'the national interests and the possibility of Labour securing a greater opportunity to mould policy and exercise executive authority in important administrative positions could not be ignored'.[101]

Henderson's entry into Lloyd George's War Cabinet entailed a commitment to fully mobilizing Britain's resources for victory. The premier promised to wage the war with 'determination, promptitude and relentness', not with the 'delay, hesitation and vacillation' which he deemed to be characteristic of Asquith's Governments. Lloyd George's approach was also very much an alternative to Lord Lansdowne's appraisal of November 1916 in which he suggested the war was destroying all the participants and suggested that a negotiated peace might be more realistic than hoping that 'the knock-out blow can and will be delivered'.

Henderson expounded the Lloyd George view of the requisite war policies with much vigour. In the first six weeks of the Government he made several speeches rebutting American and other suggestions for an early negotiated peace. He welcomed efforts 'to bring about a council of the league of nations ... that would lay down the principles but not now ... to talk about peace with the most unscrupulous military forces ... would be a step to having the whole thing fought over again'. Henderson argued, 'Indemnity for the past was not enough unless we had guarantees for the future; and guarantees for the future were not enough without ample reparation for all that Belgium, France, Serbia and Poland had suffered'.[102]

Henderson spoke publicly of the need for a better organization of manpower shortly before Asquith fell. On 1 December 1916 he said,

> We must organise as we have never yet organised... There is nothing we need so much in this country as the entire organisation of its manhood and womanhood to be placed at the service of the nation for winning the war. That can only be accomplished smoothly and speedily with the co-operation of organised labour. Trade union leaders should be used for that purpose not only in an advisory but in an executive capacity... Let us cease playing at this business.[103]

On 19 December, within Lloyd George's War Cabinet, Henderson

managed to amend proposals for industrial conscription to an agreement
to give a voluntary enrolment policy a chance. In this way, as with the
Derby scheme before the introduction of compulsory military service,
Henderson urged that voluntary methods must be seen to be exhausted
before compulsion was introduced. When the national service campaign
to enrol volunteers got underway, he chaired the meeting to launch it,
and then spoke at a series of major meetings in Manchester, Newcastle,
Sunderland, Swansea and Reading. He made it clear that he felt there
was an 'obligation, if we are opposed to compulsion, to do everything
we possibly can to make the voluntary scheme ... such a success that
there will be no need to resort to powers of compulsion'. However if
the scheme was not sufficient and he had to break his pledge against
the introduction of industrial conscription, given at the time of the coming
of military conscription,

> ... he was prepared to do the honourable thing—that was to go to his consti-
> tuents and ask to be released from the pledge. He would not be worthy
> of his position as a member of the Labour movement if... he shrank from
> saving the nation from disaster by adopting another course.[104]

However, by mid-March, even though the national service campaign
was clearly failing, Lloyd George and the War Cabinet had decided that
the introduction of industrial conscription was impractical, given the hostility of organized labour. Henderson publicly stated the case against
industrial conscription when heckled with the cry of 'traitor' at an enrolment meeting in Reading: 'It is one thing to go in for compulsion for
men to join the Forces to protect their country, but it is another thing
to go for compulsion to make profits for private employers. The government are alive to that fact'.[105]

The members of Lloyd George's War Cabinet were assigned to look
into particular problem areas. National service was one area that Lloyd
George often assigned to Henderson. As well as his active support for
the voluntary enrolment campaign, he also undertook an investigation
of the departmental conflicts which were obstructing manpower policies.
Later he and Milner became the arbiters of interdepartmental disputes
involving manpower. Lloyd George also gave them the similar task of
investigating the clash of responsibilities for labour matters between various government departments.[106]

The Government's continuing need for manpower both for industry
and for the Western Front led to major engineering strikes in May 1917.
These stemmed partly from a wide range of social grievances but were

sparked off by proposals to abolish the trade card scheme of exemption from military service enjoyed by many skilled workers and to introduce dilution of labour on non-government work. His last major roles in industrial relations for the Government were, with Addison, to consult the unions over the withdrawal of the trade card scheme and later to try to resolve the strikes. Henderson firmly warned the War Cabinet before the strikes began that 'the situation was one which would need careful handling'. He noted that there was 'grave unrest in the country, which had been deepened by the Russian Revolution'. Once the strikes were under way, Henderson joined Addison in negotiations to settle them. His role was marked by his vigorous condemnation of actions led by shop stewards against the established trade-union leadership. Thus on 10 May he told one gathering of trade union representatives,

> I have no hesitation in saying that the government would be prepared to go any length—at any rate, any reasonable length—with you to assist you to stamp this pernicious influence and policy out of the ranks of organised labour, because it is going to be disastrous to the country and disastrous to organised labour ... I have set my face like flint against anything that is going to undermine the discipline and executive authority of the respective trade unions.[107]

A month later, Henderson was to be faced with other 'unorthodox' militant workers, but this time in Russia. His wish to strengthen the moderate democratic-socialist Kerensky and his government was to lead to his enforced resignation from Lloyd George's Cabinet and his return to favour with most of the British Labour movement.

6
Preparing for a Labour Government

Henderson's attempts, simultaneously, to serve Lloyd George and the Labour movement finally failed in the summer of 1917. This arose from the issue of whether Labour should support a proposed international socialist conference at Stockholm. Henderson's enforced departure from the Government gave him much more time to devote his considerable organizing abilities to the Labour party and to assist in establishing it as the main opposition to the Lloyd George coalition. Thereafter he was a solid bastion of constitutional moderation amidst the immediate post-war industrial and social tumult, and as such he was one of several sureties that Labour in office would behave 'responsibly'.

His break with Lloyd George in August 1917 brought him to the same side of a growing chasm in wartime politics as the bulk of the Labour movement's activists. While most trade-unionists continued to back the war effort, there was growing unease as to whether there was equality of sacrifice among all classes in pursuit of victory and as to what were Britain's war aims. The Liberal journalist, A.G. Gardiner, observed of Henderson's time in Lloyd George's War Cabinet 'there was a feeling that his hold over Labour was passing'. However, he noted in an article on Henderson, published a year after the latter's resignation,

> It may be said that he was made great by his fall. No man in public life certainly ever grew more sensibly in stature as the result of resignation. The Russian episode converted him from a commonplace figure on the political stage into a man of capital significance.[1]

Henderson was acutely aware of the damage being done to his standing in the Labour movement by his role as Lloyd George's chief apologist on Labour matters. However his commitment to the war effort and his great appetite for more responsibility kept him in harness until the differences between him and Lloyd George over the Stockholm conference made a break inevitable. Henderson did not manoeuvre for a pretext for resignation. He stayed on in office too long in early August for that to be likely. But he clearly was determined to follow the course he believed to be right on Stockholm regardless of whether he had to leave the Government. As J.R. Clynes had commented of him at the 1917 Labour party conference, he was a man of 'the most stubborn kind' and once he took a stand on a major question he was 'immovable'.[2]

There were tensions between Lloyd George and Henderson before Henderson's visit to Russia. Lloyd George could admire Henderson's courage in doggedly standing up for conscription when he became convinced it was necessary, in spite of the opposition of the majority of the Labour movement, yet be irritated by what he took to be narrow-minded obstinacy on other labour matters.[3] Henderson was his own man and prone to represent organized labour's objections to various government proposals more than the other Labour ministers. The Unionist ministers found George Barnes more amenable than Henderson.

Both as a union official and as Labour party secretary Henderson was criticized for being overbearing. There are suggestions that this trait was present when he was a labour adviser in the Government during the First World War. Addison, admittedly a man who himself was always prone to stand on his dignity, continued to resent Henderson's role as overseer on labour matters when Henderson was in the War Cabinet. Thus in mid-May 1917 he noted in his diary,

> After lunch I had a few faithful minutes talk with L.G. on the subject of the methods of dealing with labour. The fact is that neither Hodge [Minister of Labour] nor myself know where we are. Henderson comes barging in with an interminable appetite for talking and a lust for deputations and conferences which is simply appalling. He sent me the instructions of the War Cabinet and we are therefore bound by the leg practically the whole time. L.G. spoke to Henderson about it afterwards and I daresay we shall have to have it out with one another.[4]

Henderson was much more comfortable with the political style of a man such as Asquith than the mercurial Lloyd George. Henderson's relationship with the latter was not improved by being the object of Lloyd George's wit on several occasions. During their trip to the Tyne and the Clyde in late 1915 their relationship was strained. Sir Ronald Davison recalled many years later that over Christmas dinner Lloyd George entertained those present by suggesting appropriate songs, and that 'For Henderson, it was "The Red Flag", another ironical dig at the mildest of trade unionists'. Then in March 1917, when he and Henderson were supporting the Electoral Reform Bill in the War Cabinet, Lloyd George, tongue-in-cheek, urged Henderson, 'You do the heavy truculent working man and then I will do my bit ...'[5] Henderson would not have taken kindly to too much of this type of banter. However he did not allow personality clashes to undermine his will to pursue what he deemed to be the right policies, as his relationship with Ramsay MacDonald clearly shows.

In spite of such occasional personal tensions, Henderson had no major policy difference with Lloyd George until he went to Russia. The prime minister, for his part, recognized that Henderson was a considerable asset to his Government. When Henderson first pressed his War Cabinet colleagues to allow him on the Labour party's mission to the Labour and Socialist representatives in Petrograd 'to impress upon them the absolute necessity of avoiding anything in the nature of a separate peace', they urged that he was needed to help resolve the serious industrial unrest in Britain.

However, Lloyd George and the War Cabinet came to the view that not only should Henderson go there, but that he should do so as a representative of the British Government. He should be authorized to replace the British ambassador, Sir George Buchanan, just as the French 'patriotic' socialist, Albert Thomas, had replaced the French ambassador. In both cases the notion was to remove establishment figures who had worked closely with the tsarist government and replace them with pro-war figures deemed likely to have greater influence on the members of the Petrograd Soviet. When the War Cabinet came to its decision to send him to Russia, Henderson was firmly against the holding of an international socialist conference, which would include representatives of all the countries at war, in Stockholm to try to formulate a general socialist policy for 'a peace without annexations'.[6]

Henderson's time in Russia had a major impact both on his career and on Labour's evolution into an independent national party. In later elections he was to be smeared for 'hob-nobbing with Bolsheviks' in Russia but, far from hob-nobbing with Bolsheviks, he had publicly denounced them. The ultra-right correspondent of *The Times* later asserted that Henderson 'was completely overwhelmed and upset by his surroundings'.[7]

He may well have been disconcerted by the scale of the problems, but nevertheless whilst in Russia he set about boosting the newly restructured

Provisional Government. Its success was crucial if Russia was to stay in the war. He wrote home,

> The new Provisional Government has had imposed upon it a task of serious magnitude, for it would have been bad enough to have had the war or the revolution, but both is almost beyond human capacity and more especially when the people are suffering from the form of intoxication that has followed upon their newly won freedom. Unfortunately both in civil life and in the armies a great percentage have no desire whatever to get on with the war. They try to excuse themselves by stating that they are prepared for a defensive war but nothing more. I think the indications go to prove that they have been permeated by pacifist theories.[8]

As for industry, Henderson was alarmed by what he judged to be 'a form of syndicalism'. He commented,

> Unfortunately there are no steadying influences akin to our trade unions and the demands that are put forward to the employers are so outrageous that it is obvious they are not prompted with a desire for economic improvement so much as with a view to obtaining complete control of the industry. Some of these demands have represented far more than the entire capital of the company.

Henderson also deplored the intransigence of the employers which he felt would leave the government 'helpless to prevent industry going over under the extreme demands made by the men'. His solution was the British one of state control, not nationalization. 'What is wanted', he argued, 'is that for all the necessary purposes of the war, industry should be controlled in the same way as we have controlled railways, mines, shipping, agriculture etc.'.[9] Henderson put this argument not only to ministers but also to financiers and industrialists. Not surprisingly, the Bolsheviks denounced him as an arch 'social traitor' and a 'British Kerensky'.

His advice from Russia to Lloyd George was to do everything possible to strengthen the Provisional Government. Hence in recommending that Buchanan not be replaced as ambassador, he wrote:

> I attach much weight to an observation of Prince Lvov [the Russian Prime Minister] that the recall of the Ambassador at the moment would be regarded as a concession to popular clamour. In other words his departure, so far from strengthening our influence here would ... actually weaken the authority of the Provisional Government, of whose desire to work in close and intimate co-operation with our own there can ... be little question.

The following day he urged again that 'our best course is to go steadily forward losing no opportunity to strengthen the hands of the government and being most careful to avoid any act or word which might give the extremists a handle against them'.[10]

Thus his actions in Russia centred on buttressing the existing regime. His conversion to supporting British participation in the Stockholm conference was largely part of this, a means of helping to secure continued Russian support for the war. He was also dismayed to find widespread suspicion among the Russian working class in Petrograd and Moscow as to the Allied countries' war aims. So he moved from his initial position in Russia of pressing the Petrograd Soviet to send delegates to a socialist conference confined to those of the Allied countries, to being a supporter of both a preliminary Allied socialist conference and the Stockholm conference. The French socialists similarly moved in favour of participation, fearing not to do so would be to risk the Russian socialists drifting in favour of a separate peace and being left to the influence of German socialists at Stockholm.[11]

On Stockholm, Henderson's and Lloyd George's attitudes reversed during the summer of 1917. Later, when denounced by the coalition candidate in the 1918 general election for supporting Stockholm, Henderson could reply that he had been opposed to it when he went to Russia but 'there was one member of the War Cabinet and only one in favour of a Stockholm conference, and that member was the present Prime Minister'.[12] Lloyd George's change of mind was due to the changing situation in Russia and the growing concern of British vested interests for their investments there. He gauged that there was less need to be sensitive to the views of the Left in Russia or Britain. As the minutes of the War Cabinet discussion on 8 August succinctly record, 'It was now clear that the influence of the Soviet in Russia was steadily declining, and that the attendance of the British delegates in Stockholm was less important than formerly'.[13] Politically, Lloyd George could not afford to be out of line with his European allies, especially the French who clearly opposed the Stockholm conference, nor could he appear to be encouraging Ramsay MacDonald's wing of the Labour movement. Moreover Lloyd George's right-wing political allies were beginning to look to the Russian military to restore 'order' and to replace even socialism of the Kerensky brand. Opposition to the meeting of Allied and German civilians at Stockholm could be argued to be consistent with support for the Russian High Command's efforts to restore discipline in the army and to stamp out fraternization with the German soldiers.

Henderson returned to Britain in late July determined to support the Stockholm conference and thereby, in his view, to strengthen the Provisional Government in Russia. Having made up his mind, he pressed on regardless of Lloyd George's or other ministers' objections. On 25 July he urged the Labour party's executive to approve participation in the Stockholm conference. It agreed to recommend this to a special Labour party conference on the condition that Stockholm be of 'the nature of a consultation and that no binding resolutions should be adopted'. Henderson then went off to Paris with G.J. Wardle (the acting chairman of the parliamentary Labour party) and MacDonald to discuss with French and Russian socialists the arrangements for the Stockholm conference.

Lloyd George later wrote, 'As a member of the British War Cabinet he had no right to go off to Paris without even consulting his colleagues in the Cabinet ...'[14] In fact, after the Labour party executive had made its decision, Henderson did inform Lloyd George (who was in Paris) by telegram that he would be coming to Paris and he did discuss the whole issue on 26 July with the other members of the War Cabinet. Faced with the latter's hostility, he even offered to resign.

On Henderson's return from Paris on 1 August he told Lloyd George that he intended to continue to work for a consultative conference in Stockholm. Lloyd George asked him to discuss the matter with his Cabinet colleagues later in the day. But when Henderson arrived, though he was still a member of the War Cabinet, he was kept outside the room for an hour while his colleagues discussed his conduct. They then sent out another Labour minister, George Barnes, to make a statement to him. Henderson demanded entry to the meeting and made it very clear that he resented being kept out on 'the doormat'.

Even after this, the War Cabinet minutes for 1 August make it clear that Henderson, as well as others, still felt it possible for him to serve two bodies, the Labour party and the War Cabinet. After admitting him, the War Cabinet debated the merits of Henderson's dual position so that a reply could be made to probable criticism in the House of Commons:

> It might be frankly admitted that on the present occasion, this had entailed some misunderstanding, but it must be borne in mind that it also possessed great advantages. It had enabled Mr. Henderson in the past to keep in the closest possible touch with the views of the Labour Party, and so, by first-hand information, to assist the government in preparing its war measures on lines which would be acceptable to labour. Moreover, it had enabled Mr. Henderson to attend the previous conferences of Allied socialists with good results. For example, only last Christmas he had attended a socialist conference in Paris, where he had met with considerable opposition, but had eventually

induced the conference to take the view which he shared with the British government in regard to the prosecution of the war ... On balance ... the dual nature of his position had been an advantage.

Bonar Law, writing to J.P. Croal, editor of the *Scotsman*, on 3 August gave as his motives that 'the main thing after all was to satisfy ourselves that Henderson is in earnest about the war, for undoubtedly his leaving the government would have had a very bad effect on Labour and might just have made the difference in turning the scale in favour of the pacifist movement. For this reason I hope that it may be possible for him to remain without too much humiliation ...'[15]

Up until the special Labour party conference on 10 August, Lloyd George appears to have been confident that Labour would reject participation in the Stockholm conference. Perhaps he was influenced by the hostility to such a conference expressed by the other Labour ministers. Certainly he underestimated the very considerable standing that Henderson had in the Labour movement and that Henderson's case for the Stockholm conference would temporarily unite all but the more vehement pro-war elements in the Labour party.

In his address to the conference on 10 August Henderson observed:

> Convinced as I was that the conference was inevitable, it was surely not unpatriotic for one who had supported the war as I had done ... to try to prevent a bad impression being continued or a worse impression being formed on the minds of the socialists of one of our Allies. In my opinion ... our case is so strong— ... the case of the whole of the Allies is so strong— that if it were presented by responsible working-class representatives it would materially assist in convincing the German people that it was the crime of their rulers that caused the war, and it is the crime of their rulers that now prevents its just settlement.

In his concluding remarks, later deliberately misquoted by the Tory press (which substituted 'supplant' for 'supplement'), he urged,

> Of this I am convinced, and I want to say this with all the seriousness and deliberation of which I am capable, that if we today ... determine for the whole period of the war, not to use the political weapon to supplement our military activities, not only shall I regret it, but I venture to predict that you as a movement will regret it hereafter.[16]

These were neither the words of a pacifist nor of one who ascribed war guilt primarily to secret diplomacy. They represent a difference of opinion between Henderson and his War Cabinet colleagues as to how to maintain Russian support for the war and a naive belief that the British establishment's war aims were not annexationist. Henderson's recommendation to accept the invitation to a consultative conference at Stockholm was endorsed to by 1,846,000 to 550,000 votes.

Lloyd George was furious. That day he had a heated meeting with Henderson and made clear that his duality of office could not continue. The War Cabinet also condemned Henderson for failing to tell the Labour party conference of its opposition to Stockholm and for failing to pass on the spurious information obtained by Lloyd George which (wrongly) suggested that Kerensky's government was also now opposed to such a conference. The War Cabinet meeting ended by instructing the Cabinet Secretary not to summon Henderson to future meetings nor to circulate documents to him. Henderson sent Lloyd George his resignation the next morning. He stated, 'I continue to share your desire that the war should be carried to a successful conclusion, and trust that in a non-governmental capacity I may be able to render some little assistance to this end'.[17]

In the War Cabinet there was some feeling that Henderson's actions should be condemned, but not too vigorously. It was deemed to be 'important, particularly in view of Henderson's offer of continued assistance, not to make a wider breach with him than could be avoided'. But in fact he was pilloried mercilessly. Lloyd George, fearing that the incident would undermine his Government, briefed the press against Henderson, and then, in the House of Commons, by mixing truth and half-truth with skill, did much to discredit him. Henderson complained bitterly about the press reports, saying

> There is no better Press Bureau in this country than the one controlled by the Prime Minister ... Before I resigned I had an overdose; since I have resigned I have had a super-dose; and though I have appealed to the Press and to the public to suspend judgement until I had an opportunity of stating my case ... in this House, I have been a subject of a shameful attack...

In the House of Commons Henderson made a lucid and telling defence of his conduct. But his belief that 'in the interests of the nation in this great crisis it is highly inadvisable that the story should be told at this moment' hampered his case.[18]

Within the Labour movement, Henderson's triumph on Stockholm was short-lived. There were very real doubts about the desirability of any Labour delegates, let alone those representing the anti-war minority, holding talks with German socialists.[19] The Miners' Federation had had reservations, and at a reconvened conference on the Stockholm issue on 21 August, it now cast its block vote against participation. Agreement to participate at the Stockholm conference was only reaffirmed by 1,234,000 votes to 1,231,000. Henderson's opponents were to make much of the fact that the Durham Miners' Association, which was the major force in his Barnard Castle constituency, was firmly against Stockholm. In the event the British Government's refusal to grant passports to delegates saved the Labour movement from further dissension.

Henderson's standing in the Labour movement, however, was boosted by the Stockholm affair. He had stood up to Lloyd George and had asserted the Labour Party's independence. He had been doggedly courageous in the face of the press onslaught on him both before and after his resignation. Lloyd George was to find that, in substituting George Barnes for Arthur Henderson, he was losing much in political weight. The shoddy way in which Henderson had been treated caused much resentment in the Labour movement at all levels. Even leading trade-unionists who had been against Stockholm were bitter at 'Lloyd George's trickeries'. Indeed, according to Sidney Webb, several trade union MPs, at the time of the House of Commons debate on Henderson's resignation, 'were furious and fierce' and declared 'that anyone taking Henderson's place would be a blackleg'. Lloyd George never recovered the trust of the trade union centre of the Labour Movement, though Labour did stay in the coalition. As for Henderson, he was adroit in capitalizing on his martyrdom over Stockholm. A few months later, one government official observed, 'a certain doormat . . . is now being very effectively used as an altar-cloth'.[20]

The Stockholm incident forced British Labour as a whole (and not just the minority) to formulate its views on war aims and a peace settlement. It also gave Henderson a new and fulfilling role, that of the international man. While he had been involved in the Second International's affairs before the First World War, he had not held the limelight, nor had such activities been his central concern. After Stockholm, both his major reorganization of the Labour party and his international concerns were in part a vindication of the role he had taken on from his visit to Russia, that of a major politician who looked beyond purely national considerations.

With regard to party organization, Henderson saw that Labour needed machinery to match its increased political and economic strength stemming from the war as well as being able to respond to the enlarged franchise after the 1918 Reform Act. After taking such posts as Asquith chose to give him, and after being subject to Lloyd George's pleasure for the tenure of his War Cabinet place, Henderson stated that he did not want to take office again 'in any government, whether in war or in peace, that was not controlled by the Labour Party'. In the circumstances of a divided Liberal party, Labour could provide the alternative government. After his Cabinet experiences, and with MacDonald in eclipse, Henderson was the key figure. Beatrice Webb noted in her diary at the time of the January 1918 Labour party conference, 'He is ambitious: he sees a chance of a Labour Party government, or a predominantly Labour government, with himself as Premier'.

In seeing the political opportunity for Labour and in having the necessary political weight to gain a majority for his reorganization proposals, Henderson was truly the refounder of the Labour party. He knew the Labour party, and the trade unions in particular, well enough to gauge how far he could go. In introducing his proposals Henderson made clear that they were a compromise. He said that whilst 'a new organisation based solely upon individual membership ... might be worth aiming at', to try to introduce it then would be a mistake. He added, 'Imagine the Executive saying to the trade unions upon whom the party had depended that they had no further use for them'. Hence he proposed to maintain the existing 'political federation consisting of trade unions, socialist bodies and co-operative societies ... but to graft on to it ... a form of constituency organisation linked up with the local Labour parties or trades councils'.

For Henderson, reorganization of the party was the first priority. Hence he told the January 1918 conference bluntly that 'it was no use the Executive issuing anything in the nature of the programme, it was no use talking about building up a new social order or reconstructing society' until 'they brought their machine up to date'. Indeed this was such a priority that it was one of two reasons why Henderson gave up the leadership of the parliamentary party in mid-October 1917. When he had joined Asquith's Cabinet Henderson had maintained the title of chairman, but first Hodge, and then Wardle, had carried out the duties as 'acting chairman'. As Wardle accepted government office on Henderson's resignation, Henderson briefly resumed the leadership. In the autumn of 1917 he stepped down in order to concentrate as secretary of the party on reorganization and to play a major part in bringing about the resumption of international socialist relationships. His single-minded dedication to this role was noted by his opponents. At the start of November, Milner's parliamentary private secretary reported, 'Arthur Henderson has not put in an appearance in the House and he and J.H. Thomas etc. seem very busy in laying the foundations of a new Labour Party organisation in the country and leave Parliament alone'.[21]

This was also one reason why Henderson made what was to prove to be the disastrous decision to give up the North-East as his political base. The 1918 Representation of the People Act split in two his Barnard Castle seat. Henderson almost certainly could have had the candidacy for either the newly formed Spennymoor seat or one of the Newcastle seats.[22] However in February 1918 he accepted the offer of the East Ham Trades and Labour Council to fight the newly formed parliamentary seat there. Henderson felt that a London seat would make life easier for him in his central role as secretary of the Labour party. In fact he was to lose in East Ham South in the 1918 general election, win Widnes in September 1919, lose it in 1922, win Newcastle East in January 1923, lose it in 1923, win Burnley in January 1924, lose it in 1931, and win Clay Cross in September 1933. These electoral misfortunes harmed his position within the parliamentary leadership. But in the autumn of 1917, when there was growing disillusionment with the war, Lloyd George soon felt that Henderson outside of his Government was a threat. At the time Milner and he were fostering Victor Fisher and 'patriotic Labour' as an alternative to the Labour party, Addison noted of their discussions,

> Henderson's movement in connection with the Labour Party is really danger-
> ous—not so much from the fact that he is organising the party with a great
> many candidates—but from the fact that his personal vanity and weakness
> might precipitate him at any time into bringing about a condition at home
> with organised labour which might make only for a patched-up peace...[23]

A month later, when considering political prospects with Sir George Riddell, Lloyd George observed that 'it may come to a fight between him and Henderson, and that all parties, including Labour, will be split and reconstituted'.[24]

Henderson's efforts towards uniting most of the Labour movement behind democratic peace proposals and reviving international socialist relations proved more successful from the autumn of 1917. The nadir had been reached with an Inter-Allied Socialist conference held in London in late August which failed to reach agreement on war aims. Beatrice Webb dubbed it 'a fiasco' and Henderson had to report, 'It cannot be disguised that the outcome ... was wholly disappointing'.[25]

At the Trades Union Congress in September Henderson spoke as fraternal delegate from the Labour party, and used the opportunity to urge that whilst the Stockholm conference might be dead the idea of an international movement of workers was not. He told them that it 'would be the finest expression of a League of Nations ... because it would be a League of the Common Peoples throughout the whole civilised world'.

Congress agreed that the Parliamentary Committee of the TUC should seek to get agreement on Allied working-class war aims and that 'an International Labour and Socialist Labour and Socialist Congress would be of the greatest service and is a necessary preliminary to the conclusion of a lasting and democratic peace'. From this resolution stemmed the co-operation between the Parliamentary Committee of the TUC and the executive of the Labour party which produced agreement on joint war aims.

Their programme stated that the most important aim was that 'there shall be henceforth on earth no more war'. To achieve this they sought 'the complete democratisation of all countries'; the 'abandonment of every form of Imperialism'; the 'suppression of secret diplomacy'; 'the universal abolition of compulsory military service'; the 'entire abolition of profit-making armament firms' and the common limitation of armaments. In addition they called for the setting up of a League of Nations, territorial adjustments to be carried out by 'allowing all people to settle their own destinies', compensation for war damage, judicial inquiries into alleged war crimes and an end to 'economic aggression, whether by protective tariffs or capitated trusts or monopolies'. This programme was endorsed by delegates representing those affiliated to the two organizations at a special conference held at Central Hall, Westminster, on 28 December 1917. It then became the basis for the agreement on war aims reached by an Inter-Allied Labour and Socialist conference held in London in February 1918.[26]

Thus Henderson succeeded in obtaining agreement on a war policy behind which the majority of the British and Allied Labour movement could unite. In January he dealt firmly with an attempt by Ramsay MacDonald to try to interpret ILP participation in a delegation set up to press other Allied socialists to accept British Labour's war aims programme as being an opportunity 'to put the views of the ILP as against the declared opinions of the Westminster conference', and thereby re-open the whole issue again.[27] The TUC in September 1917, in trying to guard against a repeat of the failure of the September 1917 Inter-Allied conference, had insisted that either 'sectional bodies within nationalities to be governed by the majority of the nationality' or the sections 'be given voting power according to the numbers of persons actually represented'. This ensured that Henderson and the trade union centre of the Labour movement were in control, not the ILP minority.

Indeed, Henderson's powerful position in the Labour movement after the Stockholm incident owed much to the increased strength gained by

the TUC during the war. The TUC had become much more active within
the Labour movement in 1916 and 1917. From the time of the September
1917 Congress the relationship between the Parliamentary Committee
and the Labour party executive became very close. In his January 1918
report to the Labour party Henderson observed, 'Probably in no previous
period of the Party's history has there been such close co-operation ...
as during the past twelve months'.[28] As secretary of the Labour party
and chairman of the Joint Board he was in a pivotal position. Moreover
as a former full time trade union official and, since 1911, president of
a major skilled union, the Iron Founders, he was an acceptable Labour
party figure to nearly all trade union leaders. He was also well able to
judge the limits to which the bulk of the movement would be willing
to go in proclaiming democratic war aims, as indeed he had been with
the revised Labour party constitution.

But if Henderson did not go far enough for the ILP, he went too
far for the 'patriotic' right of the Labour movement, which was committed
to 'the knock-out blow'. His attitude in the last year or so of the war
is well summarized in the report of a speech he made to a Scottish co-
operative conference on 10 November 1917:

> While he would not interfere with the military operations of the Allied
> nations,he saw that the consequences of the war were so appalling that if
> he could supplement the military effort by moral, political or diplomatic
> means, and if there was a door even a little open by which he could get
> through to a lasting peace, he was not going to rest satisfied until the day
> came when the knock-out blow would be given.[29]

In late 1917 and early 1918 events were going Henderson's way. The
October Revolution in Russia, followed by Lenin's truce with Germany
and the Treaty of Brest-Litovsk in mid-December, enabled Henderson
to claim that his policy of support for Kerensky had been vindicated
by events. The Bolshevik's publication of the Allies' secret treaties on
22 November 1917 ensured that public discussion of war aims could not
be avoided by Allied leaders. Moreover, Lord Lansdowne's letter on war
aims, published in the *Daily Telegraph* on 29 November, showed that
concern about war objectives stretched well beyond the Labour Left and
the pacifists. Lloyd George himself, faced with the need to respond to
statements by Trotsky and Count Czernin (for the Central Powers) and
to gain trade union support for new manpower measures, now made
a unilateral declaration of war aims, which went some way to Labour's
proposals, at a conference of trade union delegates on manpower on

5 January 1918. This came only a few days after he had rebuffed Labour at its special conference on war aims on 28 December by saying that war aims could only be revised with the agreement of Britain's allies.[30] Three days after Lloyd George's statement, President Woodrow Wilson made his 'Fourteen Points' address to Congress.

Henderson, acting with the Labour party executive, the Parliamentary Committee of the TUC and the Co-operative Political Committee, promptly welcomed both Lloyd George's and Wilson's statements as transforming the international situation. Their statement was near to eulogy in its praise of Wilson's programme which they deemed to be 'in essential respects so similar to that which the British Labour Party has put forward'. They praised it for its 'moral quality and breadth of vision' and for its condemnation of Old Diplomacy. Henderson again warmly commended Wilson's 'magnificent statement' at the January 1918 Labour party conference.[31] By linking Labour's war aims to President Wilson's ideals, he was attempting to secure a stamp of wider respectability for policies which had been readily portrayed by his opponents as unpatriotic, and was thereby appealing to a broader electorate than organized Labour.

However, the German offensive on the Western Front in late March 1918 swung much of the British public behind the policy of the knock-out blow. For a while Henderson himself swung back to saying military victory was required to carry out the ideals of Labour and President Wilson. At the London Wesleyan Mission on 8 April he stated:

> The latest act of military aggression on the part of the German government placed under temporary suspension the moral, political and diplomatic effort ... That spirit must be destroyed, for it threatened everything that counted in the development of national and international life.

Nevertheless he still saw Labour's war aims as the prime political issue, commenting that should Lloyd George's Government fall and a new Asquith coalition be put together, their acceptance would be the major policy and minimum conditions for taking office.[32]

In the last months of the war, as stalemate in the trenches ended, Henderson was subjected to the hostility of the Government, the press and 'patriotic Labour'. In August 1918 the Government refused him and C.W. Bowerman, the secretary of the TUC, passports to go to Switzerland to discuss with neutral socialists the German attitude to the Inter-Allied war aims. Lloyd George, Milner and their 'patriotic Labour' supporters made much of the vehemently pro-war stance of the American Labour leader, Sam Gompers, and the Australian Labour Prime Minister, Billy Hughes. They also launched another campaign for a trade union Labour party, spearheaded by Havelock Wilson of the Seamen's Union.[33] When Henderson set off to Paris on 25 October 1918 for a meeting aimed at rebuilding the Second International, his opponents struck. The crew at Folkestone refused to sail with Henderson and his companions on board and on leaving the harbour for the station they were harassed by a threatening crowd.[34] This incident was directly organized by Captain Tupper of the Seamen's Union—but given the nearness of a general election it is quite probable that it was encouraged by members of the Government, possibly even Milner or Lloyd George.

Captain Tupper went on to announce his candidature as National Democratic and Labour candidate against Henderson in East Ham South. There he vigorously smeared Henderson as unpatriotic and suggested that he had fled Barnard Castle because of the unpopularity of his views with the miners. Tupper stood down ahead of the close of nominations in favour of Frank Hamlett, the Conservative candidate who initially described himself as the 'Win the war to end the war candidate'. In withdrawing Tupper stated that 'he did not wish the patriotic vote to be split. . . A three-cornered contest here might let Mr. Ramsay MacDonald's friend in'. Henderson responded by stating that Tupper had withdrawn after Lloyd George had asked him and Hamlett to do so in favour of Clement Edwards, the Coalition Liberal candidate.[35]

After the withdrawal of Tupper, Edwards continued to attack Henderson as a friend of the Russian Bolsheviks. Henderson protested repeatedly that 'no man in this country has more strongly condemned [them] since my return from Russia than I have' and that he was a friend of Kerensky. Given his controversial invitation to Kerensky to address the June 1918 Labour party conference his case was clear. Nevertheless, however much he pushed other themes—no more war, a League of Nations, pensions for demobilized soldiers, housing, 'employment or maintenance', and a shorter working day—these were swamped under the 'patriotic issue'. Even with the support of Jimmy Clynes (a government minister until the election), John Clifford, T.P. O'Connor, J.H. Thomas and George Lansbury, Henderson lost heavily.[36] Edwards polled 7,972, Hamlett 5,661 and Henderson only 5,024.

Though Henderson and other leaders were defeated in the 1918 general election, the Labour party increased its number of seats from 42 to 57 (or 61 if associates are counted). With its new constitution and its programme for social reconstruction, *Labour and the New Social Order* (which had been approved at the June 1918 conference), Labour had emerged as a national party and as the main alternative to Lloyd George's coalition Government. Indeed, as Henderson rightly judged in early 1920, in the 1918 general election Labour had 'polled its minimum vote'.[37] During 1919 Labour made major gains in the county and district council elections. It also enjoyed three by-election victories and came close to winning such unlikely seats as Bromley in Kent.

Henderson himself was the second of Labour's victors in by-elections in 1919. In August 1919 he entered the contest at Widnes with hesitation, partly because as President of the Iron Founders he was committed at the time to help resolve a major national dispute over wages, and partly because Widnes, a traditionally Conservative seat, was not that promising for Labour. The by-election was due to the Conservative MP being elevated to the peerage, and the Conservatives ensured that there was only a short campaign period. According to the local press, Henderson brought 'expert political organisers to Widnes with him' and his supporters were 'leaving no stone unturned on his behalf'. He also benefited from T.P. O'Connor's efforts to get Irish voters to back him, and eventually won by 11,404 to 10,417, with the Labour vote going up by 4,108 since the general election. Afterwards, he said that 'no honour had come to him in his public life of nearly thirty years which he appreciated so much' and emphasized that he had only had eight days in which to conduct the campaign. He also was delighted that renewed attempts to smear him with 'the most wilful and unscrupulous misrepresentation' over his visit to Russia had failed.[38]

Before the Widnes by-election Henderson had briefly been gloomy about Labour's fortunes. In May he had confided in Sidney Webb,

> The divisions in our ranks which show themselves not only nationally but internationally are very trying. When the party in the House is doing so badly I sometimes think that the measure of solidarity necessary for success will never be forthcoming. What with the prospect of a revival of Asquithian Liberalism and so many of the right of our own party changing to the Coalition, the prospects of the next election, which may be in less than a year, are not good. We appear to be leaderless in the House and no better in the country and nobody in the executive or out of it seems to care about this aspect of the case. I have felt strongly inclined to get out altogether.[39]

On returning to Parliament, he continued to concentrate on his tasks as secretary of the Labour party, putting much effort into both his organizational work and his international endeavours. He did not take up a parliamentary Labour party post again until that of Chief Whip became vacant in February 1921. Adamson remained chairman until then, when he was succeeded by Clynes.

In spite of such occasional uncharacteristic despondency, for most of 1919 and until his illness at the end of February 1920 Henderson appears to have been very elated at Labour's progress. Both in regard to domestic developments and international ones his dominant tone was of enthusiastic optimism. He certainly enjoyed his new eminence as a socialist of major international standing. Mary Hamilton wrote of his outlook after his visit to Russia:

> The ideas he had learned to apply in industrial negotiations and conciliation, he now began, slowly and steadily, to apply to the larger field of international relations. His international outlook, before dim and conventional, now gradually became vivid and personal, and never again left him.[40]

The ideals and aims expressed in the Labour movement's 28 December 1917 programme were to be the basic foundations of his international endeavours for the rest of his life.

Henderson had understood his appointment to Lloyd George's War Cabinet to carry with it the right to represent Labour at the Peace Conference. Even after his withdrawal from the Government Henderson still had hopes of being present at the Peace Conference. The Inter-Allied Labour and Socialist conference of February 1918 set up a commission of three, namely Albert Thomas of France, Emile Vandervelde of Belgium and Arthur Henderson of Britain 'to secure from all the governments a promise that at least one representative of Labour and Socialism will be included in the official representation' at the Peace Conference, and to organize a Labour and Socialist conference 'to sit concurrently with the official conference'.[41] When arrangements were made for the Peace Conference in Paris Lloyd George's gesture towards a Labour presence was merely to take Barnes with him. Henderson's sole official involvement was to go to Paris at the end of January 1919 at Balfour's (the Foreign Secretary) request to advise the British members of The Allied Commission which was formulating the International Labour Charter.

Henderson concentrated his energies on vigorously promoting the alternative Labour and Socialist peace conference. In early December 1918 he secured Lloyd George's agreement that such a conference might take place before the peace treaty was signed, but only if it was held in neutral country and not in Paris. Once Henderson was confident that passports would be forthcoming he issued an enthusiastic press release through

Reuter's Agency on 1 January 1919. Henderson succeeded in bringing French and Germans together at Berne. But though he tried hard, he was unable to persuade either Gompers and the American Federation of Labour or the Belgian socialists to participate. Before the conference met and during it, he made clear his pleasure that the Bolsheviks and other European Left socialists were boycotting the conference.

Thus he set about constructing a moderate version of the old Second International. At Berne he reiterated the Labour party's peace policy and pressed for international labour agreements to achieve uniform industrial conditions in different countries. He also took pleasure afterwards in noting that 'the proceedings... proved that the failure to hold the Stockholm conference was a serious political error' as it would have 'hastened the downfall of the criminal conspirators who brought ruin upon the world'. But, above all, he firmly differentiated his international associates from the Bolsheviks. The majority at the Berne conference looked to President Wilson and the League of Nations, not to Moscow, for a future better world. Whilst the conference avoided outright condemnation of the Russian Bolsheviks, Henderson made his position abundantly clear. *The Times'* correspondent reported:

> He considered that the Bolsheviks were substituting a tyranny of anarchism for the tyranny of capitalism. He objected to oppression, suppression and repression whether from above or below. Bolshevism was a practical negation of constructive socialism. Before attempting to construct a new International they must decide what its policy was to be. Unless it was definitely opposed to anarchy he was sure he would say that the socialists of Great Britain would stand aloof and this would make it very ineffective.[42]

Henderson was quick to realize the key role of British Labour, and thereby himself, in international democratic socialism. As Arno Mayer has written, 'Before the war the German Social Democrats had been the single most influential national party in the international; at Berne, British Labour assumed the pivotal position'.[43] Henderson continued to play a leading role in the reconstruction of the Second International. The Berne conference set up a Permanent Commission with an executive of three—Hjalmar Branting (the Swedish socialist), Henderson, and Huysman (the Belgian socialist)—to supervise the implementation of the conference's resolutions and to organize a full scale Second International congress.

Henderson and MacDonald were among its delegation to present the Berne decisions to the Big Four at the Paris Peace Conference. On 21

February they saw Lloyd George and Curzon. But though Lloyd George then was full of praise for the work of the Berne conference, hopes soon dwindled that it would greatly influence the peacemakers. Two months later, when the Permanent Commission met in conference at Amsterdam, Henderson moved a resolution expressing disappointment with the peacemakers' Covenant for the League of Nations and demanding total disarmament. The actual Peace Treaty brought greater disillusionment. A week before it was formally signed at Versailles, Henderson declared at a miners' demonstration, 'The Peace Treaty is not our treaty, and we shall never accept it. We shall never rest satisfied until it has been fundamentally restructured'.[44]

For a while, Henderson had more to show for his efforts to reconstruct the Second International as a major Labour and Socialist bloc representing an intermediate position between the views of Gompers and Lenin. Gompers remained very hostile to Henderson after the armistice. When Henderson went to the United States in May 1919 to consult American labour, Gompers put out very hostile statements in which he emphasized that he was 'opposed to the direct participation of trade unions in politics'. According to one of his associates Gompers 'was concerned that Henderson would stir up class feelings' at a time when he himself was experiencing some inability to contain the militancy of many unionists'.[45]

As for Moscow and the Third International, which was formed in March 1919, Henderson always took pains to distance himself from the Bolsheviks. He tried hard to bring all non-Bolshevik socialists and labour organizations into the ambit of the Second International, initially making considerable concessions in an attempt to accommodate Gompers. At an Inter-Allied Labour and Socialist conference in September 1918, Henderson moved a resolution which, whilst expressing sympathy for the labour and socialist organizations and condemning the Treaty of Brest-Litovsk, only warned 'the workers of the allied countries ... against the tremendous dangers of a policy of intervention'. In so doing Henderson, with the approval of the executive of the Labour party, said that then there was insufficient evidence for a clear declaration for or against the Allied intervention in Russia. However, again Kerensky was given a platform, and received warm cheers for his declaration, 'I remain in favour of intervention because I am persuaded that the democratic forces of the Allies must come to the aid of the democratic forces of the Russian people'.[46] At Berne in March 1919 Henderson and his international associates made very clear their hostility to Bolshevism, even if that conference postponed judgement on Russia.

However, Henderson's attempt to create a moderate consensus failed to include Gompers and, more seriously, over Russia, it immediately alienated a substantial minority. Later some of these formed their own grouping, often known as the Vienna Union or 'the two-and-a-half International'. The struggle of Lenin's government to survive the counter-revolutionary invasions ensured that the Second International steadily lost credibility other than with Henderson and the British Labour party and the German Socialist Right.

Henderson and the other moderate Labour party and trade union leaders tried to combine vigorous denunciation of Bolshevism with comments that its character did not justify armed intervention. The ILP and the rest of the Left, however, concentrated on robustly condemning the Allied intervention. At the June 1919 Labour party conference the mover of a resolution calling on the executive to consult with the Parliamentary Committee of the TUC as to taking effective action against intervention 'by the unreserved use of their political and industrial power' bluntly stated that 'this was the first war that had ever been declared by the ruling classes against the working classes of another country'. Another socialist speaker observed that 'they did not want to ask the soldiers and the Navy to be degraded into becoming fighters for the bond holders of Russian stock, neither did they want them to be the hired assassins of the tsarist regime'. Though Clynes argued against 'direct action', saying that the Labour party had preached parliamentary democracy in the 1918 general election and should abide by the electorate's verdict, the resolution was carried by a two-to-one majority.[47]

Faced with the conference decision, Henderson and the other moderate leaders continued to argue the case against 'direct action'. Writing in his union journal, he warned,

> To endeavour to force upon the country and upon the government by illegitimate means the policy of a section of the entire community... involves the abrogation of Parliamentary government, establishes the dictatorship of the minority and might easily destroy eventually all our constitutional liberties. Labour, by taking such a course, might be the authors of a doubtful precedent today, and its victims tomorrow.[48]

At the international level, Henderson maintained the Second International's line of treating the Bolsheviks as political lepers. In his presidential address at the Permanent Commission's conference at Lucerne on 2 August 1919 he urged that while there were 'serious differences of opinion... regarding the theory and practice of Soviet government...

there was no difference with respect to the reactionary tendencies of armed intervention in Russia's internal affairs'. He urged the carrying out of policies considered at Berne, namely that:

> Steps must be taken to ascertain how far the Russian government was pre-
> pared to modify its present attitude and abandon some of its methods...
> Diplomatic relations with them would then be possible and the International
> must renew its efforts to obtain facilities for duly accredited commissions
> to visit Russia and Hungary ...[49]

However, until April 1920, even this was thwarted by Lloyd George, in conjunction with the Italian and French governments, continuing to refuse to grant passports to MacDonald and the others. Eventually a Labour party and TUC delegation did go in 1920.

By then Henderson was leading a diminishing band of anti-Bolshevik international socialists. By late 1920 a much reduced Second International transferred its headquarters to London. The 1921 Labour party confer-ence pressed for an amalgamation of the Second International with the Vienna Union. Henderson remained critical of such move which weakened his anti-Bolshevik stance. However by mid-1922 the tough line taken by Lenin as to possible death penalties for the Social Revolutionaries who were on political trials in Russia helped move the non-communist international socialist groups together, and in May 1923 they set up a new Labour and Socialist International.[50]

As well as trying to reconstruct the Second International on non-Bolshevik lines, Henderson also made strenuous efforts to champion the League of Nations as a better way in international relations than either the Old Diplomacy or the revolutionary ideals of the Bolsheviks. In Britain a League of Nations Society had emerged in early 1915, and this attracted moderate Liberal support. The movement was acceptable to many who could not support the Union of Democratic Control. The idea of a League gained ground in Britain with the stalemate continuing on the Western Front and with President Wilson endorsing the idea of League to Enforce Peace in May 1916. The Labour party, at its January 1917 conference, unanimously passed a motion supporting the formation of such a League. When the League of Nations Society in May 1917 launched a major campaign to win general support for its aims, Henderson—then still in the War Cabinet—had responded by saying in a public speech that of all the suggestions to accomplish future peace 'none appealed to him with greater force than the proposal for a League of Nations to enforce peace', though he added that 'an indispensable condition to its success' was that 'it must be a League of free peoples'.[51]

The notion of a 'League of Free Peoples' was prominent in Labour's 1918 general election manifesto. After the election Henderson, Mac-Donald and other Labour leaders took part in a campaign organized by the Parliamentary Committee of the TUC and the Labour party for the immediate establishment of a League of Nations as a major feature of the peace treaty. In February 1919, with the Allied leaders moving towards the creation of an inadequate League, Henderson, at the Berne conference, demanded 'such a League of Nations as would be a general expression of the universal will to a permanent peace'.[52]

After the draft Covenant of the League was published, the TUC and Labour party held a special conference on 3 April 1919 to consider it. This conference, though suggesting a list of twenty-two amendments, welcomed the Covenant. Henderson, in moving the main resolution, observed that,

> The final safeguard of peace did not lie in machinery of judicial arbitration or conciliation, however skilful it might be devised, security could only be permanently realised in the spirit of friendship and co-operation amongst all the peoples, based upon the fundamental identity of the people's interests. Labour wanted to build up the international law to regulate all intercourse between states and to substitute popular control. Henceforth there must be no profiteering in the armament industry . . .

Later that month, at Amsterdam, a motion moved by him, which expressed disappointment at the final version of the Covenant, was criticized as weak and vague by Dutch and French socialists.[53]

With the publication of the peace treaty, the Labour party and the TUC took the stance that the League should be broadened to include Germany and other defeated nations in order to avoid being 'a restricted instrument of the victorious coalition'. From the autumn of 1919 Labour, whilst calling for changes in the League, campaigned with the League of Nations Union to get public support for the League. In mid-January 1920, just before the formal inauguration of the League, Henderson shared a platform in Widnes with Lord Robert Cecil, and said that 'the Labour Party regarded Lord Robert as an ally' who would be 'the champion of revision of the League' in Parliament. Henderson had worked with Cecil before, including pressing the case for women getting the vote when Henderson had been in Asquith's Government, and they had maintained contact during the peace-making.[54]

The League of Nations cause was one which Asquithian Liberals and much of Labour shared. Similarly Henderson maintained a belief in Irish Home Rule that stemmed from his Gladstonian Liberal days. When he had been chairman of the parliamentary Labour party in March 1909, Henderson had presided over the first joint Labour and Irish Nationalist meeting. At this gathering John Redmond, the Irish Nationalist leader, had stated that Labour had been reliable in giving its support to Ireland and that the Irish Nationalist MPs 'were friends of the Labour cause in this country'.[55] Henderson had also been involved in discussions about the trade union and Labour party dimensions of Home Rule. In July and September 1913 he took part in talks with representatives of the Irish TUC to form a separate trade-unionist based Irish party and to arrange that a proportion of the affiliation fees paid by unions covering Ireland as well as Britain should go to the Irish party. A separate Irish Labour party was set up in 1914.

Henderson also had become involved in the autumn of 1913 in trying to arrange a settlement in the bitter Dublin transport dispute between Jim Larkin's Irish Transport Workers' Union and the Dublin employers. Henderson was outraged by the civil rights aspects of the lock-out. After the police had acted with extreme brutality in dealing with crowds following the breaking up of a meeting addressed by Larkin on 31 August, he spoke with other British Labour figures at a mass rally in Dublin on 7 September. Henderson, who had been in Dublin in connection with the Parliamentary Land Committee, denounced the police's actions more emphatically and aggressively than any other speaker. Also, given Unionist speeches of the time, he condemned as class-biased the locking up of Larkin and not Ulstermen or their supporters, and pressed all the parliamentary Labour party to sign a petition to Asquith demanding Larkin's release. Larkin was freed on 13 November.

Henderson's experiences in trying to achieve a settlement were less happy. He and TUC representatives had met the Dublin employers in early September. Within a few days he wrote to Middleton, observing, 'It will take a stiff fight to get sense into both sides'.[56] The TUC sent the 25,000 Dublin workers food and £93,637 in cash. Its support did not, and probably could not, run to encouraging sympathetic strikes. Larkin, however, appears to have expected this. After his release from prison, Larkin gave a series of fiery speeches in England in which he called for trade union action there to back the locked-out Dublin workers. His vigorous condemnation of prominent British trade union and Labour leaders, including, later on, Henderson, as 'the men who were not out to fight capitalism in this country' antagonized those whose support he needed. After a special conference organized by the TUC on 9 December turned down a proposal for British transport unions to black all Dublin traffic, Henderson made a final effort to mediate in Dublin. Shortly before Christmas, he had to admit the failure of his efforts. With a little bitterness, he observed that he was 'not altogether convinced that either party fully appreciated the motive and spirit' in which he, on behalf of the Joint Board, had intervened.[57] By the start of February 1914 the Dublin workers' resistance had collapsed.

Henderson's experiences in the Dublin transport dispute of 1913 reinforced his preference for supporting the Irish Nationalist party rather than the more militant nationalist groups. By the end of the First World War, developments in Ireland, along with the postponement of Home Rule, had undermined the Irish Nationalist party. The Easter Rising of 1916 was one such major development. Henderson, as a member of Asquith's Cabinet, was condemned thereafter in some Nationalists' eyes. Walton Newbold, a follower of James Connolly and a Communist MP, 1922–3, had a special loathing for Henderson for this reason. He later recalled, of what he termed 'the Asquith–Henderson coalition', '*They shot Jim Connolly*. I drove Henderson wild by reminding them of the responsibility in a speech in the House of Commons!' When Henderson was adopted as parliamentary candidate for Newcastle in December 1923, the only opposition came over the 1916 executions. He responded then, and on other occasions, by stating, 'Connolly was executed before I knew anything about it'.[58] However, on another key wartime issue, the plan to apply conscription to Ireland, Henderson and the British Labour movement firmly supported Irish nationalist sentiment in opposing the measure.

In 1919 British rule in Ireland came under increasing attack by the Labour movement. At the Amsterdam conference in April 1919 the British Labour delegates had readily accepted a declaration that 'the principle of free and absolute self-determination shall be applied immediately in the case of Ireland'. In July the National Union of Railwaymen demanded the withdrawal of the armies of occupation from Ireland as well as Russia, and talked of Triple Alliance strike action to enforce this policy.

In January 1920 Henderson and Adamson led a Labour deputation to Ireland. Speaking in Dublin on 26 January, Henderson said they were 'under the gravest apprehension that if the Irish question were not settled with the utmost speed on constitutional lines, it would settle itself on unconstitutional lines'. Three days later at Bishop Auckland, he observed,

> The majority of Irishmen ... declined to place further reliance either in the veracity or the honour of British statesmen. In the south and west of Ireland it was safe to say the political creed of the majority might be summed up in two words—'Clear Out'. They were frankly declaring for a separate republic. This spirit was not confined to Dublin.

Though Henderson and his colleagues saw Sinn Fein and Irish Labour and heard their arguments for an independent republic, they remained hopeful of a settlement keeping Ireland within the Empire and so without the link with Britain being completely severed. Irish republicans put pressure on Labour to move from this position when a by-election occurred in Stockport in March 1920. When Labour failed to give an unequivocal pledge that a Labour government would recognize the Irish Republic, would withdraw the British army and release all political prisoners, a Sinn Fein candidate was nominated and at the poll received 2,336 votes.[59]

By this time Henderson's hitherto robust health had broken down. He was taken ill at the end of a speech at Wellington on 31 January 1920, soon after his return from Ireland. He started work again on 5 March, but suffered a relapse on 21 April. In mid-June he underwent a major operation for gallstones. When he resumed his political activities in the autumn, he again took up the issue of justice for Ireland. Henderson still wanted Ireland to remain part of 'a British Commonwealth of free nations'. When, in October 1920, *The Times* invited him to comment on key issues which would come before the next session of Parliament, he responded by floating his own solution to the Irish crisis. He suggested that the Speaker of the Commons call a conference of thirty representative Members to come up with a proposal for Irish government which would be acceptable to the Irish people and which would operate for three years. During that time the 'Irish Parliament (or Parliaments)' would prepare a permanent constitution which would include provision '(a) for the protection of minorities and (b) for the protection of the essential security of the British Empire.'[60] Two days after his proposal was published, Henderson took part in a joint conference between the Parliamentary Committee of the TUC and the executive of Labour and their Irish counterparts. Following that, Henderson moved in the House of Commons a motion of censure on the Government over its policy of reprisals in Ireland. Five days later he moved a further motion calling for 'an independent investigation... into the causes, nature and extent of reprisals on the part of those whose duty is the maintenance of law and order'.

The call for an independent investigation was defeated in Parliament, but Labour set up its own investigation under Henderson. The Labour party executive and the parliamentary Labour party also issued a joint manifesto on Ireland in which they recognized 'the futility of seeking to set limits to the Irish in framing for themselves the constitution to which they aspire' and called for the withdrawal of all British troops, the responsibility for law and order to be transferred to local authorities and 'the immediate election, by proportional representation, of an entirely open Constituent Assembly ... which could devise without limitations, or fetters, whatever constitution for Ireland the Irish people desire'. Thus the attachment to the old formulae of Home Rule died.

Henderson was appalled at what was happening in Ireland. Speaking at Hough Green, Lancashire, on 9 December 1920, he said that 'a state of war prevailed'.

> By their actions the government's agents had produced in the minds of the Irish people the same effect as a mad dog loose in the public streets would produce... They had made the forces of the Crown, which existed only to maintain law and order, the instrument of a blind and ruthless vengeance. This was not 'resolute government' but primitive barbarism.[61]

Henderson and Adamson also pressed for a truce between the Government and Sinn Fein, during which negotiations for a settlement should take place. The report of Labour's Commission was approved at a special Labour party conference on 29 December. Labour then launched a national campaign on Ireland on 17 January 1921, one which filled halls across the country. For Henderson this campaign had something of the quality of Gladstone's great crusades. He observed, 'The moral fervour and the deep indignation displayed by the throngs who gathered to the meetings recalled the happier times when the chasm between morality and politics was not so wide as in recent years'. In the ensuing months Henderson and his parliamentary colleagues continued to condemn the Government for its complicity in murders in Ireland and to call for negotiations with Sinn Fein. When at last Lloyd George did enter into negotiations, Henderson made it plain that Labour would give its 'unqualified support in regard to the conference', and when the settlement was reached Labour supported Lloyd George against the opposition from within the coalition government's supporters.[62]

Henderson's attacks on the Lloyd George coalition Government went far beyond the inadequacies of the peacemaking, the intervention in Russia and atrocities in Ireland. With the ending of the post-war boom, unemployment rose sharply from April 1920. That autumn, on his return from convalescence Henderson took up unemployment and 'the impending

slump in trade' as a key issue, along with Ireland and Russia. As well
as calling for higher unemployment benefit, he called for the re-
establishment of trading relations with Russia which he argued would
lead to more employment in the engineering, textile, clothing and boot
and shoe industries. By the end of the year Labour was asking the Government to take action to restore European trade generally and was making
its old demand for the state (or local authorities) to provide work or
adequate maintenance.

In the House of Commons (on 21 December 1920) Henderson
demanded that the Government set up an inquiry into unemployment.
But this demand rebounded on Labour when the Government did set
up two committees of inquiry, albeit within very restricted terms of reference, and invited Labour to participate in one. On 11 January 1921 the
Parliamentary Committee of the TUC and the executive of the Labour
party rejected the Government's invitation on the grounds that the terms
of reference were too restricted and that the Government hitherto had
only been talking in terms of 'the universal extension of short time [work-
ing]'. Henderson added to this the view that Labour had been duped
too often by Lloyd George's Government and they were not going to
provide 'this government with a smoke screen to guard itself against the
temper of the people'. However this refusal to participate in an inquiry
was used by Labour's critics, not only coalition politicians but also civil
servants.

Along with Sidney Webb and other representatives of the Joint Committee, Henderson revised Labour's wartime proposals and those which
it had put to the National Industrial Conference in April 1919. This report,
Unemployment—A Labour Policy, was endorsed at a special joint TUC–
Labour party conference on 27 January 1921. As well as calling for the
improvement of international trade, the conference asked for the current
government policies which restricted building and local government
expenditure on local works to be dropped and listed a range of 'necessary
works' which should be undertaken immediately. In so doing it clearly
stated 'that such a policy is preferable to that of relief works, which
are wasteful and demoralising, extravagantly costly to the ratepayer and
taxpayer'.[63]

Henderson never saw himself as an economic thinker in the way that
Philip Snowden did. During 1921 Henderson proclaimed Labour's package of remedies and condemned the Government when it raised its out-of-
work donation from working-class people still in employment and not
from the rich. Yet though Labour's remedies were shown to be inadequate

in 1924, they were more positive than the ideas of the coalition Conserva- tives. Men such as Henderson knew from experience of their lives what unemployment meant to the families affected, and could convey this know- ledge to the electorate.

Henderson lost his seat at Widnes in the 1922 general election. In 1919 the Liberals had supported his candidature, in 1922 they supported the anti-Labour candidate and Widnes reverted to having a Conservative MP. Henderson then fought the first by-election of the Parliament, which fortuitously arose in his home city of Newcastle. His campaign concen- trated on the issue of unemployment. George Lansbury, who with his fellow Poor Law Guardians in Poplar had defied central government on behalf of the unemployed, was an early major outside speaker. Hender- son, Lansbury and their supporters paraded in Newcastle East with a banner bearing the skull and crossbones and the slogan 'Fighting 1914. Starving 1922'. Henderson also reaffirmed his belief in the Capital Levy as a means of setting Britain's war debts and called for 'the removal of slumdom'. Against Liberal and Conservative candidates, Henderson won with an increased majority. However the local Liberal newspaper, commenting on the result, observed that whilst the Tory leaders 'pretend to be gravely perturbed by the advance of political Labour', they fail to take action to keep Labour candidates out. At the general election of December 1923 Conservatives did take such action. They chose not to run a candidate in order 'to defeat the socialist candidate', and in a straight fight the Liberal candidate defeated Henderson. Both the Liberal candidate and Sir Walter Runciman ascribed Henderson's defeat to the Capital Levy.[64]

Though Henderson's own electoral fortunes were mixed between 1918 and December 1923, the Labour party in these years moved firmly into the position of being Britain's alternative government. In the general elec- tions of 1922 and 1923 Labour's vote rose from the 2,244,945 in 1918 (in 361 seats) to 4,236,733 in 1922 (in 414 seats) and 4,348,379 in 1923 (in 427 seats), with 142 MPs in 1922 and 191 in 1923.

In these years Henderson not only played a major role in the organiza- tion of the party, but also in setting its tone. For much of the period MacDonald and many other ILP leaders were eclipsed as a result of their defeat in the 1918 general election. Henderson's strong position stemmed from the continuing support he had from most of the trade- unionists who dominated the party. At the height of his powers, he used his strong political position to assert moderation with great vigour. Two American writers, Paul Kellog and Arthur Gleason, commented of him:

Unlike some men who compromise differences, he doesn't do it by soft soap
and gentle conciliation. He uses a cast-iron voice and a bull vitality to pound
in the sensible central interpretation of a plain man, and he does it with
all the energy and noise of an exhorter of the extreme left.[65]

In the years when 'direct action' ran strongly in the Labour movement,
Henderson was a leading proponent of the counter-current of co-
operation in industrial relations. The war had reinforced his pre-war belief
in joint committees of employers and trade unions as being the way forward in British industry. Thus in January 1917, at a Brotherhood meeting,
he had expressed the hope that

> ... the fellowship and comradeship which had been so marked a feature
> of our war experiences might so continue that they would find an expression
> in the removal of class distinctions, the lessening of glaring social and
> economic inequalities, the development of mutual confidence and closer co-
> operation between employers and employed, and the fuller and more complete
> recognition of community of interest and responsibility between the state
> and the people.[66]

He saw the state as a benevolent force which could help resolve working-
class injustices. When the Iron Founders presented him with a portrait
on 17 February 1917, he said that the working classes must not revert
to their pre-war position but should benefit from the 'co-partnership
between the state and the majority of the people'. He hoped that co-
partnership 'would grow closer and closer, stronger and stronger' and
'would be so extended that it would be recognised that the strike and
lock-out, if they came at all, would be the very last thing to be associated
with industrial life'.[67]

He continued to pursue his ideal of co-operation rather than confrontation in industry through the turbulence of 1919 and 1920. While others
were warmly cheered at 'direct action' meetings, Henderson won his
applause at Christian-organized meetings, as well as at regional or national
Labour and trade union conferences. He was the leading trade-unionist
in the National Alliance of Employers and Employed, formed in December
1916 'to promote the active co-operation of employers and employed
in the treatment of questions generally affecting labour and employment'.
Hence he was an eager participant in the National Industrial Conference,
made up of representatives from both sides of industry, that Lloyd George
called in February 1919 as a response to the then serious industrial unrest.
While Henderson was aware that Lloyd George acted from short-term
considerations, he clearly believed that the Conference could develop

into an instrument to improve working people's industrial conditions. After its first report was endorsed by the National Alliance, Henderson publicly 'rejoiced', observing that 'the report was a symbol of the good relationship that could exist between employers and workers in a country like England'.[68] Even when the industrial threat of Labour had diminished, and with it any interest the Government had in the National Industrial Conference, Henderson continued to urge its merits. Thus in early 1922, when arguing for its revival, he wrote that 'the main work of the Parliament of Industry would be directed to the solution of those problems which gave rise to conflict and render the use of the strike weapon necessary'.[69]

As for political change, he took his stand on democratic socialism. Thus in mid-September 1919 he stated, 'The problem was to restore popular confidence in representative institutions and to guide the mass movement along the path of constitutional change and equable democracy to become master in its own house without violence and disorder'. In condemning 'direct action', Henderson made the old Radical case that too little democracy had been responsible for aberations elsewhere. Thus in Russia, Hungary and Germany 'constant frustration of democratic demands' had led to soviets, a system which had 'nothing in common with Parliamentary democracy' being 'avowedly in the interest of class dictatorship'. Speaking at the TUC that month, he warned against turning away from constitutional action when many people in the country 'believe that on the next appeal to the country Labour is going to triumph'.[70]

Henderson was very much a key figure in ensuring that the Labour party remained a party committed to the parliamentary route to socialism, and he was usually successful in opposing extra-parliamentary or illegal action. Arthur Gleason observed in 1920,

> Labor at home is in agitation; in Britain it is forming public opinion... The great trade union socialists are successfully fighting the sweep of anarchy from Eastern and Central Europe and the murderous bitterness of American industrial relations.[71]

Henderson was committed to constructing a democratic British alternative to Bolshevism. At a conference of the Second International in London in June 1922 he was loudly cheered when he remarked that 'the difference between British Labour and the Moscow Communist Party was the difference between democracy and dictatorship'.[72]

He was inevitably a strong opponent of both Communist party affiliation to the Labour party and of individual Communists becoming members of the Labour party. At the 1921 Labour party conference he argued vigorously that 'Moscow had no intention of allowing any of its affiliated organisations the liberty either to come into conformity with the constitution of the Labour Party or any other constitution that was opposed to the theories and the thesis laid down by Moscow'. The Russians had never stood 'for constructive socialism and for real political democracy'. He went on to show how the Communist party had denigrated MacDonald and thus had contributed to the smear campaign against him in the Woolwich by-election of March 1921, when MacDonald had failed to hold Crooks's old seat. *The Times'* reporter deemed this speech by Henderson to have 'largely contributed to the Labour party conference rejecting links with the Communist party'.[73]

While Henderson was determined to exclude the Communists, he was eager to include in his construction of a broad mass of support for Labour all others whose aims were not in conflict with the Labour party's constitution. Hence from 1917 onwards he actively courted the Co-operative movement. In October 1917 he even went as far as to say that 'he would be prepared that the Labour Party as now known should cease, if by so doing they could combine the whole of the democracy into a great people's party'.[74] In the 1918 general election, Co-operators were given a clear run in ten seats, and won one. Similarly he was careful to try to extend Labour's appeal to rural voters and to disillusioned Liberals. In January 1920, when surveying the intellectual bankruptcy of coalition Liberalism, he observed with relish,

> They have to tolerate the Anti-Dumping Bill, which violates the principles of Free Trade, they have to tolerate a policy of coercion in Ireland that would have made Gladstone sick with horror; they have to tolerate a scheme of Home Rule for Ireland which Gladstone would not have looked at for a moment.[75]

By the autumn of 1923 the character of the Labour party owed much to Henderson and he was a dominant figure within it. He was the embodiment of working class nonconformity and of skilled trade-unionism. He rejected Communism and convincingly appealed as a successor to the old Liberal values. He had improved the party organization and had smoothed the way for Ramsay MacDonald's return as the charismatic leader. When Baldwin provided an early general election on the old favourite issue of 'Free Trade or Tariffs' and claimed that tariffs were essential for fighting unemployment, it enabled Henderson and the Labour party to put at the forefront of their campaign Labour's traditional demand of 'Work and Wages'. After the turmoil in the party in the war and immediate post-war years, Labour almost did appear—as a journalist commented of it at the time of the October 1922 Newport by-election —'a party in perfect accord with its national leaders', in contrast to the dissensions within Liberal and Conservative parties.[76] When Baldwin lost his majority and when Labour emerged as the second largest party in December 1923, it seemed truly that Labour's hour had come.

7

Labour's International Statesman

In the last twelve years of his life, Henderson consolidated his position at the heart of the Labour party. Molly Hamilton wrote that 'everybody felt him as... the incarnation of the Party as a Party. He was there as representative, more representative than any other, of that entity'.[1] Moreover, in the arena of foreign affairs he went on from his Second International concerns to be a success as Foreign Secretary in the second Labour Government, and to become the embodiment of Labour's commitment to the League of Nations and to securing peace.

However, the period of the first Labour Government, 22 January to 5 November 1924, did not prove to be Henderson's finest hour. His role in that Government can at best be described as undistinguished. In spite of his close contact with the party machine and with the trade union leadership, he was at times surprisingly insensitive to the views of the Labour movement. As Home Secretary, he went to a department where caution was the established tradition. It was a post which accentuated his own characteristic desire always to move forward with great caution, seeking compromises rather than confronting opposition. While Henderson was not under the thumbs of his Home Office officials, he was susceptible to 'nothing can be done' arguments on such controversial issues as the reinstatement of the police who had gone on strike in 1919. Both the Labour party and the TUC were fully pledged to reinstating policemen sacked in the summer of 1919. Yet on 7 April 1924 the Cabinet appears to have readily agreed to Henderson's recommendation not to reinstate them. He took a high-handed attitude to the dismissed men in his Cabinet paper on the subject. While asserting 'My natural sympathies would be with the strikers' he concluded, 'I could not assume the responsibility of suggesting, or even countenancing, the reinstatement of the dismissed strikers without most seriously compromising my position'. Henderson had no qualms in supporting the Police Federation, and in taking a stern view of the 1919 strike which was indistinguishable from that of right-wing Tories:

> The sudden withdrawal from duty with the avowed object of forcing the hand of the government on a matter before Parliament must be regarded as such a breach of discipline and of the obligations of the policy to the public as would in any circumstances have merited dismissal, and it was committed in breach of the agreement which the Police Union representatives had entered into and in disregard of the plan warning of the consequences that would ensue.[2]

It was hardly surprising that, when Henderson told J.H. Hayes, who was Secretary of the remains of the Police and Prison Officers' Union and Labour MP for Liverpool (Edge Hill) of this decision, uproar followed. On 11 May, when addressing a rally of dismissed policemen, Hayes read Henderson's letter of 12 April, in which Henderson put the emphasis on 'the legal and practical difficulties in the way of reinstatement'. The policemen demanded government action and not excuses, and their case was taken up by the Labour party's executive. Lord Parmoor brought it back to the Cabinet on 14 May 'as a matter of urgency'. The Cabinet members clearly still hoped to avoid the Labour movement's commitment to the men. At first they considered justifying not reinstating the men on the grounds that a minority government could not command the necessary support in the House of Commons. Instead they would offer 'a most sympathetic inquiry into the possibility of the gradual absorption of the men into other branches of government service'. In the end they were forced to recognize that what had been promised and what was demanded was reinstatement, and they deputed the Prime Minister, Parmoor and Henderson to see representatives of the Labour party's executive.[3]

At that meeting, which lasted an hour and a half, Henderson made much of the Home Office's list of practical difficulties which prevented reinstatement. These included the fact that it would need decisions by the Police Council and local Watch Committees, and the claim that most other courses of helping the dismissed men would require special legislation. After the meeting the Cabinet agreed that when addressing the House of Commons Henderson should speak of the possibility of help other than reinstatement in police forces and that he 'should be authorised, if he considered it necessary, to offer a Committee of Inquiry'.

Henderson did offer an inquiry. But his remarks beforehand were extremely unsympathetic. He not only made clear his distaste in principle of police strikes, but also appeared not to be fully briefed on the subsequent suffering of the dismissed strikers. Henderson declared,

> I have been a trade unionist for 41 years, but . . . I draw a very wide distinction between an ordinary industrial dispute and a strike in what is a disciplinary service like the policy force. Those of us who are prepared to bring about changes, either political or industrial, on constitutional lines, cannot make too clear the difference between the position of the military, . . . the police force or . . . the fire brigade, so far as taking a "down tool" policy is concerned.

His remarks drew interruptions and bitter criticism from his own side, notably from the Clydeside MPs. George Buchanan upbraided him and the Cabinet for making pledges without 'sincerely intending to carry them out'.

After that the Cabinet became locked into a dispute with the executive of the parliamentary Labour party as to the precise wording of the terms of reference of the inquiry. Both sides, however, could agree that it should be 'to ascertain how best to meet the request for reinstatement and to deal with pension difficulties' and not to 'deal with the merits or demerits of the strike or the conduct of the men'.[4]

All in all this was a shabby affair, Henderson was forced to climb down from his original negative position. But the Labour Government still avoided the Labour movement's commitment to the dismissed men. The promise of an inquiry merely shunted the issue away beyond the concern of a minority government whose existence would be short. In so doing, the Government followed Henderson's earlier action over a controversial police case; that of the former Inspector Syme, whom many in the Labour movement felt had been the victim of harsh discipline. In the case of the dismissed striking policemen, when the committee of inquiry reported in December 1925, the majority on it advised against reinstatement.

Henderson's role in passing their case to an inquiry which would have an anti-Labour majority (as such inquiries reflected the composition of the House of Commons) was not forgotten. Some of the dismissed men and their wives vented their wrath on Henderson in June 1925 by shouting him down at a Labour demonstration at New Brighton. Henderson was prevented from saying even one sentence, amidst shouts at the platform such as 'Practise what you preach, you gang of traitors'. In October the Labour party conference unanimously passed a motion calling for 'something substantial' to be done for the police strikers.[5]

Henderson was also unsuccessful in maintaining good relations between the Government and the trade unions. Given his very powerful link role between the Labour party and the TUC in the First World War, it is surprising that he did not play a similar role on behalf of the first Labour Government. Haldane, the Lord Chancellor, complained to Beatrice Webb in June 1924 that the trade union Cabinet ministers—Henderson, Clynes and Shaw —- were 'frightened of their own people'. His complaint was made in the context of productivity.[6] But in the area of industrial relations the Government rode roughshod over trade union susceptibilities. This was one of several cases in which the Cabinet ministers set out to demonstrate that they were playing 'the part of a National government and not a class government'. According to Clynes, 'an understanding had been arrived at by members of the government that its trade union members would keep to politics only and not take sides in industrial disputes'.[7]

Even so, this decision need not have excluded better co-operation with the TUC. MacDonald, reticent in consulting senior Cabinet colleagues, did not see the TUC secretary during his first premiership. Henderson, who surely should have been more aware of TUC sensitivities, endorsed the Whitehall view that the General Council should not be given an early sight of unemployment insurance, factory or other bills before the final version went to Parliament. The Cabinet decision to uphold that view outraged the TUC leaders, who eventually did manage to persuade MacDonald to break with Whitehall tradition on this. Generally both the Labour ministers and the TUC weakened links rather than worked together during the lifetime of the Government.[8]

Though Henderson was not Minister of Labour, he did become involved in industrial relations from the outset. One day after the Government was formed, he reported to the first Cabinet meeting on the effect of an unofficial railway strike on food and fuel supplies. He and J.H. Thomas had tried to settle the dispute before a strike had occurred. Fortunately it did not last long. However, faced with a serious dock dispute in February, the Labour government soon turned to emergency measures. Henderson chaired a meeting of a Cabinet committee which resuscitated the Supply and Transport Organization (STO) which Lloyd George had created to ensure the supply of food and other essentials in the event of major strikes. Then the Labour movement had condemned it as a strike-breaking organization. Now the Cabinet supported the recommendations reactivating the STO 'for dealing with emergencies arising out of industrial crises', and put Henderson's committee (with increased membership) in charge of it. Thus Henderson remained still involved, though Josiah Wedgewood took on the role of Chief Industrial Commissioner.

In the case of the dock dispute, on 16 February—the day the national strike began—he authorized the Admiralty to arrange the collection of a supply of yeast from Ireland. But that apart, the emergency organization was not put into operation as the strike ended after ten days.[9] Henderson became involved again when Ernest Bevin extended a tram workers' wage dispute first to bus workers and then to underground workers. On 26 March Henderson chaired a meeting of the Emergency Committee which recommended proclaiming a state of emergency and, if necessary, using naval ratings in power stations. As for transport, it agreed after a long discussion, that 'the government should confine its activities to providing means for the transportation of government employees'. The next day the Cabinet accepted these recommendations, though widening the provision of transport to cover 'hospital patients and similar essential services'. On 28 March the Privy Council approved the proclamation of emergency, but a settlement was arranged before the proclamation was announced or exceptional measures were taken.[10]

The readiness to use the Emergency Powers Act and the STO shocked many active trade-unionists. When the Emergency Powers Bill had been introduced in 1920 Clynes and Henderson had been critical of its scope, but not of there being some such provision. Henderson had expressed concern that under the proposed legislation transport workers who were engaged in a constitutionally called strike could find that they had lost their trade union rights under the 1871 and 1906 legislation. Clynes had declared 'provisions must be made in an exceptional way in order to meet the life needs of the nation. I do not regard steps of that kind as breaking a strike'.[11] In the case of the STO, the Labour leadership's willingness to use it in 1924 made it that much harder for them to criticize the Baldwin Government's strike-breaking activities during the 1926 General Strike. Lloyd George delighted in rubbing this point in soon after it when he wrote a forward to an account of the emergency transport organization. He observed, 'Mr. Ramsay MacDonald and his Ministry not only took it over, but were ready and even anxious to make use of it... in the two threatened emergencies of 1924'.[12]

MacDonald and his senior colleagues were not only eager to show that the Government was immune from pressure from 'turbulent strikers and foolish-speaking trade unionists' (as Sidney Webb later bluntly put it), but that they were also disposed to be tough as they saw communist agitation contributing to the causes of the labour unrest. A discussion in the Cabinet on 2 April recognized 'that the present industrial unrest is partly the result of a reaction after a long period of trade depression, accompanied by wage reduction and a lowering of the standard of living'. But it still focused on 'recent instances of sectional strikes, not recognised by the trades unions concerned, among the shipyard workers of Southampton and the builders at the British Empire Exhibition at Wembley, as well as symptoms of communist agitation and propaganda'. Either during that Cabinet discussion or immediately after, Henderson apparently said 'that the epidemic of labour revolts reminds him ... of what was happening in Russia in 1917 against the Kerensky government'.[13] The Cabinet on 2 April took the decision that some of its members should see TUC General Council members 'for an informal discussion on the industrial position'. It also readily agreed that the Government itself in dealing with its employees should take care to 'deal with representatives of the trades unions concerned, rather than with shop-stewards and others of their employees who at present were accustomed to represent the workers and who made claims in excess of what were recognised by the trade unions concerned'.[14] However when an Industrial Unrest Committee of the Cabinet looked into communist activities in industrial unrest, it found them to be of minor significance.

Both as a trade-unionist and as an MP Henderson had often been active in pressing for safer and better working conditions. As Home Secretary he had the opportunity for constructive action. He had overall responsibility for one of the Government's major proposed measures— a wide-ranging Factory Bill of 143 clauses. This Bill was intended to amend and consolidate past provisions in a way which had not been done since the major Factory Act of 1901. He made capital out of the issue by carrying out a well-publicized tour of textile mills both in his own constituency of Burnley and other parts of Lancashire. Having personally inspected working conditions in the mills, he organized a joint conference of employers and operatives to be held in Manchester to discuss items for possible inclusion in his Factory Bill.

In such a compendious measure he had the opportunity to try to meet the needs of a wide range of trade unions and factory workers. One element of the Bill would have prohibited night baking, a long-standing grievance in Britain and one that the International Labour Organization took up in the summer of 1924. When the Cabinet considered the draft Bill, Henderson warned that a clause on holidays with pay might jeopardize the whole measure, but he also gave the opinion 'that the time has come, and that the opportunity presented by the Factory Bill should be taken to give legal force to the practice for factory workers generally'. The Cabinet took the option of caution, and approved the Bill minus the clause for holidays with pay.[15] In fact their caution was unnecessary. The Bill was lost along with much else when MacDonald called a general election and subsequently lost office.

Henderson also tried to secure more factory inspectors, a long-standing personal cause. In March 1924 he responded to a friendly House of Commons question on the subject by writing, 'I am not entirely satisfied with the present position, and I propose to review it at the earliest possible opportunity'.[16] When the Cabinet had approved his draft Factory Bill, it also agreed that should the measure become law Henderson could appoint a committee to consider the case for additional inspectors.

For all these opportunities at the Home Office, Henderson would have much preferred another department, quite possibly the Foreign Office. Though he had not established himself as Labour's expert on foreign affairs to anything like the extent that Snowden had done on finance, nevertheless he had gone some way to establishing that foreign affairs were not the preserve of those such as E.D. Morel, who had been prominent opponents of the First World War. From 1918 Henderson had become one of the major figures in the Second International. In the immediate post-war year Henderson was prominent in repeatedly condemning the Versailles Peace Treaty, in calling for better relations with Russia and in advocating support for the League of Nations. He also spoke out for Labour on the international issues of the day, such as the Chanak crisis of 1922 and the French occupation of the Ruhr in 1923, and occasionally, as on 30 January 1922 in a by-election, he made a major pronouncement on Labour's foreign policy as a whole. However when MacDonald formed his Government he gave the Foreign Office to neither Henderson nor J.H. Thomas, from the trade union wing of the party, nor to E.D. Morel, from the ILP wing, but he took it himself.

Whether or not Henderson expected the Foreign Office is debatable, but what is clear is that he expected to be offered a Cabinet post. At first MacDonald considered either excluding him altogether or appointing him Chairman of the Ways and Means Committee in the House of Commons. This attitude was viewed with distaste by other leading Labour figures. Sidney Webb later wrote that in this MacDonald had acted 'with fundamental ingratitude, unfriendliness and discourtesy'.[17]

Having lost his seat in the general election, Henderson gave the impression to others that he was resigned to not taking ministerial office. He told his family that he was keen to stay out of the Government and would devote himself to improving the Labour party organization in the country. After speaking with Henderson on 18 December, Beatrice Webb noted in her diary, 'considering that he has lost his seat and has no immediate prospect of getting back again in time to be included in the Cabinet he is amazingly cheerful, good-tempered, and determined to do his level best in organising for the next general election'.[18] However he appears to have made it clear to MacDonald on 12 December that he expected Cabinet office. MacDonald noted in his diary, 'H. evidently very sore at being out. Spoke of what he wd. sacrifice if he attended to the country and was not in and asked for a safe seat'. By 3 January 1924 Sidney Webb was also aware of Henderson's expectation of 'high office'.[19]

MacDonald's conduct stemmed from more than insensitivity. It probably revealed elements of jealousy towards Henderson. MacDonald himself had never held a government post, let alone been in the Cabinet. Henderson had served both in Asquith's Cabinet and Lloyd George's War Cabinet. Whilst others such as Clynes had held office before, none of the other Labour members of the Cabinet MacDonald formed in 1924 had ever been in the Cabinet (the other exception being Lord Haldane, brought in in spite of his Liberal pedigree). Perhaps MacDonald even harboured resentment that Henderson had discussed possible Cabinet lists for a Clynes government in June 1921 when there was a chance of Lloyd George resigning and when MacDonald was out of Parliament. Then, however, MacDonald would have been included, along with the non-Labour party figures, Parmoor and Haldane.[20] More likely he still bore grudges arising from the divisions in the Labour party during the First World War.

MacDonald behaved maladroitly when the press and the Opposition made an issue out of one of Henderson's speeches while he was fighting a by-election in Burnley in February 1924. On 23 February Henderson condemned the Peace Treaties, declaring that 'all... who valued world peace and desired to see the inauguration of a new era of international co-operation and good will must insist, as an absolute essential, on the revision of the Treaty of Versailles with all expedition possible, and a solution of the vexed problem of reparations'. *The Times* thundered in an editorial, 'Nothing more unwise or more inopportune could be imagined... at the precise moment when his leader is making every effort to work once more with France in settling the European problem'. Lloyd George and the Conservatives raised it in Parliament as evidence of a divided government. Even though it was three days before polling in Burnley, MacDonald made an evasive answer, which only encouraged

Labour's opponents to make more of Henderson's speech. MacDonald was trying to improve relations with France, but as Prime Minister he had a duty of loyalty to a colleague and could have been expected to dampen down the issue with greater skill.[21]

As for Henderson, he said no more than he had done in numerous speeches since 1919. According to Jim Middleton, the assistant secretary of the Labour party, Henderson's controversial denunciation of the Versailles Treaty was 'an old speech from the last election but one, written by [Herbert] Tracey [who worked for the Labour party]'.[22] Moreover, Labour had fought the general election on a programme which included the pledge, 'the immediate calling by the British government of an international conference (including Germany, on terms of equality) to deal with the revision of the Versailles Treaty, especially Reparations and Debts'. MacDonald's embarrassment stemmed mostly from Henderson so bluntly upholding the Labour party's long-standing policy on the Treaty at a time when MacDonald was seeking to achieve French co-operation for less sweeping revision of it. There was also an element of MacDonald being annoyed at a Cabinet colleague speaking out on MacDonald's preserve of foreign policy, albeit in a by-election.[23]

Towards the end of the Government, Henderson and MacDonald differed again as to the extent of their commitment to another of Labour's foreign-policy objectives—disarmament. Henderson had been to the fore in advocating an effective system of arbitration to make the 1919 Covenant of the League of Nations a reality. He had urged that a binding system of arbitration should be set up for certain types of international dispute when he had addressed the World Peace Congress at the Hague on 11 December 1922.[24] This became the Labour party's key to the problem of achieving agreement on security with disarmament. The Labour Government had its opportunity to press ahead with such a policy at the League of Nations in Geneva in September 1924.

MacDonald addressed the fifth Assembly of the League on 4 September, and called for a system of arbitration as well a for the admission of Germany and Russia to the League. After he and the French Prime Minister left, the various national delegations spent the rest of September preparing the draft of a 'Protocol for the Pacific Settlement of International Disputes'. Lord Parmoor (a former Conservative, a distinguished lawyer and a pacifist, who was Lord President and spoke for the Government on foreign affairs in the House of Lords) and Henderson led the British delegation in the detailed negotiations. Henderson played his part on the committee dealing with security and the reduction of armaments, where, according to Parmoor, he acted with great ability. Henderson successfully argued for a scheme of collective security. He urged,

> ... to deal with war, to get rid of it root and branch ... requires a scheme by which arbitration takes the place of war for the settlement of disputes; by which armaments ... are limited and cut down to the lowest level on which we can agree; by which the sense of insecurity is removed through mutual undertakings to support a state which is the victim of unlawful aggression.[25]

The draft Protocol was discussed by the Cabinet on 29 September, and it decided that Parmoor should ensure that the decisions took the form of recommendations. While the representatives of France and nine other countries signed the Protocol, Parmoor could only praise the proposals and say that he and the British delegation were 'prepared unhesitatingly, and with all the influence at its command, to recommend to the British government the acceptance for signature and ratification of the proposed Protocol'. MacDonald dodged the decision of either supporting or opposing the Protocol by pointing out the likely impending defeat of the Government in the House of Commons when Parmoor pressed issue. Although MacDonald had outlined the broad elements of the policy in the Protocol during his few days in Geneva, he appears to have prevaricated in the face of opposition. This included some of his Cabinet colleagues, especially those representing the armed services. The Conservatives and much of the press wrongly tried to suggest that the Protocol threatened the autonomy of the British navy. Much of the Foreign Office and Whitehall appear to have been willing to undermine Labour on this, as on its Russian policy. Parmoor later complained that the Foreign Office failed to correct false impressions about the Protocol and that its members, other than those at the very top level, made clear their disapproval of Labour's peace policies by treating him 'as a strange animal who had found his way within a sacred enclosure'.[26]

Henderson lost little time after his return from Geneva in proclaiming the merits of the Protocol. He gave a major speech in his own constituency on the subject on 12 October 1924. In it he declared that 'the Protocol ... was an instrument which made reason, justice and law—not force and might of armaments—their first line in disposing of the differences between nations'. But he also warned that 'they were solemnly pledged that their force should be used to make the decisions effective, if sanity, reason, right and justice failed and these sanctions had to be employed'.[27] As Professor Winkler has observed Henderson's position was as close to the concept of collective security as anyone came before the emergence of Hitler, and his emphasis on the final sanction of force was a point that MacDonald and most other Labour leaders were reticent in making. Yet it was a position that Henderson had adopted explicitly from at least late 1917 when, in *The Aims of Labour*, he had written,

> ... moral support must be supplemented by a joint organised power—military, economic and commercial—capable of enforcing the decisions of the League on any recalcitrant member, and of defending any member which may be attacked by a non-adhering nation that may refuse to refer the dispute between them for settlement by pacific means.[28]

After the Labour Government's fall, Henderson rallied the Labour movement behind the Geneva Protocol. The General Council of the TUC and the executive of the Labour party at a meeting on 25 January 1925 urged that 'this country should do everything in its power to obtain the acceptance of the principles of the Protocol and the holding of the disarmament conference'. In the campaign to press the Baldwin Government to ratify the Protocol, Henderson starkly contrasted the Conservative Foreign Secretary's words at Geneva at the sixth Assembly of the League in 1925—'Brute force is what the nations fear, and only brute force can give security'—with the Protocol, which he said recognised 'the fact that as there can be no disarmament without security and arbitration so there can be no security or arbitration without disarmament'.[29] A Swedish delegate to both the fifth and sixth Assemblies of the League wrote in despair to Henderson,

> The gulf between the fair and generous work of the British Delegation at last year's Assembly and the sterile opposition on the part of your compatriots this year is immense. Last year there was an international spirit—now there is a spirit of negation, of selfishness and of isolation!... The scrapping of the Geneva Protocol was a mortal blow.[30]

For Henderson the aims of the Protocol, including its commitment to an international disarmament conference, remained a central cause for the rest of his life.

In spite of MacDonald's insensitive treatment of Henderson during the formation of the first Labour Government, and friction between them on several occasions subsequently, Henderson continued to support Mac-Donald as leader after the 1924 general election. MacDonald's failure to control the Foreign Office over the Zinoviev letter (a forgery which was embarrassing for Labour's policy towards Russia), or to limit the damage once it was published during the election campaign, added further to doubts about his performance as premier and resulted in moves being made to replace him. These moves were made not only by the left wing, but also by Snowden (by now hardly of the Left) and by a leading trade-unionist, Ernest Bevin of the Transport and General Workers' Union. Snowden and others saw Henderson as the alternative leader.

Henderson not only declined to act on such suggestions but actually rallied support for MacDonald. In early November he presided over a dinner given by the General Council of the TUC and the executive of the Labour party in MacDonald's honour. At the dinner Henderson condemned the press campaign against MacDonald, saying this was similar to the 'Balfour Must Go' campaign which had succeeded in ousting Balfour as Tory leader in 1911. He declared that 'the spirit and unity of that gathering represented the spirit and unity of the entire movement' as to confidence in MacDonald's leadership.[31]

Henderson had come to see MacDonald as 'the indispensable leader'. He felt that had MacDonald not returned to Parliament in 1922 he (Henderson) could have outshone Clynes and have unified the Labour party better. But with MacDonald back the party had a leader whose charisma and platform oratory made a bigger impact on the electorate than he himself could achieve. Moreover, Henderson felt that prickly figures such as Snowden would serve loyally under MacDonald but not under himself. For all his failings, MacDonald represented moderation in leadership and a better chance of maintaining party unity than any other person. Henderson had become accustomed to working with MacDonald and, if he was to serve under anyone, much preferred him to others such as Snowden or Thomas.[32]

Henderson continued to support MacDonald as leader until his defection in 1931, in the face of all pressures. After the experience of Labour in office in 1924 the ILP developed its own distinctive programme, 'Socialism in Our Time', formally adopted in 1926, and also shed many of its former leading figures, including Snowden. In the case of MacDonald the ILP conference in 1927 decided not to nominate him again as treasurer of the Labour party, given his opposition to the 'Socialism in Our Time' programme. Henderson responded with vigour, declaring at a Labour School at Oxford, 'Well Mr. MacDonald is still treasurer of the party, and I will promise the ILP that, after the next annual conference, he will remain treasurer of the party'. For good measure he added something of a warning to the left wing of the ILP,

> I want to say quite frankly that had the ILP as an organisation, and had
> certain prominent members of the ILP, some of whom are in the House
> of Commons, been dealt with according to the measure applied to Mr. Mac-
> Donald, neither the ILP organisation members, nor its members in the House
> of Commons, would be members of the national Labour Party. I know of
> no organisation that has had more tolerance shown to it by the national
> Labour Party, the Parliamentary Labour Party and the national executive
> than the Independent Labour Party.[33]

This reflected a basic element in Henderson's outlook—a firm belief
that elected leaders in the unions or the Labour party must be supported.
Henderson's support, given his influential position in the trade union
movement, his control of the Labour party machine and his resumption
of the post of Chief Whip until February 1927, made MacDonald powerful. However by the mid-1920s onwards MacDonald was not an effective
leader of a party of the Left, not least because of his increasing tendency
to be embarrassed by socialist and even fairly moderate Labour party
objectives. Viewed with hindsight after 1931, it was, as Margaret Cole
has suggested, 'at least arguable that Henderson's obstinate and ill-repaid
fidelity to MacDonald was a mistake for which the Party paid dearly'.[34]

MacDonald, for his part, found that from 1924 he had to take more
notice of Henderson's importance in the Labour movement. After some
early parliamentary blunders stemming from lack of overall planning in
the early weeks of the first Labour Government, MacDonald consulted
some of his major colleagues over Monday lunches at 10 Downing Street.
Henderson, Clynes, Snowden, Webb, Thomas and Ben Spoor, the Chief
Whip, were regular attenders at these.

After the fall of the Government MacDonald reluctantly gave way
to Henderson's demand that Labour should formulate a clear policy to
put to the electorate. The result was the statement, *Labour and the Nation*,
adopted by the 1928 Labour party conference. MacDonald generally took
Henderson's loyalty for granted and was infamous for his failure to reci-
procate even with praise. Though one notable exception occurred when,
in July 1928, he presided over a dinner at the House of Commons to
mark the twenty-fifth anniversary of Henderson's arrival in Parliament.[35]

Labour and the Nation, like much else in the Labour party in the 1920s,
bore the stamp of Henderson's moderate politics. Though it had been
intended to be an election programme, the document ended up as a
seventy-two point statement of Labour's aims, replacing that of 1918,
Labour and the New Social Order. Much of its contents had been the
regular substance of Henderson's speeches around the country in the

preceding years. This was especially so not only of the section 'International peace and Co-operation' but also of those passages on factory legislation, agriculture and rural life, and the importance of the co-operative movement in the creation of 'the socialist commonwealth'. Henderson saw to it that while the programme would make it harder for Tory propaganda 'to make a bogey of socialism' at the next general election as a result of there being no clear and approved party objectives, it did not tie the hands of a future Labour Cabinet too firmly. In the debate at the Labour party conference, John Wheatley, the leading Clydeside left-wing MP, pointed out that it was a programme which might take forty or fifty years to enact in Parliament and that even then socialism would not be achieved. Indeed, Wheatley suggested, some of the proposals were such as could be adopted 'by any advanced Liberal in this country, and which might therefore make the basis of a working arrangement between Liberalism and Labour for probably a quarter of a century'. Wheatley argued, 'No one suggests that you are doing anything more than undertaking to run capitalism successfully where other people equally qualified have failed to run capitalism in the past'.[36]

As well as ensuring that a broad and moderate programme was ready, Henderson, in the years between the first two Labour governments, did all that he could in other ways to try to widen Labour's appeal. In a speech in Torquay in April 1925 he optimistically tried to woo such sectors of the electorate as rural workers, co-operators and women. In the course of it he observed that Labour 'had rallied to their support so large a number of the electors of the country that a very slight change in the balance of voters would place them in office again, and with a majority'. However he did draw firm lines beyond which he would not go for support. Thus where party policy clashed with the wishes of such electorally powerful groups as the Catholics and temperance organizations, Henderson was more ready than Snowden or MacDonald to take a firm stand in defence of party policy.[37]

Henderson also worked hard to ensure that Communists were kept out of his broad Labour church. He worked against their influence in either the Labour party or the trade unions. At public meetings, when heckled by Communists, he retorted that 'there was no room for men who stand for bloodshed and revolution in a democratic movement like the Labour Party'. Similarly, in March 1926, he was equally direct in opposing ILP proposals for talks with the Communist International about creating an all-inclusive International. Then he wrote for the Labour Press Service that the Labour party could not consider many of its differences with the Communist International to be 'negotiable issues', nor was the party 'ready to bargain about political democracy or the inevitability of armed revolution'.

Henderson was eager to win over Liberal voters but was firm in ruling out deals with the Liberal party, at least ahead of the general election. He firmly rebuffed suggestions of possible pacts when floated by Dr Thomas MacNamara (a former coalition Liberal minister) in September 1925, Lloyd George in January 1926, or the press in July 1927. Instead Henderson made much of any Liberal pacts with the Tories in by-elections and local elections, and pressed hard the argument that Labour was the only real alternative to Baldwin's Government.[38]

Henderson's lifelong view of the desirability of co-operation rather than confrontation in industry was another aspect of his appeal to moderate voters in the late 1920s. Both before and after the 1926 General Strike he was a major proponent of settling industrial differences by discussions and compromise. During the General Strike and coal lock-out, as with the 1921 mining dispute, he tried to mediate between the miners and the Government. Clynes later recalled that in late April 1926, 'Thomas, Snowden, Henderson, MacDonald and I moved behind the scenes, trying to find some way out of the impasse, hindered on the one hand by the armed preparations of the government, and on the other by the ferocious statements and wild promises of Cook [the Secretary of the miners' union] and his following'. Henderson's last-minute efforts to promote a compromise formula that Ernest Bevin and others had devised, and to which the TUC had agreed, came to nothing. Thereafter, having failed to prevent the General Strike occurring, Henderson and MacDonald acted as political advisers to the General Council of the TUC, with MacDonald as its main spokesperson in Parliament.[39]

Like MacDonald, Henderson was not sympathetic to what he saw to be the miners' intransigent stand. But he was angered by the Baldwin Government's apparent willingness to ensure that there was confrontation. Henderson informed Walter Citrine, the acting secretary of the TUC, that Arthur Steel-Maitland, the Minister of Labour, had told him that 'it was about time we were put in our places' and Churchill had replied to Henderson's comment, 'It seems to me, Winston, that you are trying to give us a dose of Sidney Street', with 'You will be better prepared to talk to us in two or three weeks'. Henderson was to see the Supply and Transport Organization, which he had revived in 1924, used against the strikers in May 1926. In 1925 he had been a member of a sub-committee of the National Joint Committee which had reviewed the Labour movement's policy towards the use of the STO. This had concluded only that Labour representatives should refuse to help the STO in such a crisis.[40] Hence his criticisms centred on the Government's unwillingness to engage in meaningful negotiations, not on its use of the emergency supply organization.

Before the General Strike had begun, Henderson, like many other moderate figures in the Labour movement, had hoped that the report on the Royal Commission on the Coal Industry, set up in 1925 under Sir Herbert Samuel, would provide the basis of avoiding a major conflict in the industry. Thus on 17 April at a Labour demonstration in St. Albans he strongly suggested that all sides should use the report's recommendations as a basis for negotiations. He observed then, as on other occasions, that he 'regretted very much that the wage question was allowed to take precedence over the more fundamental and vitally important question of reorganising the mining industry'. He argued that increased efficiency in the coal industry was a prerequisite for resolving the industry's bad industrial relations. It would meet Labour's demand 'that a living wage for all miners must be a first charge upon the industry'.[41]

After the miners were starved back to work, Henderson continued to urge that some measure of reorganization be carried out based on the recommendations of the Samuel Commission. When charged with dropping Labour's commitment to nationalization, he responded by saying that was the long-term aim. But in the short term they needed 'something immediately practicable, even under the present government, to lighten the load of unemployment, care and misery among the mining population'. In so far as he had any notions as to how to organize a nationalized coal industry, he appears to have envisaged a role for consumers as well as producers. Thus he spoke of applying 'the co-operators' principle as an integral part of a national and unified system of coal, power and transport to be carried on as a great public service'.[42]

Henderson also continued to argue the case for co-operation between both sides of industry. Speaking at Burnley on 6 January 1927 he commented:

> The most important question at the moment is how can all the talk about a new spirit in industry be translated into concrete proposals such as will command the confidence and goodwill of men and women of the highest type in all classes? Recriminations about the failure to apply the decisions of the Industrial Conference in 1919, the Sankey Commission of the same year, and the Samuel Commission of last year will not improve the position.
>   ... co-operative effort for the re-establishment of our economic life can

... be made possible on the basis of a frank recognition by employers that
the workers are to be admitted to a fuller partnership in the conduct of
industry, and given, through their organisations, a higher status in the productive enterprises by which the nation lives.[43]

Four days later, at Falkirk, Henderson called on the Speaker of the House
of Commons to convene and preside over a conference of representatives
of the National Confederation of Employers' Organizations (NCEO),
the National Joint Council of the TUC and the Labour party 'to meet
for an informal non-committal discussion of the whole industrial situation'. He suggested that at such a meeting the effectiveness of joint councils
should be discussed. Henderson also called for a permanent body like
the National Industrial Conference to be established.

His views on how 'an Economic Council or Parliament of Industry'
might develop reflect a powerful faith in corporatist solutions to Britain's
economic ills. He was a firm believer in the efficacy of discussion based
on sound facts. He urged,

> Such a body, equipped with a competent technical staff for the examination
> of industrial problems and fully representative not only of the parties respon-
> sible for the conduct of industry, but including representatives also of econ-
> omic science, financial authorities and other interested parties, would be
> able to give full consideration to every question arising in industry and to
> evolve appropriate policies for dealing with them.[44]

However his campaign for such a development had to be halted for
several months, given the Baldwin Government's action in bringing forward tough trade-union legislation. This also had the effect of lessening
recriminations within the British Labour movement as to who was to
blame for the failure of the General Strike and the miners' struggle and
brought all together to defend the trade unions' existing rights. Henderson
played a leading role in the TUC and Labour party's major campaign
in the country against the proposed legislation. He vigorously condemned
it as 'class legislation of the worst type' and warned that it would 'destroy
all hopes of improved industrial relations'. He reserved special venom
for the clause affecting the political levy of trade unions, denouncing
it as 'a deliberate attempt to strangle the political activities of the entire
trade union movement ... The trade unionist was to be treated as a sort
of political leper, segregated from the rest of his fellow citizens by special
regulation and regimentation'.[45]

By the autumn of 1927, however, both sides of industry were moving
again to engage in talks which would cover the 'entire field of industrial

reorganisation and industrial relations'. From such moves sprang the Mond–Turner conferences, involving a group of leading industrialists led by Sir Alfred Mond and the TUC led by its president for the year, Ben Turner. Welcoming these talks in a speech in his Barnley constituency, Henderson pressed the need for British industry to adjust to the changing international market. He pointed out that 'the main development of British industry and trade seemed to be in what might be described as the luxury trades, rather than in those basic productive and heavy manufacturing trades and industries which in the past had given the country the title of 'the world's workshop''. As the representative of a cotton town he was very aware of the urgent need for industrial readjustment.[46] Here he was expressing views he shared with the TUC's general secretary, Walter Citrine, and many of its General Council.

The Mond–Turner talks ranged widely over such matters as industrial rationalization, trade union recognition, victimization and the impact of the gold standard. One of the issues on which there was agreement was the desirability of setting up a National Industrial Council, which would have half its representatives from the TUC and half from the FBI and the NCEO. As one would expect, Henderson publicly pushed this issue. He deemed it to be 'in many respects the most important constructive project evolved by the industrial conference':

> It would be nothing short of a national tragedy if it should fail to materialise. He refused to believe that any responsible body of employers would fail to associate themselves with it; he was sure that public opinion would sharply condemn any employers' association which stood aloof and thus jeopardised the hopeful and promising development rendered possible by these joint discussions.
>
> The success of the TUC General Council's policy would open a new era for British industry, and lead to a fruitful expansion of the influence and authority of the trade unions in the organisation and control of industry . . .[47]

Such an enhancement of the trade unions' status, however, was not something that the two employers' associations would promote, and they rejected the proposed National Industrial Council. Thereafter Henderson's efforts in promoting co-operation were most conspicuous in the area of foreign affairs.

After the fall of the first Labour Government Henderson continued to show considerable interest in foreign policy. Until he took office again in the second Labour Government in 1929, he remained President of the Labour and Socialist International. In this capacity and as a very prominent Labour front-bencher, he made numerous pronouncements on the problems of securing world peace. During the 1920s Henderson was, as Henry Winkler has observed, 'one of the major architects of Labour's foreign policy'.[48]

Along with other Labour foreign affairs specialists such as Ponsonby and Trevelyan, Henderson warned against the creation of new systems of alliances and urged that a policy of securing peace should be grounded on the League of Nations. In April 1925 he told a meeting at Exeter that 'the attitude of the Labour Party towards foreign policy was to bring it under the control of popularly elected assemblies, to maintain a vigilant watch over the activities of diplomats and the agents of international finance, to secure publicity for all agreements between states, and to destroy the evil influence of the International Armaments Trust'.[49] To this old Union of Democratic Control line, Henderson added the importance of ratifying the Geneva Protocol and holding a disarmament conference.

He and the Labour party were shocked at the extent to which the Baldwin Government consistently undermined moves to make the League of Nations effective in securing international peace. Austen Chamberlain's approach as Foreign Secretary was to enter into multilateral pacts to offer France and other powers security without becoming committed to compulsory arbitration and the other elements of the Geneva Protocol. Chamberlain's main achievement was the Locarno Pact of October 1925. This, as F.S. Northedge has observed, 'avoided the payment of any price for European security other than the lowest possible one'. Henderson accepted Locarno with 'strong reservations'. He pointed out that such treaties 'did not outlaw war, nor did they take any definite step calculated to lead to the abolition of war as a method of settling national disputes'. Indeed he warned that 'the restricted security provided might make the holding of an early disarmament conference no longer possible, and, if held, the fears and apprehensions of the unprotected countries might render it abortive'.[50] Thereafter he found even less to welcome in Chamberlain's foreign policy. He complained that 'the government had departed from the much-claimed policy of continuity in foreign policy ... Owing to this ... the moral leadership held by this country had been deflected ...'. In his major BBC radio broadcast before the 1929 general election Henderson ended on a high note of commitment to the League of Nations and a pledge to 'endeavour to harness the spirit of goodwill in the world ... with a view to the establishment of law and order in place of the arbitrament of war'.[51]

With Labour's victory in the summer of 1929, Henderson was the most obvious choice for the Foreign Office. He had groomed himself for the position. He was eminent figure in the Labour and Socialist International, and in 1926 and 1927 had made lengthy visits to Canada, the USA, Australia and New Zealand. Above all he was a major front-bench figure. Along with Snowden and Thomas, Henderson was one of three with whom MacDonald discussed possible Cabinet positions in April, and again after the general election results were known (this time with the addition of Clynes).

As Snowden recalled, 'We knew that Henderson had set his heart upon this post'. MacDonald noted in his diary for 1 June, 'Henderson told me some weeks ago he would not return to H.O. but would put in a plea for F.O.'.[52] Yet MacDonald's first choice was J.H. Thomas. His initial rejection of Henderson for the post provoked a major and bitter row between them. Thomas was not an absurd nominee. He had been a leading Labour figure for over a decade. H.N. Brailsford, when speculating on possible nominees for Foreign Secretary in a Labour Government in 1928 had named him as one, along with Oswald Mosley, but had seen Henderson and Hugh Dalton as more likely candidates.[53] Yet for all his popularity with opponents and the press, Thomas was a much less weighty figure in the Labour movement than Henderson.

MacDonald always underestimated Henderson's abilities and yet was jealous of the prestige he gained from participation in the wartime governments and the Second International. Conversely, MacDonald had a high opinion of his own abilities as an international statesman and hoped, like Lloyd George, to intervene frequently in foreign affairs as Prime Minister, especially in relations with the USA. For him Thomas was likely to be more congenial and acquiescent as Foreign Secretary than Henderson, who was much more his own man. Yet Henderson had worked loyally with MacDonald for so many years. In opposition in 1927 and 1928 MacDonald had led for Labour on foreign issues, and Henderson had diligently followed. Thus, as secretary of the Labour party when drawing up the executive committee's resolutions for the 1927 party conference, he wrote to MacDonald,

> With regard to the one on arbitration and disarmament, I think we have sufficient in your recent statements to guide us, and we will, therefore, amend the resolution of last year to bring it into harmony with recent developments
> . . .
>   I find it difficult, however, to fix the line upon which the resolution on the Chinese situation should go, as there has been such kaleidoscopic change. If there were any lines upon which your mind is running, and you will send

me a rough note, I will see that the resolution is brought into harmony
with it.[54]

This tone was very different from that of Snowden, who did not hesitate
to differ from his colleagues in their own special areas, as on the Geneva
Protocol, let alone on his own area, notably on the proposed surtax.

It is possible that MacDonald feared that Henderson might be too
radical as Foreign Secretary. He did not share the latter's fervour for
the Geneva Protocol, though he was willing to publicly support it. Hence
in September 1927 he informed Henderson that 'in view of what has
happened at Geneva, I think we should welcome the revival of the Protocol
and declare that only in accordance with its ideas and policy can peace
be secured'.[55] Henderson was also vigorous in condemning the Whites
in Hungary, and the Horthy government in particular. In this he was
expressing the policy of both the Labour and Socialist International and
the Labour party's executive committee. His actions were denounced by
the Hungarian government. MacDonald may well have been uneasy at
such blunt carrying out of party policy: indeed he himself was by no
means antagonistic to the Horthy government. On visiting Hungary, he
observed in a letter to Jim Middleton, 'The whole situation in Budapest
is one of baffling insincerity and propaganda manoeuvring'.[56]

Indeed, MacDonald had a rather elitist attitude to foreign affairs. He
felt that it should be conducted by the able few. The German commentator,
Egon Wertheimer, wrote perceptively in 1930 that MacDonald was 'a
conservative in his innate historical sense, in his profound respect for
the monuments of the past, in his instinctive understanding of the traditions of the nation and in his persistent yearning for the idyllic peace
of a quiet life'. As such MacDonald was not deeply sympathetic to
Labour's notions that the Foreign Office should be brought into line
with Labour party conference decisions. Thomas was always seen as something of a maverick in the Labour movement, whereas Henderson, like
Clynes—as Wertheimer perceived in 1930—belonged 'to the sympathetic
class of Labour leader, who in spite of their social advance, have never
lost real contact with their movement'.[57]

Thus it was in spite of MacDonald's considerable reluctance to give
him the post, that Henderson took on the office that greatly enhanced
his reputation. Indeed, at the time and in retrospect, Henderson has been
widely recognized as the most successful member of the second Labour
Government. Molly Hamilton, herself MP for Blackburn between 1929
and 1931, recalled,

... at the time we felt that, at home, the 1929 government did not even try to do the right things. The foreign success ... was Henderson's; he knew what he wanted to do, and did it. If MacDonald knew what he wanted it was not what we wanted. I am inclined to think that he did not know.[58]

Henderson's conduct of foreign affairs was much admired at the time, both by Labour party figures (excluding probably a jealous MacDonald) and by the press. Dalton, who served under Henderson at the Foreign Office, later testified: 'I. . . learned much from him, not only in his untiring pursuit of international peace but in his most competent handling of a great government department'.[59]

Henderson managed the Foreign Office with quiet firmness. He had confidence in his own abilities and judgement; based on long experience as secretary of the Labour party, his past trade-union posts, his Cabinet experience under three Prime Ministers and his position in the Labour and Socialist International. Thus, as Lord Robert Cecil later recalled, when Henderson wanted Cecil to have a room in the Foreign Office he 'summarily overruled the departmental objections'. Beatrice Webb felt that men such as Henderson, MacDonald and Snowden had a talent for foreign affairs deriving from the fact 'that the principal men in the Labour movement have probably travelled far more widely and in a far more effective way than the members of the Conservative government. It is one thing to go touring about two continents, and another thing going as a delegate to important international assemblies, as these men are constantly doing'. Major A.C. Temperley, the British chief military adviser at Geneva, in recalling Henderson's strengths as Foreign Secretary, observed,

... he was a man of decision and once he had taken a line he stuck to it. He was genial by nature but apt to get irritable and shout at people, yet the Foreign Office loved him.[60]

Throughout his career Henderson won respect for his judgement. He was not quick witted. He mulled information over and came to his conclusion after careful reflection. Like Lloyd George, he did not work long hours on departmental memoranda but preferred issues to be explained verbally to him and to then ask questions. Lord Robert Cecil recalled of Henderson at the Foreign Office,

At first one was inclined to doubt whether he appreciated what was being said to him, and very often an interview ended rather inconclusively. But by the next day it was clear that the arguments had been understood and weighed, and a decision was given.

Hugh Dalton, his Parliamentary Under-Secretary, and Philip Noel Baker, his Private Secretary, both confirmed that by these means he achieved a good 'grasp of the problems he faced and ... [an] ability to cut to the heart of an issue without burying himself in the minutiae of detail'.[61]

In regard to policy, Henderson told the 1930 Labour party conference that he 'was trying religiously to stick by *Labour and the Nation*'. Henderson had played a major role in drawing up that document. It represented a radical approach to many foreign policy issues, but did not go far enough for some in the party, notably ILP members, who wanted more far-reaching action on disarmament. At the 1929 party conference Henderson bluntly responded to the call for 'total disarmament within the lifetime of the present Parliament' by observing that 'we are only deceiving ourselves by expounding such ideas' and claimed that 'there is no member of this conference who, if placed in a position of responsibility, would ever seek to persuade the public ... that it was within the power of his or her government to carry such a policy into operation'. In office he held firm against unilateral action. He stood by the policy of 'the general and progressive reduction of armaments by international agreement'. The Labour Government, he reminded delegates, was committed to 'strengthening the League of Nations and all its machinery, using it as speedily as they possibly could towards the goal ... of universal disarmament'.[62] This, as he commented on many occasions, was a policy which had been developed since 1919.

Aided by Dalton, he tried to ensure that the Foreign Office did not gratuitously deviate from the policies laid out in *Labour and the Nation*. They circulated two dozen copies in the Foreign Office after spending much effort redrafting answers to parliamentary questions so that they would be in line with these policies. Dalton recalled Henderson saying 'with a slight tone of surprise in his voice, "I don't believe some of these chaps have ever read any of our Annual Conference Resolutions"'.[63]

Henderson also was faced with MacDonald's habitual attempts to manoeuvre round, or totally ignore, party policy. MacDonald was easily rattled by the Tory press or the establishment making a fuss as to the wisdom of actually carrying out some item of party policy. In early September Henderson, when speaking at the Assembly of the League of Nations in Geneva, welcomed the Convention for Financial Assistance to States in Danger of Aggression and declared, subject to certain limitations, that Britain would adhere to it. The Convention strengthened the machinery for arbitration, by increasing the financial penalties for international aggression. This was clearly in line with Labour's commitment in *Labour and the Nation.*

However MacDonald raised Henderson's statement and the press response in the Cabinet. He wrote a letter to Henderson stating that the Cabinet was concerned and that the Convention should be examined in Whitehall before being approved. An enraged Henderson replied that it had already been examined by the Treasury and that, moreover, it had been 'submitted to you personally, and returned to the Foreign Office ticked by you'. He chided MacDonald for flinching in the face of opponents' attacks and he complained that 'there is not that confidence when working in the international sphere [that] one is entitled to expect'.[64]

MacDonald was also lukewarm in support of Henderson's achievement in getting widespread support at the League of Nations for the Optional Clause which accepted compulsory arbitration in legal disputes between governments. It was an integral part of the Geneva Protocol. As Dalton later wrote, this was seen to be 'the first step towards an orderly system of predetermined procedures for settling all disputes between nations. "Law, not war", we said'. Henderson was pressed by leading figures in the Foreign Office and Whitehall, as well as by the dominions, to compromise on this commitment. MacDonald, who was being briefed against this policy by the Permanent Under-Secretary at the Foreign Office, equivocated and at one stage withdrew his support, but he came back into line with Party policy 'under pressure from Henderson'.[65]

Henderson's foreign policy followed faithfully the ideals that he and the Party had expounded in the 1920s and which had been set out in *Labour and the Nation.* After the horrors of the First World War, this policy aimed to build collective security through the League of Nations. It was to be a step-by-step policy towards 'Security, Arbitration and Disarmament'. As Foreign Secretary he expressed at Geneva his long held faith in arbitration. In putting the case for the Optional Clause he told the League of Nation's Assembly,

> A nation which relies on arbitration and is ready to accept the verdict of an impartial judge does not rely on the use of armed force. Its national mind is turned in a new direction, and it is precisely in this new spirit which the practice of arbitration may induce that lies perhaps the most powerful single factor in bringing the nations security from war.[66]

The key to peace was to change attitudes. But he was not unaware that this would take time. His was a 'policy that recognises that you must have progressive disarmament down to a reasonable standard of policing forces'. As he told the 1929 Labour party conference, 'The world will have to be very much more advanced and human nature very much more perfect before you will be able to do without policing forces'.[67]

After succeeding in getting Britain and many other nations to sign the Optional Clause, Henderson worked to build up the League of Nations in other ways, including strengthening the League's Covenant. He unsuccessfully sought to amend the Covenant to outlaw war by bringing it into line with the Kellogg Pact (or 'Pact of Peace'). But he successfully fulfilled Labour's election pledge to accede to the General Act of Arbitration, Conciliation and Judical Settlement. This took the application of arbitration beyond cases which could be settled by international law to other classes of dispute, with the intention thereby of avoiding resort to war. Henderson signed the General Act on 21 May 1931.

After the Labour Government had fallen, Hugh Dalton could tell the 1931 Labour party conference 'that so far as the objectives laid down for foreign policy in *Labour and the Nation* are concerned ... we had already carried out ... all those objectives except one, and that one was general disarmament'. Cecil had been exploring the ground for disarmament throughout the existence of the Labour Government, but increasing tension between Germany and France, as well as between Italy and France, lessened whatever likelihood there was of any successful moves. However in January 1931 at last a date was agreed on which to hold a world disarmament conference, namely in February 1932. In May the League of Nations delegates unanimously invited Henderson to be president of that conference. This was due to it being Britain's turn to take the presidency, but the warmth of support for Henderson as the nominee stemmed from his ability as chairman. Temperley later testified that 'the Council had been impressed with the way that he had discharged his duties, cutting short discussion and stopping irrelevancies with an efficiency unheard of among League chairmen'.[68]

The issue of Germany's position in international affairs created difficulties for Henderson as Foreign Secretary. From the outset, he tried to end Germany's position as a pariah nation and to bring her back into good relations with the other European nations. Labour was committed to the 'immediate and unconditional' withdrawal of all foreign troops from the Rhineland and 'a complete and definite settlement of the German reparations problem'. Evacuation depended on agreement on reparations, and the French were not easily satisfied. At the Hague in August 1929 Henderson put strong pressure on the French to make an agreement on reparations by announcing that regardless of the outcome of the discussions British troops would begin to withdraw in September. Thus he fulfilled Labour's election promise and gained considerable prestige for playing a major part in securing a solution to the issue of the Rhineland. Afterwards he commented with satisfaction that the conference had 'at long last taken the final step for bringing the world war to an end'. However, whilst his success at the Hague was widely recognized, it was overshadowed by Snowden's successful yet belligerent, even jingoistic, fight for more money for Britain during the accompanying negotiations on reparations.[69]

Labour was also committed to improving diplomatic and economic relations with Soviet Russia 'on the basis of reciprocal recognition of non-interference with each other's internal affairs'. In spite of opposition from much of the press and the King, Henderson refused to be deflected. However, MacDonald caused delays in July 1929 by unwisely promising the House of Commons in effect that there would be no exchange of ambassadors until October. This gratuitous delay enraged many Labour back-benchers. Outside of the Cabinet, Henderson loyally supported MacDonald: Dalton noted Henderson's response in his diary,

> Uncle ... takes the view that he can't now go back on J.R.M.'s supplementary answer, wrong though it was. We should have all the Press against us and the danger of 1924 all over again. 'Russia has brought us down once. We can't afford to let it happen twice.' Russia, after all, is not the only pebble on the beach.[70]

In the Cabinet, however, he complained, and later at the Labour party conference on 2 October he made it clear that he would be delayed no further, 'At the general election we made it unmistakably plain that if we formed a government one of the first things we would do would be to bring about a resumption of diplomatic relations with Russia'. In the interim, he had personally conducted many of the negotiations, and he concluded them at a meeting with the Russian envoy at the unusual venue of the White Hart Inn at Lewes where Henderson was staying during the Brighton party conference.[71]

Henderson also pressed ahead with negotiations for a trade agreement with the Soviet Union. This was signed on 16 April 1930. In the first year of resumed trade, Russia took £6 to £7 million of British goods, mostly engineering, electrical and chemical goods and Britain took £34 million of Russian goods. Henderson was no more enamoured of dealing with the Soviet government in 1929 to 1931 than he had been in his contacts with the Bolsheviks in 1917. Indeed in December 1930 he complained to the British ambassador to Russia, 'I am bitterly disappointed at the results of one year's experience of renewed relations with the Soviet government whose actions seem designed deliberately to play into the hands of the opponents of continued Anglo-Russian relations'.[72] Yet, as in other areas of foreign policy, Henderson loyally carried out Labour's election policy.

Henderson also maintained a relatively enlightened policy towards areas under the League of Nations Mandate system. In the case of Iraq he was unequivocal that his policy was 'the early establishment of Iraq as an independent and self-reliant state'. Under an unratified Anglo-Iraq treaty of 1927 Britain was to support Iraq's entry to the League of Nations in 1932 providing the rate of progress in Iraq was maintained. This proviso created suspicion in Iraq. So Henderson authorized the High Commissioner there to announce that Britain would back Iraq for membership of the League of Nations 'without proviso or qualification'. As a result, Henderson told the 1929 Labour party conference, 'Distrust and suspicion at once gave place to mutual confidence and good will'.

With regard to Palestine, Henderson acknowledged the desirability of a Jewish homeland. In his foreign policy speech to the Labour party conference he declared,

> There is no question of altering the position of this country in regard to the Mandate or the policy, laid down in the Balfour Declaration of 1917 and embodied in the Mandate, of supporting the establishment in Palestine of a National Home for the Jews. This policy is still, as it always has been, subject to the condition that the civil and religious rights of all the inhabitants of Palestine, irrespective of race and religion, must at all times be safeguarded.

The problems and dangers of such a policy were to be experienced by the next Labour Foreign Secretary, Ernest Bevin, in 1945. Henderson himself felt the political sensitivity of the issue when, as chairman of a Cabinet committee, he rescued the Government from Jewish wrath over equivocal support for the terms of the Mandate expressed by Sidney Webb, the Colonial Secretary.[73]

As for Egypt, a case where Henderson personally conducted negotiations, he was willing to do much to improve Anglo-Egyptian relations. But he was committed to a British military presence in the area of the Suez Canal and he was unwilling to support Egyptians' demands for a unified Egypt and Sudan. Yet Henderson was radical compared with MacDonald. His moves to withdraw troops from the cities to the Suez Canal area and generally restore relations to what they were before an uprising in 1924 alarmed not only the King, the Tories and the leaders of the armed forces but also MacDonald. Over this issue, Henderson's Principal Private Secretary observed to Dalton, 'The P.M. has a diehard streak, you know'. According to Dalton, Henderson was exasperated at the pressure from both the Palace and 10 Downing Street. MacDonald may even have encouraged hostile articles in the press against Henderson's handling of Egypt. Dalton noted, 'Uncle says that if he is to be pulled about much more, he will suggest that J.R.M. should become Foreign Secretary himself, and be done with it'.[74] Henderson realized that any agreement needed the support of the Egyptian people. Hence he made it subject to approval 'by a freely elected and properly constituted Egyptian Parliament'. When a left-wing trade-unionist demanded at the 1929 Labour party conference, 'why the Labour government should not clear out of Egypt altogether and leave the Egyptians to manage their own business?' Henderson replied in his best 'tough Uncle' manner, '... I have already stated that I have given a set of proposals to the people of Egypt. It is for them to decide, and not Mr Gossip, as to what should be done with them'.[75]

Labour's Egyptian policy earlier had led Henderson to take the decision to dismiss Lord Lloyd, the British High Commissioner in Egypt. He felt that Lloyd was not the person to carry out a more sympathetic policy towards democratic forces in Egypt. This caused a sensation, delighting Labour's supporters and enraging most of its opponents. But in dismissing Lloyd he was moving in step with the mandarins of the Foreign Office. As Dalton put it, 'Lord Lloyd ... was, from their point of view, an "outsider", not a professional diplomat but a Tory politician, who had been a thorn in their side under the late government, and well to the Right of Sir Austen Chamberlain'. What transformed this episode into a major triumph for Henderson was the fact that Winston Churchill, backed by much of the Tory press, chose to make a major issue of it in Parliament while Austen Chamberlain chose to say nothing in Lloyd's defence. Henderson, skilfully using details of clashes between Lloyd and Chamberlain during the previous Government, demolished his opponents. Dalton noted in his diary for 26 July 1929, 'An overwhelming triumph for the government... Tremendous elation in our Party... "If only the other Departments can do as well as the Foreign Office", said one'.[76]

Within the Labour movement, Henderson's great reputation as Foreign Secretary rested, in part, on the fact that he carried out party policy proudly and without any apologies. Drawing on his long experience in public life and as a trade union and political party organizer, he administered with confidence. He showed common sense and wisdom in handling diplomatic difficulties. This drew admiration from non-Labour people, both civil servants and figures such as Lord Robert Cecil. In his auto-biography published in 1941, Cecil gave the verdict,

> He was the most successful Foreign Minister we have had since 1918, with no brilliant and showy qualities, but with that faculty for being right which Englishmen like the Duke of Devonshire of my youth, possess. His political courage was great—almost the rarest and most valuable quality for a states-man.[77]

Cecil, of course, also believed deeply in the League of Nations. Part of Henderson's laurels were won at Geneva. For this major area of his policy he was the right man at almost the right time. The late 1920s had seen a reaction in Britain against war, marked by autobiographies and works such as R.C. Sheriff's *Journey's End*. Henderson was thus in tune with the spirit of 'Never Again' and with the widespread idealistic faith in the League of Nations. However while he was in office the internal politics of Germany were becoming more menacing. The slump in the international economy de-stabilized Henderson's politics of peace and hope. It also swept away the second Labour Government.

Henderson, based at the Foreign Office, avoided direct implication in the calamities which overtook the second Labour Government's economic policies. Yet as a major figure in the Government he was involved in other areas. Beatrice Webb noted in her diary in December 1929 that Henderson was enjoying the Foreign Office:

> But he is also supervising the Labour Party office and preparing for the next general election, and trying to lead a helping hand to the P.M. in Cabinet business ... What worries Henderson is the lack of any organisation of Cabi-net business, especially with regard to finance. Ministers come, one by one, with demands for money to successive Cabinet meetings. There is no kind of survey of their respective demands with a view of discovering which of the proposals are most important![78]

Nominally, he gave up the secretaryship of the Labour party after taking office. However he continued to supervise Labour's headquarters, calling in daily. In June he had taken back the post of treasurer of the party, which he had held in 1904—5 and from 1906 to 1911, when MacDonald accepted it. Henderson also maintained a high profile in the House of Commons, being present more often than any minister other than Lansbury. With Clynes he served on the Consultative Committee, which as in 1924 was a link between back-benchers and the Cabinet.[79]

He was also frequently involved in negotiations with the Liberal MPs, on whose general co-operation the minority Labour Government depended. This was a delicate relationship and the Liberals often reasonably felt that they took many knocks but gained little credit. Henderson was one of five Labour ministers who negotiated with Lloyd George and his colleagues in December 1929 over the Government's proposals to reorganize the coal industry. It soon became apparent that Lloyd George in fact wished to bargain support for the Government's coal reorganization plans to extract electoral reform, preferably the introduction of proportional representation. On 3 February 1930 MacDonald noted in his diary,

> Ll.G. came and talked with Thomas, Snowden, Henderson and myself about an agreement to keep us in office for from two to three years. Turned upon whether we would give him a bargain on Electoral Reform.

On 18 November 1930 Henderson became involved in further talks, this time just with MacDonald, Lloyd George and Sir Herbert Samuel. MacDonald had been fending off the Liberals with vague promises for months. Henderson, however, was willing to offer the Liberals the alternative vote (whereby in three-way contests electors indicate a second preference) in return for their support in repealing the hated 1927 Trades Disputes Act. Indeed he remonstrated with MacDonald for trying to equivocate further, pointing out the needs of a minority government for support and the 'very definite promises made at the two interviews with the Trades Union Council and with the committee presided over by the Lord Chancellor on the Trades Disputes Bill' to introduce both bills before Christmas, albeit in 'dummy' form. He pointed out that no Labour party meeting had taken exception to a commitment to electoral reform made a month earlier in the King's Speech to Parliament. Later in the month both Labour's executive committee and the parliamentary party agreed to the alternative vote being included in the electoral reform proposals.[80]

His role in this was pragmatic. He was deeply committed to repealing the post-1926 trade union legislation. He was also aware that if the alternative vote had been in force in the 1929 general election, it would probably have resulted in about fifteen extra seats for Labour and over forty for the Liberals at the expense of the Conservatives. Henderson had expressed reservations about proportional representation but spoken in favour of the alternative vote in the House of Commons before the outbreak of the First World War. He had again called for the alternative vote at the time of the debates on what was to be the 1918 Representation

of the People Act, and with Asquith unsuccessfully moved an amendment
for its trial in one hundred constituencies. Indeed before the First World
War there had been considerable support for both the alternative vote
and proportional representation. Later, in the 1920s, this support lessened
as Labour became the second strongest party and benefited under the
existing electoral system from its concentrated support in working-class
areas and in certain parts of the country.[81] However, as far as the Trades
Disputes Bill was concerned, all the negotiations in 1930 proved to be
in vain, for the Bill was withdrawn after the Liberals carried a hostile
amendment to it. Though the Government nevertheless continued with
electoral reform, that was lost with much else in the 1931 political crisis.

MacDonald felt that Henderson wanted to supplant him as leader in
1931, and others have suggested that their differences over foreign policy
between 1929 and 1931 contributed substantially to making the breach
between the two men in the 1931 crisis.[82] Certainly ill feeling continued
between them over foreign affairs virtually to the end of the Government.
Thus in July 1931 in trying to arrange the settling of differences between
France and Germany over reparations Henderson acted on his own initiative, sometimes in conflict with MacDonald's plans thereby bringing, as
David Carlton has shown, 'his relations with MacDonald almost to breaking point'.[83]

Yet, even when MacDonald's interference in foreign affairs was most
exasperating, Henderson remained loyal to the Prime Minister. On at
least two occasions during the Government he rebuffed suggestions from
Labour MPs that he should replace MacDonald as Prime Minister. Henderson's faith in MacDonald as the essential leader led him to swallow
many slights. The premier's moderate approach to politics was close to
his, and he was not likely to throw him over at the behest of an Oswald
Mosley anymore than he had responded to the calls of Ernest Bevin
and others after the first Labour Government. Indeed Henderson tried
to keep the Labour door open for MacDonald after the formation of
the National Government just as he had done after the split following
the outbreak of war in 1914. In March 1931 MacDonald appears to have
been treating Henderson as his deputy Prime Minister, asking him to
deal with anything that might turn up when he was away. Henderson's
thoughts, however, were on a quieter time, as Foreign Secretary in the
House of Lords.[84]

He had no distinctive economic policy of his own. He subscribed to
Labour's broad belief in the need for public works and the restoration
of trade which had been disrupted by the First World War and by the

Bolshevik revolution in Russia. Before the 1929 general election he had responded to the Liberals' 'We can Conquer Unemployment' package with the claim that there was nothing new in their proposals and that they were Labour's long-held schemes for 'national development and economic reconstruction'. By the end of 1929 Henderson was well aware that Thomas was not up to the job of dealing with the worsening problem of unemployment, and advocated that MacDonald himself should 'take the subject in hand', helped by G.D.H. Cole with Oswald Mosley (under supervision) 'to carry out agreed plans'.[85] It is quite possible that Henderson had reservations about Snowden's abilities to deal with the worsening economic situation and since he had no alternatives himself, he may well have been genuinely willing for Mosley's proposals to be properly assessed.

Henderson became involved in the Government's response to the developing economic crisis as a member of the Cabinet Economy Committee. Following a run on the pound, this held emergency special meetings from 12 August 1931. During this series of meetings the inner ring of the Cabinet considered ways of achieving major savings in order to gain the confidence of the international money markets. Henderson appears to have been willing to accept the introduction of a tariff, some cuts in unemployment benefits and some raising of taxes. As the archetypal Labour party loyalist, he was willing to swallow a good deal to keep a Labour government in office. He had not felt the issues concerning Egypt or Anglo-Russian relations were in themselves so vital as worth endangering the existence of a Labour government. Similarly he appears to have felt that it was better to have some labour cuts to demonstrate equality of sacrifice in the community and so maintain Labour in office than to reject all cuts and end up with a Conservative government which would introduce massive cuts falling mostly on the unemployed and wage earners. In addition, as he said at the time, he was torn between 'loyalty to my Cabinet colleagues and loyalty to the Movement outside'.

Hence Henderson, with his usual sensitivity towards those Labour bodies to whom he felt accountable, suggested at the second special meeting of the Cabinet Economy Committee on 13 August that it should consult the General Council of the TUC and the Labour party's executive committee and not just the opposition leaders and the Bank of England. When the delegation from the TUC saw the Cabinet Economy Committee on 20 August Henderson was undoubtedly impressed by its rejection of the proposed cuts and its suggestion of new taxation and the suspension of the Sinking Fund. Probably this made him feel that no further cuts for working people should be suggested. As a skilled worker who had experienced lengthy unemployment he was more sensitive to the impact of ten-per-cent dole cuts than MacDonald and Snowden. When the Opposition leaders rejected the government's package of cuts as inadequate, it is likely that Henderson came to feel as Andrew Thorpe has argued, that the Opposition leaders 'were seeking to gain the utmost political advantage from the crisis, in that they wanted to split the Labour movement by gradually increasing the stakes'.[86]

In these circumstances Henderson thought that the Cabinet should propose its package of economies and, if the Opposition parties rejected these, the minority Government should resign. Tom Johnston said of Henderson's role in the Cabinet that 'he never finally assented to anything. He always said he must get the complete picture. Then at the end he dug his feet in against the dole cut'.[87] Henderson took his stance on 22 August when he was in the minority opposing sounding out the Opposition as to further possible levels of cuts. He again opposed further cuts the next day. On 24 August the Cabinet met for the last time. Although there had been much talk of a National Government, including by MacDonald, Henderson was shaken when MacDonald informed them that the King had invited him to stay on and form such a government. Raymond Postgate, George Lansbury's son-in-law, has written,

> As he left the meeting, Lansbury looked white, but the face of his most powerful ally was ghastly. An onlooker said that Henderson seemed shrivelled and bowed, and his usually ruddy face was yellow. Disloyalty was a thing he could not understand ...; he looked like a man who had been given a mortal wound.[88]

Unquestionably, Henderson remained shaken for several weeks. A friend who saw him three weeks after that last Cabinet meeting felt that he was 'not only suddenly aged but broken'. However there was a general feeling in the Labour movement that he was 'now the only possible leader'. But it took several days of pressure for him to accept the nomination at the parliamentary Labour party meeting. He expressed his unwillingness to take it on to Dalton,

> He says that he is now 68; that they wouldn't have him fifteen years ago; that he must look after the party organisation, in view of an early election; that we musn't drive J.R.M. and the others out; that this is only an interlude in the life of the Party, like the war; that Clynes is Deputy Leader and must not be pushed aside...[89]

There was much in what Henderson said. He was tired and his health was weakening. He still hoped for MacDonald's return. He did not share Bevin and other trade-union leaders' thirst for a fight. In the weeks before the general election, his actions did not echo Bevin's vigorous assertion, 'This is like the General Strike. I'm prepared to put everything in'. Yet Henderson was the only Labour figure then big enough in the public eye to be leader. He was quick to decline the peerage that MacDonald offered on 25 August. At the same time he made it clear that he would keep the Labour party on the path of moderation. He could build on the party's solid trade-union base, and prevent it from following what he deemed to be the wild policies of the ILP. It was in this spirit that a few years later he responded to Lansbury's comment that he hoped Stafford Cripps would succeed him (Lansbury) as leader, with the heartfelt comment, 'If that happened, I would feel that all that I have worked for had gone for nothing'.[90]

In the immediate aftermath of MacDonald's departure, Henderson was pushed along by the trade union leaders in support of a policy of 'vigorous opposition' to the National Government. On 27 August the leaders of the parliamentary Labour party, the General Council of the TUC and the Labour party executive agreed to a manifesto which endorsed the TUC delegation's proposals of 20 August. Henderson, who had been willing to accept the first proposed package of economies, was embarrassed by this outright condemnation of all cuts.

In Parliament and outside, Henderson avoided bitter attacks on his former colleagues. Henderson was rightly reluctant to subscribe to the view that MacDonald had cold-bloodedly planned in advance the replacement of the Labour by a National government. Similarly he declined to join Dalton and others in proclaiming the change to be the result of a bankers' plot. Until about 21 September 1931 Henderson appears to have tried not only to keep the door open for MacDonald's return but even to have considered bolstering a reconstructed National Government in its struggle to cope with the financial crisis. On 20 September Beatrice Webb wrote of him, 'he is not thinking of himself ... but of the country first and the Party second'. The next day she noted, 'Henderson is quite determined that he will do nothing without the approval of the three Executives and the PLP [Parliamentary Labour Party]. Otherwise he will keep "an open mind"'. However, that evening in the House of Commons, when he maintained his talk of unity and failed to attack the Government for abandoning the gold standard, he found a majority of his supporters took a more vigorous line. At a meeting of the parliamentary Labour party the next day he was strongly criticized. He denied that he was negotiating Labour support for the Government—and offered to resign as leader. He was talked out of that. On the 28 September the Labour party's executive committee expelled MacDonald and all his supporters from the Labour party. So, in spite of Henderson, a clear break was made between Labour and its former leaders.[91]

In addition to his concern to follow a moderate policy at a time of economic crisis, Henderson was very anxious about an early general election. After a lifetime as a political organizer, he knew that the consequences for Labour would be bad. Hence while he may have believed MacDonald's talk of the National Government being only a temporary expedient before those involved returning to their party politics, he may also have felt that it was best to act on that premise in order not to give MacDonald an excuse for an early general election. If so, he was to be disappointed. On 5 October the Cabinet agreed to call a general election for 27 October.

Henderson launched Labour's campaign at the party conference, held at Scarborough from the 5 to 8 October. He had scored a triumph at the 1929 Labour party conference in his speech as Foreign Secretary. He did so again in 1931 as leader. Henderson gave the conference the speech it wanted, and needed, to hear. He told the delegates,

> We are convinced that the decaying fabric of capitalism cannot be patched up any further. We must go forward ... courageously to try to realise the Socialist State.

To those who said their policies were extreme and would lead to disaster, he replied 'that it is only such constructive action as we propose that can save us from the chaos which now undoubtedly exists and save us from the anarchy which in itself contains the gravest possible threat of revolution'. Henderson's speech received loud and prolonged cheers. He responded by thanking them and then making a statement which came from the heart,

> I am under no illusions as to the task which I personally have in hand, but with all the strength that God gives me I will try to lead, not unconscious of many limitations. Though I may not be able to rise to standards of brilliance, I will yield to none in my fidelity to the ideals and principles of our great Movement.[92]

Henderson perhaps did not realize just how tough a fight he faced. Labour had been slipping badly in the by-elections even before the economic crisis. With the departure of most of its leaders and with its election programme still relying much on *Labour and the Nation*, its campaign was concerned with trying to hold on to the seats it had won in 1929. Henderson responded to bitter attacks on himself by pointing out that those most responsible for the Labour Government's economic policy— MacDonald and Snowden—were now leading the National Government. In a BBC radio broadcast on 23 October he reiterated the commitment to the *Labour and the Nation* programme and called for 'the banking and credit system ... to be made a national service'. He urged Liberal voters that the only way to avoid Tory tariffs was to vote Labour.

Early on he realized that he would probably lose his own seat at Burnley. After an exhausting speaking tour in the Midlands and the North, he went to his own constituency. There he caught a chill and ended the campaign in bed. When Henderson's defeat in Burnley was announced, his agent vented the bitterness that Henderson himself had always avoided. In his comments he truly expressed the resentment of the Labour party's activists:

> They had had the party machines against them, all the monied people against them, and they had had two of the finest 'ratters' they had ever known— MacDonald and Snowden—who would never have been Prime Minister and Chancellor of the Exchequer respectively had it not been for the Labour Party, and the sooner they were rid of such rubbish the sooner would the Labour Party make real progress.[93]

Out of Parliament, Henderson was left to pick up the pieces after the results across the country were known. All Labour's leaders except Lansbury were defeated, and only fifty-two (of whom forty-six were officially approved) MPs were returned in contrast to the 287 of 1929. On 3 November the parliamentary Labour party confirmed Henderson as Labour party leader, but elected Lansbury to be chairman of the parliamentary party and to lead in the House of Commons.

After this electoral disaster Henderson determined that Labour must remain on the path of moderation. Lansbury found him to be uneasy at the more advanced policies of the 1931 Labour party conference. Lansbury reported to Cripps, 'He talked of miners and others demanding something to go with, and not being content to wait for Socialism; this seemed like our old friend Gradualism with a vengeance'. Lansbury's verdict was,

> ... that A.H. is terribly worried about the party, that he feels Labour is in the wilderness for a long period unless we can trim our sails so as to catch the wind of disgust which will blow Mac and his friends out, and that he is not too anxious for us to be too definite about Socialist measures

as our first objectives. Put them in our programme but be sure when we come to power we keep on the line of least resistance. He is not dishonest or to be blamed for this attitude; like me he has spent his whole life doing small things while advocating his 'changes'. You must make him see the movement he has done so much to foster will perish if once again it gets lost in the morass of opportunism.[94]

Henderson's health was very poor after the election. He had ended the campaign suffering from a chill. However it seems that his old gallstone complaint kept him low until mid-1932. He convalesced at home and then at Tring, before going to Cannes for the sunshine from 10 to 27 December 1931. On his return to London he saw specialists, who, after tests, felt that he could be treated medically, without another operation. He continued to receive medical treatment until he left for Geneva on 28 January 1932. Yet in spite of his health, Henderson was determined to take up his role as president of the World Disarmament Conference. In December he had informed Burnley Trades Council and Labour party that he would not be standing there for Parliament again. He also let it be known that he would not be looking to contest a by-election until after the Disarmament Conference had ended. Given his state of health and the importance he attached to the Disarmament Conference, this was eminently sensible. It also defused part of the press campaign against his taking up the post—though, of course, arguments that as he was no longer Foreign Secretary but leader of a shattered Opposition and so should not go to Geneva as his circumstances had changed, were another matter. However his commitment to the Disarmament Conference, and the fact that the conference dragged on longer than expected, made it inevitable that he should give up the leadership of the party to Lansbury at the start of the October 1932 session of Parliament.[95]

In devoting himself to the Disarmament Conference, some have seen Henderson to have been an unrealistic 'martyr' to a hopeless cause. This is to use the benefit of hindsight and to ignore that this was the best option for Henderson after the crushing 1931 general election defeat. The Disarmament Conference gave him the opportunity to pursue Labour's one outstanding specific foreign policy commitment of 1929. It also gave him a final leading role on the international stage, when he cannot have had realistic hopes of ever returning to office in Britain. Above all it gave him the opportunity to work for, and to publicize internationally, the cause nearest to his heart.

The World Disarmament Conference, at least in its early stages, caught public attention in Britain as well as internationally. Henderson's speech at the opening of the conference on 2 February 1932 was broadcast on BBC radio and was published in full in several newspapers. One of his main resources in pressing governments to keep talking was the general awareness that there was a sizeable sector of public opinion in most countries which was strongly committed to the success of the conference and which would be outraged if its government was to blame for the conference's failure. This attitude is well exemplified by the Archbishop of York who, in a message to a Women's Peace Crusade meeting in June 1932, warned that the Disarmament Conference might break down 'over technicalities', and deemed that such an outcome would be 'both wicked and infamous'. Henderson had strong support from the churches, League of Nations Unions and many other bodies in Britain.

However even before the Disarmament Conference got underway, international events were making disarmament less likely than rearmament. In Germany the Nazis were increasingly prominent after their success in the September 1930 Reichstag elections, when their seats increased from twelve to 107. In the Far East, war in Manchuria overshadowed, and indeed even caused an hour's delay to the opening ceremony of the Disarmament Conference. After the conference had failed, Henderson admitted that the major political problems in Europe were responsible. He wrote, 'It was soon evident that, unless those problems were previously solved, the initial impetus of the conference would spend itself in a series of fruitless discussions. Indeed, time after time, the progress of the conference was checked, because the settlement of these political questions had not been sufficiently prepared in advance'.[96]

Henderson presided over the first stage of the conference in extremely poor health. The League of Nations' Secretary General later recalled, 'We thought he might die in the chair'. Henderson's constitution recovered somewhat after Easter 1932, and he was indefatigable in chairing meetings and lobbying for the conference's success. In July 1933, on one of the occasions when the talks were deadlocked, Henderson took on an arduous tour of Paris, Rome, Berlin, Prague and Munich to lay the groundwork for the resumption of talks at the conference. Such activities further undermined his health and may well have hastened his death.

Beatrice Webb wrote of him soon after his return from his European tour that 'he absurdly overrates the binding value of *signed documents*, however vague the words are, whatever the character of the individuals are'. She rightly pointed to the particular worthlessness of agreements with 'half-wits and scoundrels, like the Hitler group'. Hence her verdict was, 'Henderson's guileless and naive dragging out of the conference for two long years has increased his reputation for dogged devotion and honesty, but diminished trust in his judgement'. Yet at the outset of his tour *The Times*, which was critical of Henderson and his disarmament work, could still express some optimism. If the right safeguards were pursued then 'there is still hope that the nations of the world will set a limit to the engines of destruction which they are preparing against each other'. Its editorial also recognized that Henderson was more versed in the intricacies of the outstanding problems at the conference 'than any other individual'.[97] However, that October Germany withdrew from both the World Disarmament Conference and the League of Nations. Thereafter rearmament, not disarmament, became a higher priority for most European countries. Henderson struggled on with the conference in 1934. It faded away in 1935, holding a final meeting on 11 June of that year. Yet even after that, at the time of the Abyssinian crisis, its Secretariat still hoped that Henderson would recover his health and chair a meeting in Geneva.[98] Henderson's last high point in his efforts for peace proved to be his receipt of the Nobel Peace Prize in the autumn of 1934.

After his tour of Europe in July 1933, Henderson did accept nomination for a by-election in the safe Labour seat of Clay Cross. When he had announced that he would not stand again for Burnley and would consider only certain seats, he had stated that 'his official duties for the party have become very heavy during a general election, and he feels that it must be for a constituency which will enable him more easily and effect-ively to discharge these and other responsibilities'. Clay Cross was very much such a seat. His main problem was that three unions felt they had a right to it: the Transport and General Workers (TGWU), the previous member being one of its officials, the National Union of Railwaymen and the Derbyshire area of the Miners Federation. At the selection con-ference Henderson secured fifty votes to sixteen for the miners' candidate, fourteen for the TGWU's candidate and seven for the railwaymen's candidate. Afterwards there was considerable ill feeling and Bevin secured a Labour party inquiry into the way the selection had been carried out.

Henderson fought the by-election with the issue of disarmament at the heart of his campaign. He declared, 'I am going to fight this by-election in regard to foreign policy, and especially the efforts I have been making for the past two years to make international war impossible',[99] though he did broaden his campaign out to encompass other issues, such as unemployment and the means test. He was returned on 1 September with a 15,638 majority over his National Government opponent.

His return to Parliament gave Labour the benefit of his long experience and his prestige in foreign affairs. Henderson set out the party's official policy on how a Labour government would 'seek to attain a permanent peace' in one of his last writings, *Labour's Way to Peace* (1935). But much of his remaining energy still went on the Disarmament Conference. Indeed Hugh Dalton noted that Henderson's absence at Geneva for much of 1932 resulted in him losing 'a good deal of his old ascendency' over the Labour party's executive committee. Dalton also felt 'it was clear that he had lost touch a little with the home situation'. This continued to be the case, with Henderson finding himself out of sympathy with the majority on several occasions. In May 1934 he agreed to stand down as Labour party secretary at the end of the year. According to Dalton, 'he had practically to be pushed out'.[100]

Henderson's decline was slow and sad. Molly Hamilton recalled of his last year or so, 'His ruddy colour was gone; instead his skin was an ashen yellow, and his face so shrunk that the deep graved lines were like furrows beneath his sunken eyes. His clothes hung loose upon his powerful dwindled frame'.[101] He was ill again in mid-1935 and on 17 September 1935, after a period of convalescing, Henderson's health deteriorated and he entered a London nursing home: he died on 20 October.

In his will, Henderson left £23,926. He had been careful, even frugal, with money all his life. He set aside what he and his family needed, and then, in best Wesleyan tradition, put some of any surplus to good causes. The Labour movement, his Wesleyan and temperance activities as well as his family were central to his life. Apart from enjoying good long walks, especially during summer when Parliament was in recess, he had very few other interests. Clynes wrote of him, 'His only luxury seemed to be work'.[102] His devotion to his union work and then to running the Labour party machine make him appear almost the stereotype of the Labour party bureaucrat. He recognized where the reins of power were, and he took them in his hands. What he secured, he held on to—and added to. His accumulation of major positions of power and influence within the labour movement was remarkable. His strong constitution enabled him to carry these out competently—at least until ill health became persistent from 1931.

This taste for power and responsibility was also marked in government. Under both Asquith and Lloyd George he pushed for larger responsibilities. In both Labour Governments he took on Cabinet committee work whilst maintaining a firm hand on parliamentary party and Labour party affairs. He took his positions very seriously and did not suffer fools lightly. After 1917 he could come close to pomposity, but this was almost always soon relieved by his bluff geniality. As Chief Whip, Labour party secretary and in other party roles Henderson could be overbearing. Lord Snell, a Labour MP from 1922 to 1931, later recalled,

> Robust in expression, a little prone to carry any disputed point by verbal assault, he was quickly roused to wrath, but was even more quickly composed. He was always approachable, always reliable, and considerate in his judgements, sometimes a little more 'Uncle Mussolini' than the 'Uncle Arthur' who was a revered friend of us all.[103]

Henderson loomed large over the Labour party from its early days. From at least 1908 he was seen as one of the Labour party's three or four key figures. Robert Michels, the German political theorist who had grown disillusioned with the German socialist party, criticized the way people came to dominate power in labour movements for long periods. 'A leader who does his duty conscientiously is more secure in his position than is a minister in the Prussian monarchy founded upon the grace of God.' Some of Michels' strictures fit Henderson very well. 'Every democratic organisation rests... upon a division of labour. But wherever division of labour prevails, there is necessarily specialisation, and the specialists become indispensable.'[104] Henderson was such a professional organizer in the Labour party; the man who had the electoral and administrative expertise, who dealt with the constituency and affiliated organizations and who controlled the nerve centre of the movement.

Henderson also played a major role, especially during 1917 to 1920, in maintaining the British Labour party firmly on the parliamentary road to socialism. Lenin was as scornful of Henderson as he had been of Kerensky. In a famous passage of his *Left-wing Communism—An Infantile Disorder* (May 1920), Lenin wrote,

> I want to support Henderson in the same way as the rope supports a hanged man—that the impending establishment of a government of the Hendersons will prove that I am right, will bring the masses over to my side, and will hasten the political death of the Hendersons and Snowdens just as was the case with their kindred spirits in Russia and Germany.

Lenin went on to argue that those who followed the Henderson line 'cannot go beyond the bounds of bourgeois democracy, which, in its turn, cannot but be a dictatorship of capital'.

Henderson's career made clear his answer to the central dilemma of British democratic socialism—whether to work with capitalism or to work to replace it. For him co-operation was a life-long principle. Henderson was firmly against the idea of a revolutionary insurrection. He himself deplored violence and bloodshed, and observed, 'Revolution . . . is alien to the British character'. He argued instead for orderly negotiations—'compromise generally represents a step forward'.[105] His attitudes stemmed from his Christian faith. This was expressed in secular form in the Brotherhood Movement and the quest for world peace. Such political and trade union moderation was a feature of the North-East, and Henderson was but one of many such figures to achieve considerable national standing. Yet he also became a socialist of international stature. As Kenneth Morgan has observed, 'his sturdy class-consciousness as a late-Victorian artisan impelled him towards a sense of international kinship'.[106] After the traumas of the First World War, Henderson's Cobdenite and nonconformist roots helped him to become the embodiment of Labour's aspirations for peace and security.

Henderson had the loyalty to the Labour movement common to many Christian socialists. Molly Hamilton commented on his 'inner security': 'He knew in what he believed—and it was not himself. . . He knew good from evil. That men must work out their common salvation in the light of certain inexorable principles was for him fact, not phrase'. In a somewhat similar vein in 1927 Beatrice Webb asked, 'Was there ever a more sterling character than his, conduct more uniformly guided by public spirit and personal devotion and good comradeship?' and added that 'he is never elated and never gloomy—he just plods on along the chosen way towards some dimly perceived social betterment'.[107]

In many respects Henderson was to the Labour party what Baldwin came to be for the Conservative party. He represented what was widely perceived to be the decent, solid and respectable face of the party—one which appealed not only to the regular Labour voter but also to a wider electorate. Throughout his career he kept close to the trade unions and to the constituency organizations. He knew of their concerns and generally shared them. He was always grounded in the trade-union approach to politics, an approach which expected its spokesmen to be accountable to the membership and loyally to follow the union's democratic decisions. He epitomized many of the strengths and weaknesses of the British Labour movement in the first third of the twentieth century. He was truly what one writer claimed in 1925: 'the most representative Labour leader of our time'.[108]

Notes

Notes to Introduction

1 Perhaps in Evelyn Waugh's eyes these qualities merited a sneer. In his *Vile Bodies*, written in 1929, there is a humdrum commercial traveller called Arthur Henderson.
2 N. and J. MacKenzie (eds), *The Diary of Beatrice Webb*, Vol. 4 (1985), pp.359 and 397: entries for 23 October 1935 and 11 November 1937.

Notes to Chapter 1

1 Friendly Society of Iron Founders' (FSIF) Monthly Report, June 1892, p.4. E.A. Jenkins, *From Foundry to Foreign Office* (1933), p.4; H.J. Fyrth and H. Collins, *The Foundry Workers* (1959), p.102.
2 M.A. Hamilton, *Arthur Henderson* (1938), pp.1–3; P. Laslett and R. Schofield, *Bastardy* (1979), especially pp.119–216; D. Marquand, *Ramsay MacDonald* (1977), pp.189–91.
3 Hamilton, pp.5–8. Jenkins, pp.4 and 9. Gypsy Smith was only three and a half years older than Henderson, and then based at West Hartlepool. Gypsy Smith, *Gypsy Smith: His Life and Work* (1902), pp.82–108.
4 Fyrth and Collins, p.99. FSIF *Annual Report for 1891*, p.29. FSIF *Monthly Report*, January 1892, p.5.
5 FSIF EC minutes, especially 4 May and 6 July 1892; MS 41/FSIF/1/4.
6 Hamilton, p.21. Fyrth and Collins, p.103. The whole district committee set-up cost the union only £53 in 1892. FSIF, *Annual Report for 1892*, pp.7–8.
7 R. Harrison, G. Woolven and R. Duncan, *The Warwick Guide to British Labour Periodicals 1790–1970* (1977), p.365. FSIF *Monthly Report*, October 1893, p.5.
8 For the background of this dispute see *Report by the Chief Labour Correspondent on the Strikes and Lock-outs of 1894*, British Parliamentary Papers c.7901, 1895, pp.28–9; *Board of Trade Journal*, Vols 16 and 17, April–September 1894; FSIF, *Annual Report for 1894*, pp.6–8 and *Monthly Reports*, April–September 1894; Fyrth and Collins, pp.101–2; and W. Mosses, *The History of the United Pattern Makers' Association 1872–1922* (1922), pp.109–13.

[9] FSIF EC minutes, 18 April 1894; MS 41/FSIF/1/5/1. FSIF, *Monthly Report*, July 1894, p.7. *Newcastle Evening News*, 2 and 3 July 1894; and Mosses, p.110.

[10] *Newcastle Evening News*, editorial, 12 July 1894. Letter by Henderson of 3 July and letter by James Robinson, Secretary of the Employers' Association of 4 July in ibid., 4 and 5 July 1894. FSIF, *Monthly Report*, June 1894, p.1.

[11] *Newcastle Evening News*, 23 July 1894. FSIF, *Monthly Report*, August 1894, pp.14–15. The Bishop's services were used in establishing the conciliation board.

[12] Ibid., 29 and 31 August, 22 October and 26 November 1894.

[13] *Report ... on Strikes and Lock-outs of 1894*, Appendix, pp.292–3. The board operated until 1903, collapsed and was resurrected.

[14] *Iron Founders' Society Conference Report 1911*, p.29.

[15] At a new branch at Wallsend. *Newcastle Evening News*, 3 December 1894. Hamilton, pp.24–5.

[16] FSIF, *Monthly Report*, June 1892, 1893 and 1894.

[17] 'The Parliament of Labour', FSIF, *Monthly Report*, October 1917, p.328.

Notes to Chapter 2

[1] Fyrth and Collins, pp.84–92.

[2] Mr Gladstone's visit to the city for the National Liberal Federation's conference was very much a major event. *Newcastle Daily Leader*, 5 October 1891. Hamilton, pp.16–17.

[3] Initially, 1886–7, it had been called the Labour Electoral Committee: H. Pelling, *Origins of The Labour Party 1880–1900* (1965 edn), pp.57–8 and 65–6; K.O. Morgan, *Keir Hardie* (1975), pp.24–30.

[4] J. Havelock Wilson, *My Stormy Voyage Through Life* (1925), p.266.

[5] The main source for my account of the by-election is the *Newcastle Daily Leader*, especially 10, 15, 21 and 22 November 1892.

[6] Fyrth and Collins, pp.90–1. FSIF executive committee minutes, 27 April 1892; FSIF/1/3/4.

[7] There were ten spoiled ballot papers and a counting error of one.

[8] This is the major theme of my 'Liberals and the Desire for Working-Class Representatives in Battersea 1886–1922' in K.D. Brown (ed.), *Essays in Anti-Labour History* (1974), pp.126–58.

[9] *Newcastle Daily Leader*, 8 December 1892, (for the proposal at its committee stage, 30 November 1892).

[10] D.A. Hamer, *John Morley* (1968), pp.255–63 and 275–7.

[11] *Newcastle Evening News*, 14 and 16 February 1895. Morley's remarks were made at the end of January.

[12] P. Corder, *The Life of Robert Spence Watson* (1914), pp.169–84, 208, 255–6 and 267.

[13] *Newcastle Evening News*, 14, 16 and 21 February 1895.

[14] *Newcastle Daily Leader*, 20, 22 and 23 February 1895.

[15] P. Corder, p.255. A.F. Purdue, drawing on E.I. Waitt's work, in 'Arthur Henderson and Liberal, Liberal–Labour and Labour Politics in the North-east of England 1892–1903', *Northern History*, 11 (1980), p.200.

[16] *Newcastle Evening News*, 29 February 1895.

[17] Ibid., 30 May and 9 July 1895.

[18] Letter of 15 July 1894. W. Stewart, *J. Keir Hardie* (1921), pp.96–7. H. Pelling, *Origins of the Labour Party* (1965), pp.164–5.

[19] 29 February 1895.

[20] J. Morley, *Recollections*, Vol. 2 (1917), p.47.

[21] *Darlington and Stockton Times*, 26 February 1898.

[22] Ibid., 5 November 1898.

[23] Ibid., 14 November 1903.

Notes to Chapter 3

[1] Friendly Society of Iron Founders executive minutes, 13 August 1902; FSIF/1/71. *Report of the Third Annual Conference of the Labour Representation Committee* (1903), pp.106 and 112.

[2] Fyrth and Collins, pp.110–111. FSIF executive minutes, 15 October 1902; FSIF/1/71. FSIF, *Monthly Report*, September and November 1894.

[3] Fyrth and Collins, pp.110–11. FSIF, *Monthly Report*, January 1903.

[4] J.A. Pease to H. Gladstone. H. Gladstone Papers, BM. MS. 46002, f.125. *Westminster Gazette*, 21 July 1903. There are valuable accounts of the famous Barnard Castle by-election in Purdue, pp.202–16; P. Poirier, *The Advent of The Labour Party* (1958), pp.196–206; and F. Bealey and H. Pelling, *Labour and Politics 1900–1906* (1958), pp.152–5.

[5] Bealey and Pelling, pp.140–59. Poirier, p.184–93.

[6] FSIF executive minutes, 25 February and 6 March 1903; FSIF/1/7/1. Henderson to MacDonald, 27 February and 2 March 1903; LRC Corres. 7/214 and 215.

[7] MacDonald to Hughes, 24 February 1903; LRC Letter book 1, f.282; *Newcastle Daily Chronicle*, 2 April 1904. FSIF executive minutes 2 April 1903. Henderson to MacDonald, 31 March, n.d. (1 April?) and n.d. (2 April?) 1903, LRC Corres. 7/216 and 217, and 6/179. MacDonald to R. Morley, 20 March 1903, LRC Letter book 1, f.331.

[8] Hamilton, p.42. Purdue, pp.204–5. S. Maccoby, *English Radicalism, the End?* (1961), p.18.

[9] J.M. Paulton to H. Gladstone, 14 April 1903, H. Gladstone Papers, 46002, Vol. 68, f.6.

[10] FSIF executive minutes, 30 April 1903, FSIF/1/7/1.

[11] J. Hodge, *Workman's Cottage to Windsor Castle* (1931), p.145.

[12] LRC NEC minutes, 7 May 1903, Vol. 1, ff.141–3. MacDonald to Henderson 3, 8, 9, 10 and 12 June and 1 July 1903, LRC Letter book 2, ff.76, 117, 124, 132, 152 and 247. Henderson to MacDonald 6 and 11 June and 2 July 1903, LRC Corres. 9/11, 183 and 188.

[13] Henderson's report on the election, n.d. (19 May?), LRC Corres. 9/333, *Westminster Gazette*, 12 May 1903, p.4.

[14] Henderson to MacDonald, 19 May 1903, LRC Corres. 9/227. See Purdue, p.208, for most of the letter. MacDonald to A. Gee, 12 May 1903, LRC Letter book 1, f.589. Hardie to MacDonald, 15 May 1903, LRC Corres., 8/186.

[15] MacDonald to Henderson, 20 May 1903, LRC Letter book 2, ff.46–7. Hughes to MacDonald, 20 May 1903, LRC Corres. 9/208.

[16] Henderson to MacDonald, 25 May 1903; ibid., 9/181. MacDonald to Henderson, 26 May 1903; LRC Letter book 2, ff.60–1. *Newcastle Daily Chronicle*, 25 May 1903. *Westminster Gazette*, 21 July 1903.

[17] Pease to Gladstone, 29 June 1903, cited by Purdue, p.210. Beaumont to Trevelyan, 3 July 1903, cited by A.J. Morris, *C.P. Trevelyan* (1977), p.59.

[18] Poirier, p.201.

[19] Jenkins, p.11.

[20] B. Pimlott (ed.), *The Political Diary of Hugh Dalton 1918–40, 1945–60* (1986), p.184. Morgan, *Keir Hardie*, p.135. Numerous letters by Henderson to MacDonald between 25 May and 13 July 1903, LRC Corres. 9/11, 9/181–8 and 10/137. Hodge to MacDonald, 16 July 1903; ibid., 10/203. MacDonald to G. Hobbs, 3 July 1903, and to Henderson 5 July 1903, LRC Letter book 2, ff.277 and 280. *Westminster Gazette*, 3–27 July 1903.

[21] Iron Founders executive minutes, 24 June and 3 July 1903, FSIF/1/7/1. The £800 came from the Belfast branch.

[22] Samuel to his wife, 23 July 1903, House of Lords Record Office, Samuel Papers A/157/127. Samuel to MacDonald, 23 June 1903, LRC Corres. 9/369.

[23] Hudson to Gladstone, 28 July 1903, H. Gladstone Papers 46021, f.14.

[24] *The Times*, 27 July 1903.

[25] Iron Founders executive minutes, 12 August 1903. Hamilton, p.44. Poirier, p.204.

[26] FSIF executive minutes, 16 and 25 September, 14 and 21 October 1903, and 2 and 9 November 1904. FISF, *Monthly Report*, February and March 1905.

[27] FSIF executive minutes, 28 October 1903 to December 1904. Memorandum on the Parlimentary Position, 6 June 1911; FSIF/1/11/6. 'Organising in South Wales', FSIF, *Monthly Report*, October 1904, p.10. *Iron Founders' Society Conference Report 1911*, pp.26–30 and 44–5.

[28] Macdonald to T. Proctor, 20 June 1904, LRC Corres. 15/206. J. Frankland to MacDonald, 28 June 1904, 15/87. The complaints came from Accrington, Barrow, Blackburn, North Staffordshire, St Helens, Stockport, West Ham, Woolwich and York. Morgan, *Keir Hardie*, p.146.

[29] *Report of the Fourth Annual Conference of the Labour Representation Committee* (1904), pp.50–1.

[30] FSIF executive minutes, 6 July 1904. 'Parliamentary Notes', FSIF, *Monthly Report*, July and August 1904. J. Maddison to MacDonald, 7 July 1904, (Henderson signed that day), LRC Corres. Misc. 1/38. Bealey and Pelling, p.208.

[31] R. Bell to MacDonald, 6 July 1904; W. Thorne to MacDonald 15 June 1904; LRC Corres. 16/6 and 15/115. G. and L. Radice, *Will Thorne* (1974), p.58.

Notes to Chapter 4

[1] M.A. Hamilton, *Arthur Henderson* (1938), pp.65–7. Henderson to Keir Hardie, 28 August 1906, Labour Party Correspondence 1906–1914, Box 7.

[2] *The Times*, 17 February 1908.

[3] K.D. Brown, 'Nonconformity and the British Labour Movement: A Case Study', *Journal of Social History* (1974), pp.113–20.

[4] *Labour and Religion by Ten Labour Members* (1910), pp.1–107.

[5] The Revd George Freeman. *The Times*, 4 January 1910.

[6] 135 *H.C. Deb 4s*, 980–82; 7 June 1904 and 137 *H.C. Deb 4s*, 1518; 13 July 1904.

[7] *The Times*, 26 October 1908.

[8] Friendly Society of Iron Founders' *Monthly Report*, July 1907, pp.9–13.

[9] FSIF, *First Conference Report 1911*, pp.27–29.

[10] *The Times*, 4 May 1908 and 5 December 1911.

[11] FSIF, *Monthly Report*, November 1908, pp.38–44. H. Llewellyn Smith to Henderson, 18 September 1908, Labour Party Corres. HEN/08/1/10.

[12] Furness to Henderson, 18 September 1908, ibid., 08/1/14. The Times, 8 October 1908. E. Bristow, 'Profit-sharing, Socialism and Labour Unrest', p.282 in K.D. Brown (ed.), *Essays in Anti-Labour History* (1974).

[13] 2 *H.C. Deb. 5s*, 2082, 26 March 1909.

[14] *Report of the Proceedings of the Forty-fourth Annual Trade Union Congress 1911*, *pp.229–31*. B.C. Roberts, *The Trades Union Congress 1868–1921* (1958), p.241.

[15] FSIF, *Monthly Report*, November 1911, pp.372–4.

[16] *The Times*, 11 October 1911. Minutes of the TUC's Parliamentary Committee, 18 October 1911. Sir G. Askwith, *Industrial Problems and Disputes* (1920), p.181. R. Charles, *The Development of Industrial Relations in Britain 1911–1939*, pp.57–74.

[17] FSIF, *Monthly Report*, December 1907, p.21.

[18] C. Wrigley, *David Lloyd George and the British Labour Movement* (1976), pp.62–5. *The Times*, 20 February and 23 August 1911. Labour Party Corres. Box 20, ff.336–9; October–November 1907.

[19] *The Times*, 21 August, 5, 6 and 23 October 1911. Henderson to MacDonald, 30 September and 7 October 1911; George Roberts to MacDonald, 19 October 1911; MacDonald Papers 30/69/1155, ff. 188–94 and 341–42.

[20] *The Times*, 6, 13 and 18 November, 5, 11 and 12 December 1911. 31 H.C. Deb 5s, 1275–81, 22 November 1911. P. Bagwell, *The Railwaymen* (1963), pp.300–04.

[21] FSIF, *Monthly Notes*, December 1910, pp.318–19. *The Times*, 30 June 1909 and 30 November 1911.

[22] *The Times*, 24 September 1913.

[23] 'Parliamentary Notes' and report of a speech at Bradford, FSIF, *Monthly Report*, April 1905, pp.14–15 and 20, and September 1905, p.17. Response to request of 1 April 1906 from editor of *Reynolds News*, Labour Party Corres. Box 3, ff.270–71. *Labour Party Annual Conference Report 1906*, pp.41–43.

[24] Minutes of the Parliamentary Committee of the TUC, 22 and 24 October and 21 November 1906.

[25] Viscount Snowden, *An Autobiography*, Vol. 1 (1934), p.126. Hamilton, p.71.

[26] H. Clegg, A. Fox and A.F. Thompson, *A History of British Trade Unions Since 1889*, Vol. 1 (1964), p.392.

[27] *Report of the Proceedings of the Thirty-ninth Annual TUC 1906*, p.144; 5 September 1906.

[28] Snowden, p.151.

[29] 'Parliamentary Notes', FSIF, *Monthly Report*, January 1907, pp.12–14; September 1907, p.17; and January 1909, p.22.

[30] K.O. Morgan, *Keir Hardie* (1975), pp.219–220. Glasier to MacDonald, 27 October 1908, MacDonald Papers PRO 30/69/1152 f.124.

[31] Snowden, pp.218 and 176.

[32] 183, *H.C. Deb. 4s*, 166–72, 29 January 1908. Farsley branch of the ILP to

MacDonald, MacDonald Papers 30/69/1152, ff.29–30. 'Parliamentary Notes', FSIF, *Monthly Report*, July 1908, p.13.

[33] K.D. Brown, *Labour and Unemployment 1900–1914* (1971), pp.95–105. Wrigley, p.30. 1 H.C. Deb. 5s, 54–56, 16 February 1909. 5 H.C. Deb. 5s, 519, 19 May 1909. H. Pelling, *A Short History of the Labour Party* (1961), p.21.

[34] 2 *H.C. Deb. 5s*, 2081–86, 26 March 1909. Hamilton, p.50. Clegg, Fox and Thompson, p.405.

[35] *The Times*, 20 January 1908.

[36] *The Times*, 23 August 1908. 'Parliamentary Report', FSIF, *Monthly Report*, May 1907, p.33; 53 *H.C. Deb. 5s*, 1635–36, 11 June 1913.

[37] 'Parliamentary Notes', FSIF, *Monthly Report*, January 1909, p.23. N. and J. MacKenzie (eds), *The Diary of Beatrice Webb*, Vol. 3 (1984), p.149 (entry for 30 November 1910).

[38] 12 *H.C. Deb. 5s*, 2069, 4 November 1909. *The Times*, 27 September 1909.

[39] *The Times*, 25 October, 22 November, 6, 11 and 15 December, 1909.

[40] Simon to Asquith, 5 February 1910, Simon Papers. N. Blewitt, *The Peers, The Parties and The People* (1972), pp.239–40.

[41] Lord Elton, *The Life of James Ramsay MacDonald* (1939), pp.189–90. Benson to MacDonald, 14 January 1911, MacDonald Papers 30/69/1155, f.56. Marquand, pp.128–30.

[42] 'Parliamentary Notes', FSIF, March 1911, pp.64–65.

[43] Elton, p.153.

[44] Henderson to Middleton, 11 February 1910, Henderson to Robinson 15 and 22 February 1910, Robinson to Henderson, 16 February 1910, Labour Corres. HEN 08/1/32 and 35–37.

[45] Hamilton, pp.55–57. R. McKibbin, *The Evolution of the Labour Party 1910–1924* (1974), p.3.

[46] Marquand, pp.151 and 153. Snowden, pp.217–18. 'Parliamentary Notes', FSIF, *Monthly Report*, April 1910, pp.98–101.

[47] *The Times*, 19 November 1910. *Report of the Proceedings of the Forty-third TUC 1910*, pp.141–2.

[48] FSIF, *First Conference Report 1911*, p.37.

[49] 'Parliamentary Notes', FSIF, *Monthly Report*, August 1911, pp.267–69. *The Times*, 25 September 1911.

[50] S. Pankhurst, *The Sufragette Movement* (1931), pp.245 and 513. *Report of the Labour Party Conference 1910*, p.75. Henderson to MacDonald, 4 April 1913, Labour Party Corres. HEN 08/1/78.

[51] Henderson's circular on the meeting with Lansbury, 15 December 1912, Labour Party Corres. HEN 089/1/68. Henderson to MacDonald, 4 April 1913; ibid., 78. *Report of the Labour Party Conference 1913*, p.82.

[52] K.O. Morgan, *Labour People* (1987), p.81.

[53] C. Howard, 'Henderson, MacDonald and the Leadership of the Labour Party 1914–1922', Cambridge University Ph.D., 1978, p.17.

[54] Minutes of the Parliamentary Committee of the TUC, 25 April 1910. R. Martin, *TUC: Growth of A Pressure Group 1868–1976* (1980), pp.113–19.

[55] R. McKibbin, 'James Ramsay MacDonald and the Problem of the Independence of the Labour Party 1910–1914', *Journal of Modern History* (1970), pp.216–35.

[56] McKibbin, *Evolution*, p.55. *The Times*, 17 and 29 July 1912.
[57] *The Times*, 2 May 1912. Henderson to Middleton 21 July 1912 and 29 October 1913; Labour Corres. HEN 08/1/51 and 93.
[58] *Report of the Special and Annual Conferences of the Labour Party 1914*, pp.76–77.
[59] N. and J. MacKenzie (eds), pp.196 and 389, entries for 18 February 1914 and 16 October 1921. Henderson's coalition account is told with other details in Hamilton, p.74 and is contested in Elton, pp.182–85.
[60] Marquand, pp.142, 150 and 159–61. *Report of the Special and Annual Conferences of the Labour Party 1914*, pp.81–82.
[61] *The Times*, 13 April 1914. Snowden, p.220.
[62] H.J. Fyrth and H. Collins, *The Foundry Workers* (1959), p.115. *The Times*, 28 January 1909.
[63] 53 *H.C. Deb. 5s*, 1641–42, 11 June 1913. FSIF, *First Annual Conference Report, 1911*, pp.77 and 80–81.
[64] 'Parliamentary Report', FSIF, *Monthly Report*, May 1907, p.33.

Notes to Chapter 5

[1] The full statement is published in G.D.H. Cole, *Labour in War-Time* (1915), pp.24–5.
[2] H.J. Fyrth and H. Collins, *The Foundry Workers* (1959), p.109.
[3] D.J. Newton, *British Labour, European Socialism and the Struggle for Peace 1889–1914* (1985), pp.46–7.
[4] T. Selby to Henderson, 6 February 1905, LRC Corres. 20/226. Keir Hardie to Henderson and Henderson to Keir Hardie, both 8 January 1907, Lab. Gen. Corres. 11/204 and 205. Edward Carpenter to MacDonald, January 1905, in J. Cos (ed.), *A Singular Marriage* (1988), pp.292–3.
[5] 175 *H.C. Deb, 4s*, 1589, 13 June 1907. Newton, pp.169–78. A.J. Morris, *Radicalism Against War 1906–14* (1972), pp.175–81. K.O. Morgan, *Keir Hardie* (1975), pp.258–9.
[6] FSIF, *Monthly Report*, August 1908, p.31. 189, *H.C. Deb, 4s*, 1118, 27 May 1908.
[7] Speech at Heywood, 29 June 1909, *The Times*, 30 June 1909.
[8] 8, *H.C. Deb, 5s*, 642–5, 22 July 1909. F.M. Leventhal, *The Last Dissenter* (1985), pp.97–8. *The Times*, 26 July and 2 August, 1909.
[9] 1 *H.C. Deb. 5s*, 50–2, 16 February 1909. 2 H.C. Deb. 5s, 1132–8, 17 March 1909.
[10] W. Brace and J. Seddon, 154 *H.C. Deb, 4s*, 166 and 156, *H.C. Deb*, 663–4, 19 March and 2 May 1906. FSIF, *Monthly Report*, May 1907, p.32.
[11] *The Times*, 20 March 1909.
[12] FSIF, *Monthly Report*, January 1909, pp.23–25. Newton, pp.300–3. E.A. Jenkins, *From Foundry to Foreign Office* (1933), p.36.
[13] Newton, op. cit., pp.259–93.
[14] Ibid., pp.265–6. D. Marquand, *Ramsay MacDonald* (1977), pp.165–6. *Labour Party Annual Conference Report* 1912, p.101. Henderson to J. Middleton, 18 January 1911, Lab. Corres. HEN/08/1/41.

[15] Lord Elton, *The Life of James Ramsay MacDonald* (1939), pp.242–7. *Lord Riddell's War Diary* (1933), pp.4–6. 65 *H.C. Deb. 5s*, 1829–31.

[16] J.M. Winter, *Socialism and the Challenge of War* (1974), pp.184–5.

[17] *Report of the Annual Conference of the Labour Party 1916*, pp.3–4.

[18] J. Hodge, *Workman's Cottage to Windsor Castle* (1931), pp.166–7.

[19] MacDonald diary, 23 September 1914, quoted in Marquand, op. cit., p.169. MacDonald to Henderson, 21 and 24 August 1914, quoted in C. Howard, 'MacDonald, Henderson and the Outbreak of War, 1914', *Historical Journal*, 20, 4 (1977), pp.882 and 884.

[20] Labour Party Executive Committee minutes, 5 August 1914, 10a.m. and 2p.m. For the importance of the Committee see also R. Harrison, 'The War Emergency Workers' National Committee 1914–1920' in A. Briggs and J. Saville (eds), *Essays in Labour History 1886–1923* (1971), pp.211–59 and Winter, pp.184–223.

[21] Interview, *The Times*, 9 November 1914. At the request of the party's executive he devoted a major part of his response to the King's Speech in Parliament on 12 November to these matters as well as to the Army's poor treatment of many recruits. 68 *H.C. Deb. 5s*, 46–52. Labour Party EC minutes, 10 November 1914.

[22] *The Times*, 13 March 1915.

[23] 69, *H.C. Deb. 5s*, 10–12, 2 February 1915. Ibid., 776–84, 11 February 1915.

[24] Cole, p.109.

[25] Quoted in Winter, p.197.

[26] Minutes of the meeting, 27 August 1914, Asquith Papers, Vol. 89, ff.156–177. £70,566 went to the cotton unions out of £84,175 paid over by the Government by the end of July 1915 when it ended the scheme. *Report of the Annual Conference of the Labour Party 1916*, pp.26–30.

[27] Cole, p.108. Howard, op. cit. is wrong to write that the Labour movement's 'co-operation in the industrial truce was secured at gunpoint' by the Cabinet.

[28] Labour party E.C. minutes, 29 August 1914.

[29] Henderson and Illingworth accepted, Talbot declined. Asquith to Venetia Stanley, 24 December 1914 in M. and E. Brock (eds), *H.H. Asquith: Letters to Venetia Stanley* (1982), pp.337–8. *The Times*, 31 May 1915.

[30] Quoted in Howard, p.887. For his valuable account of MacDonald's position, see ibid., pp.884–9.

[31] *The Times*, 8 October 1914.

[32] Cole, pp.55–7 and 33–5.

[33] Henderson to MacDonald, 19 October 1914, printed in Marquand, p.177.

[34] Ibid., pp.178–9.

[35] 68 *H.C. Deb. 5s*, 44, 12 November 1914.

[36] *The Times*, 21 September 1915.

[37] Quoted, p.86, in R. McKibbin, 'Arthur Henderson as Labour Leader', *International Review of Social History, 23 (1978)*, pp.79–101.

[38] *The Times*, 19 May and 26 June 1916.

[39] *The Times*, 8 January and 17 February 1915.

[40] Asquith to Runciman, 4 February 1915, Ministry of Munitions Papers, MUN 5–8–171/29.

[41] Henderson to Asquith, 2 March 1915, Lloyd George Papers C/6/11/35. (The letter was passed on to Lloyd George before the conference.)

[42] Memorandum, probably by Runciman, forwarded by Llewellyn Smith to Lloyd George, 16 March 1915, LG C/7/5/10. Llewellyn Smith to Lloyd George, 17 March 1915, C/7/5/11.

[43] Transcripts of the proceedings of the Treasury Conference, 17–19 March 1915, MUN 5–10–180/17.

[44] Balfour to Bonar Law, 3 April 1915; Balfour Papers, Add. MS. 49693, f.206. Minutes of the War Committee, third meeting, 26 April 1915, MUN 5–8–172/1

[45] *The Times*, 26 March 1915.

[46] Henderson to Lloyd George, 3 May 1915, LG C/11/3/60.

[47] 71, *H.C. Deb 5s*, 1044, 4 May 1915. Lloyd George was slow to set up the committee. W. Mosses to Lloyd George, 19 June 1915 and Lloyd George to Mosses, 21 June 1915, LG D/11/1/4 and 5.

[48] Asquith Papers, Vol. 27, f.206. *The Times*, 26 and 31 May 1915.

[49] Labour party E.C. minutes, 19 May 1915.

[50] Steel-Maitland to Bonar Law, 21 May 1915, Bonar Law Papers 50/3/25.

[51] 72 *H.C. Deb 5s*, 1554–5 and 1574–5, 28 June 1915.

[52] C. Wrigley, *David Lloyd George and the British Labour Movement* (1976), pp.122–8. B. Supple, *The History of the Coal Industry*, Vol. 4 (1987), pp.64–7. *The Times*, 1, 19, 20, 21 and 22 July and 1 September 1915.

[53] At a meeting with the ASE, 17 September 1915, MUNS 5–570–320/4.

[54] Diary entry, 19 September 1915. C. Addison, *Four and A Half Years* (1934), p.126.

[55] Conference minutes, 13 September 1915, MUN 5–57–320/3. NAC minutes (34), 13 September 1915, MUN 5–22–242–1/100.

[56] NAC minutes (35), 16 September 1915, MUN 5–22–242.1/100. Lloyd George saw the ASE separately on 17 September. Minutes, MUN 5–57–320/4.

[57] Conference of Ministry of munitions officials, 13 August 1915, MUN 5–73–324/15/4.

[58] An account of a deputation to Newcastle, 10–14 June 1916 in a memorandum sent by Henderson to Montagu, 20 November 1916, MUN 5–44–264/2

[59] Sir Ronald Davison, 'A Reminiscence of Lloyd George', *Manchester Guardian*, 12 May 1945.

[60] *History of the Ministry of Munitions*, Vol. 4, 4 (not published), pp.102 and 176–80. *Report of the Annual Conference of the Labour Party 1917*, pp.105–06.

[61] Ibid, pp.106–12. Sidney to Beatrice Webb, 24 January 1917 in N. MacKenzie (ed.), *The Letters of Sidney and Beatrice Webb*, Vol. 3 (1978), pp.79–80. *Report of the Annual Conference of the Labour Party 1918*, pp.146–9.

[62] Unpublished diary, 8 March 1916; Addison Papers, Box 97. *History of the Ministry of Munitions*, Vol. 4, 4, pp.131–35.

[63] Asquith's Cabinet report to the King, 30 March 1916, Asquith Papers, Vol. 8, ff.154–5. Addison's diaries, 31 March and 3 April 1916, Addison, p.188.

[64] 83 *H.C. Deb. 5s*, 257, 4 May 1916.

[65] Letter to Mr. Dawson, 20 January 1916, *The Times*, 22 January 1916.

[66] 73 *H.C. Deb. 5s*, 106–13 and 144–50, 5 July 1915.

[67] Wrigley, pp.165–77. R.J.Q. Adams and P. Poirier, *The Conscription Controversy in Great Britain (1987)*, pp.114–15.

[68] Labour party EC minutes, 15, 27 and 29 September 1915. *The Times*, 29 October 1915. *Report of the Annual Conference of the Labour Party 1918*, pp.5–7.

[69] Talbot to Bonar Law, 16 October 1915; Bonar Law Papers, 51/4/16.

[70] *Times Educational Supplement*, 2 November 1915, p.130. Samuel to his wife, 22 December 1915, Samuel Papers A157/801. Runciman to his wife, 28 December 1915, Runciman Papers, Box 18.

[71] *Report of the Annual Conference of the Labour Party 1916*, pp.6–8. Labour Party EC minutes, 5 and 6 January 1916. Diary entries, 2 and 6 January 1916, N. and J. MacKenzie (eds), *The Diary of Beatrice Webb*, Vol. 3 (1984), pp.244–6.

[72] Henderson to Asquith, 10 January 1916, Asquith Papers, Vol. 16, f.8.

[73] Runciman to his wife, 10 January 1916, Runciman Papers, Box 18. Labour Party EC minutes, 12 January 1916. Asquith's speech was printed in the Parliamentary Recruiting Committee's pamphlet, *Guarantees of the Government on the Military Service Bill*, copy, Asquith Papers, Vol. 30, f.114.

[74] *Report of the Annual Conference of the Labour Party 1916*, pp.117–24.

[75] Entry for 13–20 April 1916, T. Wilson (ed.), *The Political Diaries of C.P. Scott 1911–1928* (1970), pp.197–200.

[76] Labour Party EC minutes, 19, 26 and 27 April 1916.

[77] Adams and Poirier, pp.154–68.

[78] The Liberal journalist, Harold Spender to Lloyd George, 21 April 1916, Lloyd George Papers D/20/2/86.

[79] 'The New Head and the Old', *Times Educational Supplement*, 1 June 1915, p.74.

[80] Addison, p.84.

[81] Henderson's speech in the debate on the Board of Education's Estimates. 84 *H.C. Deb. 5s*, 869–89; 18 July 1916. L. Andrews, *The Education Act 1918* (1976), p.16.

[82] 'National Union Notes', *Times Educational Supplement*, 7 September 1916, p.115.

[83] R. Barker, *Education and Politics 1900–1951* (1972), pp.26–7. *Times Educational Supplement*, 2 November 1915, p.130.

[84] Henderson to Asquith, 26 July and 8 August 1916, Asquith Papers, Vol. 17, ff.27–9 and 45. Hamilton, pp.105–7.

[85] Unpublished entries in Addison's diaries, 1 October 1915 and 13 July 1915, Addison Papers, Box 97. Also entry of 8 March 1916, Addison, p.180. Henderson also expressed his dissatisfaction to Lord Crewe. Crewe to Lloyd George, 3 April 1916, LG D/16/9/8.

[86] Unpublished entry in Addison's diary, 13 July 1915, Addison Papers, Box 997. Montagu to Henderson, 4 August 1916, Asquith Papers Vol. 17, ff.40–41.

[87] 'Political Notes', *The Times*, 15 August 1916.

[88] 'Political Notes', *The Times*, 4 and 7 October 1916. Sir George Askwith, *Industrial Problems and Disputes* (1920), p.412.

[89] Unpublished entries in Addison's diaries, 4 and 5 August 1916, Addison Papers, Box 99. Primrose (Ministry of Munitions) to Addison, 29 September 1916, Addison Papers, Box 37.

[90] Asquith's letters to the King, 5 and 19 September 1916, Asquith Papers, Vol. 8, ff.195 and 197–8. Memorandum of interview with Sir Sam Fay, 23 October 1916, Labour Party Papers HEN 2/2.

[91] Montagu to Henderson, 6 November 1916 and Ministry of Munitions minutes of 15 and 17 November 1916, MUN 5–79–328/1.

[92] His reply to a letter by the MP J.M. Hogge, *Yorkshire Post*, 4 September 1916.

[93] Derby to Lloyd George, 19 August 1916, LG E/1/1/2.

[94] Henderson to Asquith, 30 October 1916, Asquith Papers Vol. 17, f.128. 87 *H.C. Deb. 5s*, 1687–92, 23 November 1916.

[95] John Lonsdale to Bonar Law, 20 October 1916, Bonar Law Papers 53/4/10.

[96] Lord Edmund Talbot to Bonar Law, 29 November 1916, ibid., 53/4/25.

[97] *Report of the Annual Conference of the Labour Party 1917*, pp.88–97.

[98] *The Times*, 2 and 12 December 1916.

[99] Diary entry, 26–30 January 1917, Wilson (ed.), p.257. Diary entry 6 December 1916, Riddell, *War Diary*, p.228. D. Lloyd George, *War Memoirs*, Vol. 2 (1933), pp.997–8 and Vol. 3 (1934), pp.1047–61. Balfour's memorandum on December 1916, Balfour Papers, Add. MS., 49692, f.201.

[100] *The Times*, 7 December 1916.

[101] *Report of the Annual Conference of the Labour Party 1917*, p.43.

[102] Speeches of 11 and 15 December 1916, *The Times*, 12 and 16 December 1916.

[103] *The Times*, 2 December 1916.

[104] 90 *H.C. Deb. 5s*, 941, 15 February 1917. *The Times*, 17 February 1917. For the national service campaign see K. Grieves, *The Politics of Manpower 1914– 1918* (1988), pp.102–13.

[105] *The Times*, 9 March 1917. Lloyd George, Vol. 3, pp.1357–9.

[106] D. Dilks, *Neville Chamberlain*, Vol. 1 (1984), pp.226–9. Labour Party Papers HEN 1/27.

[107] Wrigley, pp.184–97.

Notes to Chapter 6

[1] A.G. Gardiner, 'Mr. Henderson and the Labor Movement', *Atlantic Monthly*, 72, August 1918, pp.221–30.

[2] *Report of the Annual Conference of the Labour Party 1917*, p.96, 23 January 1917.

[3] *Lord Riddell's War Diary* (1933), p.149 (entry for 16 January 1917). D. Lloyd George, *War Memoirs*, 627.

[4] Addison's (unpublished) diary entry, 16 May 1917. Addison Papers, Box 98.

[5] Sir R. Davison, 'Reminiscence of Lloyd George', *Manchester Guardian*, 12 May 1945. A.J.P. Taylor (ed.), *Lloyd George: A Diary by Frances Stevenson* (1971), p.148, entry for 2 April 1917.

[6] On the Stockholm incident see especially J.M. Winter, 'Arthur Henderson, the Russian Revolution and the Reconstruction of the Labour Party', *Historical Journal*, 15 (1972), pp.753–73 and D. Kirby, 'International Socialism and the Question of Peace: the Stockholm Conference of 1917', ibid., 25, 3 (1982), pp.709–16. The Labour Party's initial decision was reported in *The Times*, 10 May 1917.

[7] Robert Wilton's letter ('Our Petrograd Correspondent') to *The Times*, 31 December 1917.

[8] Henderson to T.W. Dawson, 19 June 1917, Labour party MS HEN 1/30.

[9] Henderson to J.G. Dale and to R.W. Raine, both 19 June 1917, ibid., 1/28 and 29.

[10] Henderson to Lloyd George, 14 and 15 June 1917, L6 F/27/3/13 and Foreign Office Papers, PRO F.O. 371–3011, ff.4–6.
[11] Henderson to G.H. Roberts, 21 June 1917, HEN 1/31. Jefferson Cohn to Haig, 30 May 1917, Haig Papers, Vol. 214, i.
[12] *East Ham Echo*, 29 November, 1918.
[13] War Cabinet minutes (WC 207), 8 August 1917, CAB 23–3–165.
[14] *Report of the Annual Conference of the Labour Party, January 1918*, pp.3–7 and 43–6. D. Lloyd George, *War Memoirs*, Vol.4 (1934), pp.1900–01.
[15] War Cabinet minutes (WC 2020), 1 August 1917, CAB 23–3–149/50. Bonar Law to Croal, 3 August 1917, Bonar Law Papers 84/6/99.
[16] *Report of the Annual Conference of the Labour Party, January 1918*, pp.50–51.
[17] War Cabinet minutes (WC 211), 10 August 1917, 6.15pm; CAB 23–3–176/7. Milner diary, 10 August 1917, Milner Papers, Vol. 280. Henderson to Lloyd George, 11 August 1917, L6 F/27/3/15.
[18] War Cabinet minutes (WC 212), 11 August 1917, CAB 23–3–177. 97 *H.C. Deb. 5s*, 909–932; 13 August 1917.
[19] T. Wilson, *The Myriad Faces of War* (1986), pp.524–5.
[20] Sidney to Beatrice Webb, 13 August 1917, N. MacKenzie (ed.), *The Letters of Sidney and Beatrice Webb*, Vol. 3 (1978), pp.92–3. R. Harrison, 'The War Emergency Workers' National Committee', p.250, in A. Briggs and J. Saville (eds), *Essays In Labour History 1886–1923* (1971).
[21] *Report of the Annual Conference of the Labour Party, January 1918*, pp.98–101. *Report of the Annual Conference of the Labour Party, June 1918*, p.32. Entry for 21 January 1918, N. and J. MacKenzie (eds), *The Diary of Beatrice Webb*, Vol. 3 (1984), p.293. W. Ormsby-Gore to Milner, Milner Papers 117, f.106–9.
[22] *The Times*, 11 December 1917. *Newcastle Daily Chronicle*, 8 February 1918.
[23] Diary entry of 28 December 1917, relating to a dinner party a week earlier. Unpublished extract, Addison Papers, Box 98.
[24] 27 January 1918, *War Diary*, p.309.
[25] Entry for 1 September 1917, M. Cole (ed.), *Beatrice Webb's Diaries 1912–1924* (1952), pp.94–5. *Report of the Annual Conference of the Labour Party, January 1918*, pp.8–12.
[26] *Report of the Proceedings of the Forty-ninth Trades Union Congress, 1917*, pp.272–7. *Report of the Proceedings of the Fiftieth Trades Union Congress 1918*, pp.65–6. P. Kellog and A. Gleason, *British Labor and the War* (1919), pp.343–51.
[27] Henderson to MacDonald, 2 February 1918, MacDonald Papers 30/69/1162, f.39.
[28] *Report of the Annual Conference of the Labour Party, January 1918*, p.16. R. Martin, *TUC: The Growth of A Pressure Group 1968–1976* (1980), pp.150–60.
[29] In reporting this *The Times* printed 'supplant' for 'supplement' and printed a correction the next day. *The Times*, 12 and 13 November 1917.
[30] A.J. Mayer, *Political Origins of the New Diplomacy 1917–1918* (1959), pp.293–328. C.J. Wrigley, *David Lloyd George and the British Labour Movement* (1976), pp.222–4.
[31] *The Times*, 10 January 1918. *Report of the Annual Conference of the Labour Party, January 1918*, p.105. He also praised Wilson's principles in his *The Aims of Labour* (n.d.), p.38, written in December 1917.

[32] *The Times*, 9 April 1918. Beatrice Webb's diary entry, 25 April 1918, MacKenzie (eds), pp.306–07.

[33] Kellog and Gleason, pp.225–304. A.J. Mayer, *Politics and Diplomacy of Peacemaking* (1967), pp.41–6.

[34] *The Times*, 10 August 1918.

[35] *East Ham Echo*, 15 and 29 November 1918.

[36] *East Ham Echo*, 6, 13 and 20 December 1918.

[37] At Widnes, 8 January 1920, *The Times*, 9 January 1920.

[38] *Widnes Guardian*, 15, 22 and 26 August and 16 September 1919. *Widnes Echo*, 29 August 1919. *The Times*, 5 September 1919. Henderson's agent was H. Drinkwater, the Midlands organizer.

[39] Henderson to Sidney Webb, 17 May 1919, Passfield Papers IIg, 133 a and b.

[40] M.A. Hamilton, *Arthur Henderson* (1938), p.166.

[41] *The Times*, 16 January 1917. Kellog and Gleason, pp.352–66. *Report of the Nineteenth Annual Conference of the Labour Party, 1919*, pp.3–10. Gompers was added as a fourth Commissioner at a further Inter-Allied Conference in September 1918, but obstructed rather than helped these aims.

[42] *The Times*, 2, 16 and 27 January and 5, 7, 10, 12 and 19 February 1919. Mayer, *Peacemaking*, pp.375–408. *Report of the Nineteenth Annual Conference of the Labour Party, 1919*, pp.11–16 and 196–205.

[43] Mayer, *Peacemaking*, p.407.

[44] *Report of the Nineteenth Annual Conference of the Labour Party, 1919*, pp.19–20 and 206–11. *The Times*, 30 April and 23 June 1919.

[45] *The Times*, 15 May 1919. W. MacKenzie King diary, 14 May 1919; quoted in H.M. Gitelman, *Legacy of the Ludlow Massacre* (1988), p.298.

[46] Kellog and Gleason, pp.293–6, and Mayer, *Peacemaking*, pp.49–51. Executive minutes of the Labour party, 18 September 1918.

[47] *Report of the Nineteenth Annual Conference of the Labour Party, 1919*, pp.156–61. S.R. Graubard, *British Labour and the Russian Revolution 1917–1924* (1956), pp.64–82.

[48] *Iron Founders Monthly Journal and Report*, July 1919.

[49] *The Times*, 4 August 1919.

[50] D. Marquand, *Ramsay MacDonald* (1977), pp.260–67.

[51] *The Times*, 21 May 1917. For a recent account of the background, see G.W. Egerton, *Great Britain and the Creation of the League of Nations* (1979), especially pp.8–13 and 49–53.

[52] *The Times*, 3 January, 7 February and 30 April 1919.

[53] *The Times*, 4 and 30 April, 1919.

[54] *The Times*, 14 January 1920. Egerton, pp.174–5. Henderson and Cecil to Asquith, 16 November 1916, Asquith Paperes.

[55] The meeting was in Sunderland, 15 March 1909. *The Times*, 16 March 1909.

[56] Henderson to Middleton, 17 September and 17 November 1913, Labour Party Corres. 08/1/89. *Report of the Annual Conference of the Labour Party, 1914*, pp.23–25. *The Times*, 8 September 1913. E. Larkin, *James Larkin* (1965), Part 3.

[57] *The Times*, 23 December 1913.

[58] Newbold to Lothian, 8 June 1937, Lothian Papers, GD40–17–341, ff.763–4. (Newbold had left the Communist party and rejoined the Labour party but

had then followed MacDonald in 1931.) *Newcastle and North Mail*, 29 December, 1922. (This is contrary to Hamilton, p.206 where she asserts 'he had striven to prevent the execution of Connolly and the others'.)

[59] *The Times*, 27 and 30 January 1920. *Report of the Twentieth Annual Conference of the Labour Party, 1920*, pp.5–7.

[60] *The Times*, 16 October 1920.

[61] *The Times*, 10 December 1920.

[62] *Report of the Twenty-first Annual Conference of the Labour Party, 1921*, pp.22–5. *The Times*, 31 October and 1 November, 1921.

[63] *Report of the Twenty-first Annual Conference of the Labour Party, 1921*, pp.25–30. *The Times*, 19 January, 1921. There are Ministry of Labour suggestions that this refusal to participate should be used in justifying not resurrecting the National Industrial conference in LAB/2/775/3 (January 1922).

[64] *Newcastle Chronicle and North Mail*, 29 December 1922 to 16 January 1923 and 27 October to 8 December 1923.

[65] Kellog and Gleason, p.95.

[66] At the annual meeting of the Croydon Northend Brotherhood, 15 January 1917. *The Times*, 16 January 1917.

[67] *The Times*, 19 February 1917.

[68] *The Times*, 5 July 1919.

[69] In his Foreword to the Secretary of the National Alliance, Arthur Paterson's book, *The Weapon of the Strike* (n.d.), pp.11–14, (published April 1922.) Also Henderson's article, 'The Parliament of Industry', *The Times*, 25 April 1922, pp.13–14.

[70] At the International Brotherhood Congress, 16 September 1919 (and at a conference on 'Labour and Religion', 4 September 1919). *The Times*, 5 and 17 September 1919. *Report of the Fifty-second Annual Trades Union Congress*, 1919, pp.310–13.

[71] A. Gleason, *What the Workers Want* (1920), p.3.

[72] *The Times*, 19 June 1922.

[73] On 22 June 1921. *Report of the Twenty-first Annual Conference of the Labour Party, 1921*, pp.165–67. *The Times*, 23 June 1921.

[74] At the Co-operative Conference, 18 October 1917. *The Times*, 19 October 1917.

[75] *The Times*, 9 January 1920.

[76] *The Times*, 29 October 1923 and 18 October, 1922. For recent assessments of his role as Party Secretary in these years, see K.O. Morgan, *Consensus and Disunity* (1979), pp.218–20 and 234, and F.M. Leventhal, *Arthur Henderson* (1989), pp.102–10.

Notes to Chapter 7

[1] M.A. Hamilton, *Arthur Henderson* (1938), p.266.

[2] Cabinet Paper C.P. 230, 31 March 1924, CAB 24–166–169/73. Cabinet meeting (25), 7 April 1924; CAB 23–47–387.

[3] *The Times*, 12 May 1924. Cabinet meeting (31), 14 May 1924, CAB 23–48–89.

[4] 173 *H.C. Deb. 5s*, 1667–1698, 15 May 1924. Cabinet meetings (32, 33, 34 and 35) 15, 21, 27 and 30 May 1924. CAB 23–104/5, 119, 139 and 146.

[5] 173 H.C. Deb. 5s, 606–7; 8 May 1924. On the case of Syme see G.W. Reynolds and A. Judge, *The Day the Police Went On Strike* (1968), pp.6–31 and 226–32. *The Times*, 22 June 1925. After the New Brighton incident Henderson issued a press release in which he recognized the suffering of the families but suggested the committee of inquiry had been a reasonable response. *The Times*, 25 June 1925. *Report of 25 Annual Conference of the Labour Party, 1925*, pp.281–3.

[6] Diary entry, 23 June 1924. N. and J. MacKenzie (eds), *The Diary of Beatrice Webb*, Vol. 4 (1985), p.30.

[7] Quoted in Bert Williams's pamphlet, *The Record of the Labour Government* (n.d., 1924), pp.12–13.

[8] Cabinet meeting (22), 26 March 1924; CAB 23–47–323. R. Martin, *TUC: The Growth of A Pressure Group 1868–1976* (1980), pp.169 and 186–8.

[9] Cabinet meetings (1 and 5), 23 January and 13 February 1924, CAB 23–47–10 and 135. Report of Emergency Committee meeting (CP102), 12 February 1924, CAB 24–165–34/41. R. Desmarais, 'Strike breaking and the Labour Government of 1924', *Journal of Contemporary History*, 8 (1973), pp.165–75. K. Jeffery and P. Hennessy, *States of Emergency* (1983), pp.78–86. R. Lyman, *The First Labour Government 1924* (1957), pp.218–23.

[10] Report of Emergency Committee meeting (CP 211), 24 March 1924, CAB 24–166–42/4. Cabinet meeting (23), 27 March 1924, CAB 23–47–328/31. A. Bullock, *The Life and Times of Ernest Bevin*, Vol. 1 (1960), pp.239–42.

[11] 133 *H.C. Deb. 5s*, 1423–29 and 1608, 25 and 26 October 1920.

[12] G. Glasgow, *General Strikes and Road Transport* (n.d., 1926), p.11.

[13] S. Webb, 'The First Labour Government', *Political Quarterly*, 32 (1961), p.24. Henderson's remark was recorded by Beatrice Webb in her diary entry, 3 April 1924. M. Cole (ed.), *Beatrice Webb's Diaries 1924–1932* (1956), p.18.

[14] Cabinet meeting (24), 2 April 1924; CAB 23–47–365/6.

[15] *The Times*, 5, 10, 11 and 17 April 1924. Cabinet Papers (CP 281 and 281A) on the Factories Bill, 2 May 1924, CAB 24–166–656/721. Cabinet meeting (33), 21 May 1924, CAB 23–48–122.

[16] *171 H.C. Deb 5s*, 1855, 31 March 1924.

[17] S. Webb, p.17.

[18] Hamilton, p.236. N. and J. MacKenzie, Vol. 3, p.432. On 12 December she noted that Henderson was 'amazingly disinterested' as to office. M. Cole (ed.), *Beatrice Webb's Diaries 1912–1924* (1952), p.256.

[19] D. Marquand, *Ramsay MacDonald* (1977), p.298. Sidney to Beatrice Webb, 3 January 1924, N. MacKenzie (ed.), *The Letters of Sidney and Beatrice Webb, Vol. 3* (1978), p.190.

[20] Ibid., p.276. N. and J. MacKenzie, Vol. 3, pp.379–80.

[21] *The Times*, 25 and 26 February 1924. Marquand, pp.333–4. Hamilton, pp.238–40.

[22] Herbert Tracey worked for the Labour party. Beatrice Webb's diary, 29 February 1924. M. Cole (ed.), *Diaries 1924–1932*, p.11.

[23] Too much emphasis should not be put on jealousy on this occasion. B. Pimlott (ed.), *The Political Diary of Hugh Dalton 1918–1940, 1945–1960* (1986), p.42.

[24] *The Times*, 12 December 1922. Also the excellent account by H.R. Winkler, 'Arthur Henderson', in G.A. Craig and F. Gilbert, *The Diplomats 1919–1939* (1953), pp.311–43, especially 314–16.

NOTES 201

25 Lord Parmoor, *A Retrospect* (1936), pp.213–64. *The Times*, 27 September 1924.
26 Marquand, p.356. Parmoor, pp.196–7 and 253. E. Windrich, *British Labour's Foreign Policy* (1952), pp.38–51.
27 *The Times*, 13 October 1924.
28 Winkler, p.316. A. Henderson, *The Aims of Labour* (n.d.–written December 1917), p.40.
29 The Labour party issued his speech in the House of Commons on 24 March 1925 as a penny pamphlet, *Labour and the Geneva Protocol* (1925).
30 Arthur Engberg to Henderson, 26 September 1925, MacDonald Papers, PRO 30/69/1170/1, ff.397–98.
31 *The Times*, 7 November 1924.
32 M.A. Hamilton, *Remembering My Good Friends* (1944), p.118. Beatrice Webb's diary, 2 December 1929, N. and J. MacKenzie, Vol. 4, p.203. Hugh Dalton's diary, 12 January 1930, B. Pimlott (ed.), *The Political Diary of Hugh Dalton 1918–1940, 1945–1960* (1986), pp.87–8. Marquand, p.391.
33 R.E. Dowse, *Left In The Centre* (1966), pp.120–27. *The Times*, 19 April 1927.
34 M. Cole, *Makers of the Labour Movement* (1948), p.266.
35 *The Times*, 28 July 1928.
36 On Tory propaganda, *The Times*, 15 March 1926. For Wheatley and the *Labour and the Nation* debate, 3 October 1928, *Report of the 28th Annual Conference of the Labour Party*, 1928, pp.212–15.
37 *The Times*, 9 April 1925. Correspondence with MacDonald, 20 February 1928 and 25 and 29 May, 1929, MacDonald Papers PRO 30/69/1173, f.592 and 1174, ff.490–95.
38 *The Times*, 3 March 1926, 12 September 1925, 26 January 1926, 30 July 1927 and 30 January 1928. *Huddersfield Examiner*, 20 June 1925. E.A. Jenkins, *From Foundry to Foreign Office* (1933), p.148.
39 J.R. Clynes, *Memoirs 1924–1937* (1938), p.76. G.A. Philips, *The General Strike* (1976), p.126. M. Morris, The General Strike (1976), p.245.
40 Lord Citrine, *Men and Work* (1964), pp.175–6. Philips, pp.92–3. Beatrice Webb's diary, 7 May 1926; MacKenzies, p.78.
41 *The Times*, 19 April and 1 March 1926 and 7 January 1927.
42 *The Times*, 12 October 1927 and 22 February 1926.
43 *The Times*, 7 January 1927.
44 *The Times*, 12 January 1927. Henderson's speech set to work Ministry of Labour officials to prepare the case against a National Industrial Council being reconstituted. Memo of 13 January 1927 by F. Leggett, PRO Lab 2/775/4.
45 *The Times*, 8 January and 30 April 1927.
46 *The Times*, 12 January and 26 March 1928.
47 *The Times*, 24 October 1928. G.W. MacDonald and H.F. Gospel, 'The Mond–Turner Talks 1927–1933', *Historical Journal*, 16, 4 (1973), pp.807–29.
48 Winkler, p.319.
49 *The Times*, 7 April 1925.
50 F.S. Northedge, *The Troubled Giant* (1966), p.269. *The Times*, 28 November 1925.
51 *The Times*, 12 January 1928 and 12 April 1929.
52 Snowden, Vol. 2, p.760. Marquand, p.489.
53 B. Pimlott, *Hugh Dalton* (1985), p.183.

54 Henderson to MacDonald, 19 September 1927, MacDonald Papers, PRO 30/69/ 1172, ff.719–20.

55 MacDonald to Henderson, 20 September 1927, ibid., f.721.

56 *The Times*, 24 August 1925, 30 July 1926 and 26 March 1927. MacDonald to Middleton, 18 November 1925, MacDonald Papers, PRO 30/69/1170, f.2.

57 E. Wertheimer, *Portrait of the Labour Party* (second English edition, May 1930), pp.174–5, 281 and 290.

58 M.A. Hamilton, *Remembering My Good Friends* (1944), p.125.

59 H. Dalton's Foreword to M. Cole, *Makers of the Labour Movement* (1948), p.vii. Dalton's diary, 5 November 1931, B. Pimlott (ed.), pp.162–3.

60 Viscount Cecil, *A Great Experiment* (1941), p.200. B. Webb to E. Haldane, 30 August 1929, N. and J. MacKenzie (ed.), Vol. 3, p.318. Major-General A.C. Temperley, *The Whispering Gallery of Europe* (1938), p.163.

61 Winkler, pp.320–21. Cecil, p.200.

62 *Report of the 30th Annual Conference of the Labour Party, 1930*, p.240. *Report of the 29th Annual Conference of the Labour Party, 1929*, p.215.

63 H. Dalton, *Call Back Yesterday* (1953), pp.223–4.

64 Henderson to MacDonald, 13 September 1929; printed in Hamilton, *Henderson*, pp.327–8. It is discussed in D. Carlton, *MacDonald Versus Henderson (1970)*, pp.79–80.

65 Cecil, p.202. Dalton's diary for 29 June, 8 July and 23 August 1929, Pimlott (ed.), pp.59, 61 and 64.

66 Quoted in Winkler, p.330.

67 *Report 1929*, p.216.

68 *Report 1931*, p.185. Carlton, pp.94–9. Temperley, p.142.

69 Windrich, pp.75–7. *Report 1929*, p.208. Carlton, pp.37–56.

70 Dalton's diary, 18 July 1929, Dalton, pp.230–33.

71 *Report 1929*, p.207. Hamilton, *Henderson*, p.311.

72 Henderson to Ovey, 3 December 1930, cited in Carlton, p.162. Northedge, pp.321–2. Windrich, pp.72–4.

73 *Report 1929*, p.206. On Webb see A. Bullock, *The Life and Times of Ernest Bevin*, Vol. 1 (1960), pp.455–7, and Webb to Amulree, 10 February 1931, N. McKenzie (ed.), pp.345–46.

74 Dalton, pp.226–7. Dalton diary, 30 July 1929; Pimlott (ed.), p.62. Carlton, pp.24 and 169–73. Temperley, p.72.

75 *Report 1929*, pp.207–11.

76 Dalton, pp.225–6. C.F. Adam, *Life of Lord Lloyd* (1948), pp.218–33. J. Charmley, *Lord Lloyd and the Crisis of the British Empire* (1986).

77 Cecil, p.200.

78 Diary, 2 December 1929, N. and J. MacKenzie (eds), Vol. 4, p.202.

79 Hamilton, *Henderson*, p.349.

80 Marquand, pp.525–31, 567–8 and 584–5.

81 *H.C. Deb 5s*, 7 April 1914. *H.C. Deb 5s*, 23 November 1917. M. Pugh, *Electoral Reform In War and Peace 1906–1918* (1978), pp.8–11 and 166–67.

82 See, for example, Carlton, p.222.

83 Carlton, pp.200–11.

84 Marquand, pp.576–8. R. Skidelsky, *Politicians and the Slump* (1967), p.270. A. Thorpe, 'Arthur Henderson and the British Political Crisis of 1931', *Histori-*

cal Journal, 31, 1 (1988), pp.117–39. MacDonald to Henderson, 31 March 1931, MacDonald Papers, PRO 30/69/1176, f.245.

85 *The Times*, 11 April 1929. Beatrice Webb's diary, 2 December 1929, N. and J. MacKenzie (ed.), Vol. 4, p.202.

86 Thorpe, p.122. Bullock, pp.480–90. Dalton, pp.267–9.

87 Dalton's diary, 27 August 1931, Pimlott (ed.), p.152. Beatrice Webb's diary, 23 August 1931, N. and J. MacKenzie (ed.), Vol. 4, p.253.

88 R. Postgate, *The Life of George Lansbury* (1951), pp.271–2.

89 Hamilton, *Henderson*, p.386. Dalton, p.274. Presumably the 'fifteen years' is a little wrong, but refers to the period 1917 to 1921 when Adamson was leader.

90 Dalton, p.274. Thorpe, pp.124–6. Postgate, p.279.

91 M. Cole (ed.), *Diaries 1924–1932*, pp.287–89. Marquand, p.657–63. Thorpe, pp.130–32.

92 *Report 1931*, pp.244–5.

93 *The Times*, 24 October 1931. *Burnley News*, 21 and 28 October 1931.

94 Postgate, pp.279–80. Lansbury probably saw him in the week from 19 January 1932, when Henderson returned to his work at Labour Party headquarters.

95 *The Times*, 5 December 1931, 1 January and 19 October 1932.

96 *The Times*, 14 June 1932. Hamilton, *Henderson*, p.441. F.S. Northedge, *The League of Nations* (1986), pp.122–36.

97 Hamilton, *Henderson*, p.408. Beatrice Webb's diary, 5 August 1933; N. and J. MacKenzie (ed.), Vol. 4, p.309. *The Times*, 10 July 1933.

98 C. Aghnides to Henderson, 31 August and 2 September 1935, Labour Party Papers HEN/A/87 and 89.

99 *Derbyshire Times*, 29 July and 5 August 1933.

100 Dalton's diary, 8 October 1932, 24 January 1934 and 1934/1935; Pimlott (ed.), pp.168, 183 and 184.

101 Hamilton, *Henderson*, p.446.

102 J.R. Clynes, *Memoirs*, Vol. 2 (1938), p.210.

103 Lord Snell, *Men, Movements and Myself* (1936), p.233.

104 A quotation by Eduard Bernstein used by Michels. R. Michels' *Political Parties* (English edition, 1915), pp.100–1 and 150.

105 A. Henderson, *The Aims of Labour* (n.d.–written December 1917), pp.57–9.

106 K.O. Morgan, *Labour People* (1987), p.83.

107 Hamilton, *Remembering*, p.251. Diary, 5 April 1927, N. and J. MacKenzie (ed.), Vol. 4, p.119.

108 H. Tracey, 'Rt. Hon. Arthur Henderson', in H. Tracey (ed.), *The Book of the Labour Party*, Vol. 3 (1925), p.151.

A Note on Sources

Unlike most Cabinet ministers today, Henderson did not keep files of his personal papers. He preferred to use the waste-paper basket, though as an *apparatchik* of the trade union movement and then of the Labour party, he was as careful to account for office correspondence as he was for finance.

The records of his regional work for his union, the Friendly Society of Iron Founders, seem not to have survived. But the national records have survived, including the handwritten minute books of the executive committee. These are located at the Modern Record Centre, University of Warwick. Particularly important for Henderson's career before 1914 are the near monthly commentaries which he contributed to the union's journal, the *Monthly Report*, from the time he was elected to be the union's nominee as a parliamentary candidate. Indeed Henderson features in the Iron Founders' (and its successor union's) journal from September 1890, when he made a presentation to a member on behalf of the union, until his death forty-five years later.

Henderson appears frequently in the Labour party's records from the early days of the Labour Representation Committee (1900–6) until near to his death. The National Executive Committee minutes are particularly valuable and the National Executive Committee sections of the Labour party's annual reports are his accounts of the party's performance during his stewardship. Given the small staff at the Labour party headquarters for most of his career, it is not surprising that the correspondence files give an impression of not only his day-to-day life at work, but often personal details as well. Thus in one letter (8 January 1907) there is an account of his getting his family out on the street at 2.30 a.m. on a Saturday morning when the adjoining house was gutted by fire.

For his time as a Cabinet minister under Lloyd George and Ramsay MacDonald there are Cabinet minutes and papers. For his time as Foreign Secretary these are complemented by a small collection of Henderson papers among the Foreign Office records. A rich source for his period in Asquith's Cabinet, when he often acted as a trouble-shooter on labour matters, is the Ministry of Munitions records. All of these are located at the Public Records Office.

Henderson's letters to other people survive in many collections. The most notable of these is the Ramsay MacDonald Papers, held at the Public Record Office. Henderson also features frequently in the diaries of Beatrice Webb and Hugh Dalton, which have been edited for publication by N. and J. Mackenzie (4 volumes, 1982—5) and B. Pimlott (2 volumes, 1986) respectively.

As for biographies, two early ones were written by Labour MPs who knew him: E.A. Jenkins, *From Foundry to Foreign Office*, 1933, and Mary Agnes Hamilton, *Arthur Henderson*, 1938. Jenkins's book, thin on Henderson's career before 1914, but more detailed on the period after the First World War, is a mediocre work. Hamilton's is much better. She knew both MacDonald and Henderson well. She was prone to eulogy — not just on Henderson but also in her earlier books on MacDonald, written in 1923 and 1925 under the pen-name 'Iconoclast'; though she became disillusioned with MacDonald after the first Labour Government. Her biography of Henderson is substantial and valuable, but there are inaccuracies, especially in the early chapters where she was more dependent on family recollections. Her own autobiography, *Remembering My Good Friends*, 1944, is of interest. Another portrait by one who knew Henderson is Margaret Cole's in her *Makers of the Labour Movement*, 1948.

Recently F.M. Leventhal has written a good brief biography, *Arthur Henderson*, 1989, which makes some use of the main political (but not trade union) archives, draws on recent secondary literature and provides shrewd appraisals of such issues as Henderson's relationship with MacDonald and also Liberal–Labour politics after the First World War. There are also perceptive portraits of Henderson by John Saville in his and Joyce Bellamy's *Dictionary of Labour Biography*, Vol. 1, 1972, and K.O. Morgan in *Labour People*, 1987.

The main secondary literature is outlined in my references to the chapters of this book.

Index

The Author

Chris Wrigley is Reader in Economic History at Nottingham University. He is a member of the Councils of the Economic History Society and the Historical Association, the executive committee of the Society for the Study of Labour History and is a Fellow of the Royal Historical Society. His books include *David Lloyd George and the British Labour Movement, A History of British Industrial Relations Vol. 1: 1875–1914* and *Vol. 2: 1914–1939* (editor), and also *Warfare, Diplomacy and Politics: Essays for A.J.P. Taylor* (editor).

The General Editor

Professor Kenneth O. Morgan, D.Litt, F.B.A., is Principal of University College of Wales, Aberystwyth, and was formerly Fellow and Praelector of The Queen's College, Oxford. He has written extensively and authoritatively on radical movements in nineteenth-century and twentieth-century Britain; his titles include *Wales in British Politics, 1868–1922* (1963), *The Age of Lloyd George* (1971), *Keir Hardie* (1975), *Consensus and Disunity* (1979), *Rebirth of a Nation: Wales 1800–1980* (1981), *Labour in Power 1945–1951* (1984) and *Labour People* (1987). His latest book, *The People's Peace: British History, 1945–1989* appears in 1990. He has been editor of *The Welsh History Review* since 1965 and was elected Fellow of the British Academy in 1983.